WALKS & HIKES IN THE

FOOTHILLS & LOWLANDS

AROUND PUGET SOUND

Harvey Manning
&
Penny Manning

Photos by Bob & Ira Spring

THE
MOUNTAINEERS

*To Leo Gallagher
and the others of the 100 club members
who loaned The Mountaineers the funds
to publish* Freedom of the Hills,
which began all this.

Published by
The Mountaineers
1001 SW Klickitat Way
Seattle, Washington 98134

First edition: first printing 1995, second printing 1997

All opinions expressed in this work are the authors'.

Published simultaneously in Canada by Douglas & McIntyre, Ltd., 1615 Venables Street, Vancouver, B.C. V5L 2H1

Published simultaneously in Great Britain by Cordee, 3a DeMontfort Street, Leicester, England, LE1 7HD

Manufactured in the United States of America

Edited by Dana Lee Fos
Maps by Gary Rands and Gray Mouse Graphics; back cover map by Gray Mouse Graphics
All photographs by Bob and Ira Spring
Cover design by Watson Graphics
Book design and layout by Gray Mouse Graphics
Typesetting by The Mountaineers Books

Cover: *border:* oak ferns; *inset:* forest trails, both by Kirkendall/Spring

Library of Congress Cataloging-in-Publication Data
Manning, Harvey.
    Walks and hikes in the foothills and lowlands around Puget Sound / by Harvey Manning and Penny Manning ; [all photographs by Bob and Ira Spring].
        p.   cm.
    Includes index.
    ISBN 0-89886-431-3 (paper)
    1. Hiking--Washington (State)--Puget Sound Region--Guidebooks. 2. Hiking--Washington (State)--Kitsap Peninsula--Guidebooks. 3. Hiking--Washington (State)--Olympic Peninsula--Guidebooks. 4. Puget Sound Region (Wash.)--Guidebooks. 5. Kitsap Peninsula (Wash.)--Guidebooks. 6. Olympic Peninsula (Wash.)--Guidebooks. I. Manning, Penny. II. Title.
GV199.42.W22P837   1995
796.5'1'097977--dc20   94-44877
                                                                   CIP

CONTENTS

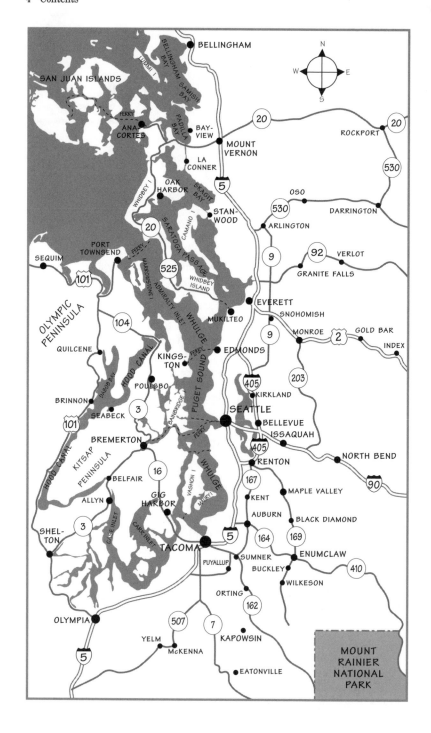

Deschutes Falls (Page 234)

INTRODUCTION

Trails for Feet

Trails. *True* trails. That is to say, trails for feet. The definition may be extended, where fitting, to include the hooves of horses and the paws of dogs. The wild things obviously are always welcome, whatever their means of locomotion, whether walking, hopping, flying, or squirming on the belly. They can be trusted to take care of their own manner of motion. Our audience here is human. Trail-walking, that's the subject of this book.

However, as our faithful readers over the past third of a century have learned, we do not do books purely or even primarily to serve recreation. Re-creation ranks higher. Highest of all is preservation—preservation of those attributes which support the human claim to be superior to the sludgeworm, of those qualities which permit us to claim for Mother Nature superiority to a dump of sludge. It pleases us that our books have serendipitous value as guides to the kinetic-esthetic pleasures of walking. However, they really are something less and something more: pamphlets, broadsides, wall posters, political manifestos. To readers' complaints that they want directions on where to go, not lessons in how to behave, we answer, "If you don't want sermons, don't go to church." To those who disagree with our politics, we say, "Publish your own books."

Since this will be the elder surveyor's final book for The Mountaineers, a peroration may be in order telling how we got where we are. To start the story somewhere this side of the Big Bang and the Garden of Eden, in 1960, when the Climbing Committee concluded a 5-year effort with publication of *Mountaineering: The Freedom of the Hills,* financed not by the impoverished club but by loans from club members who expected never to be more than partly repaid, we were startled by the commercial success. We had thought there were only hundreds of us climbers, never dreamt (nightmared?) thousands and, before long, tens of thousands. The profits (which were a conversion to cash of the unpaid labors of a hundred writers, reviewers, editors, and helpers) were an embarrassment. We saw them, too, as a danger, since they were all too likely to be exploited in ways that would fail to keep faith with us climber-volunteers, not to mention the quarter-century of the Climbing Course on whose experience the book was based. The Board of Trustees agreed and established the Literary Fund to receive income from and publish new editions of *Freedom* and to finance other books, including those that never would be undertaken by commercial publishers because by definition they would

11

be furthering the purposes of The Mountaineers enunciated in 1906 and, thus, would very probably lose money.

To pass over the brothers and sisters, cousins and nieces and nephews of *Freedom,* in 1964 Tom Miller brought to a meeting of the Literary Fund Committee (the LFC, our unpaid, volunteer directorship) an English guidebook which served as our model for *100 Hikes in Western Washington.* This epochal volume, published in 1966, was the first guidebook ever to top the Seattle bestseller list. It begat a half-dozen successors in our *100 Hikes* series and golly knows how many imitators across the nation.

The original plan of the LFC was for a book that would sample every manner of Mountaineers pedestrianism not entailing three-point suspension and rope and dynamic belay. We quickly saw, however, that the University of Washington Arboretum would not be displayed to proper advantage side by side with the Hoh River rain forest. Yet to publish walking books that failed to honor the arboretum was to deny an essential of our club heritage.

As chance would have it, the *Seattle Times* Sunday magazine was just then paying the first journalistic attention to walking any of us ever had seen. We recruited the author of these "Footloose in Seattle" articles, Janice Krenmayr, and in 1969 published her *Footloose Around Puget Sound: 100 Walks on Beaches, Lowlands, and Foothills.* A federal official addressing a national conference on the subject of urban and urban-edge outdoor recreation held up a copy of Janice's book and declared, "Every city in the nation should have a book like this." Before long, just about every city did.

Janice revised the book several times before being drawn to other enthusiasms. Having been her editor, I loved *Footloose* as dearly as if it were mine own and couldn't endure watching it slip away. One thing led to another. From the spring of 1976 to the fall of 1978, I walked some 3000 "extra" miles, over and above normal backpacks in the high country and on the ocean beaches and exercises in my backyard Issaquah Alps. Between the front ridges of the Olympics and front ridges of the Cascades, on beaches, lowlands, foothills from Bellingham to Olympia, were born the "Sons of Footloose," the four volumes of *Footsore: Walks and Hikes Around Puget Sound.*

Revisions, new editions, more thousands of miles, and suddenly it's the 1990s and a decision from the Bottom Line to put to death the *Footsores.*

The execution has been only partly fatal. From the ashes rose, phoenix-like, the "Sons of Footsore." The 1993 *Hiking the Mountains to Sound Greenway* rescued the Snoqualmie Valley portion of the defuncted *Footsore 2.* The 1995 *Walks and Hikes on the Beaches Around Puget Sound* assembled all the saltwater shores of *F-1, F-3,* and *F-4.* That left in limbo the large inland residue of the four volumes, to be covered by the single volume here in hand.

In 1976 I had set out for a comfortably finite updating of Janice's book.

But as a few hundred miles of walking grew into a thousand, then two, and at last three thousand, I was gripped by an obsessive compulsion. My resolve became to comprehensively inventory the entirety of "the wildness within," to set forth a trails-preserving agenda for the citizenry and government. Periodic front-to-back revisions over the years kept the inventory reasonably current.

The political agenda is now even more urgent as we run out of open space, as every remaining patch of green is eyed by dollar-greedy trammelers. More surveyors are needed to publicize threatened lands and water. More publishers free from the tyranny of the Bottom Line. More amateurs.

If not a comprehensive inventory, this book is a useful sampling, an outline of what needs to be inventoried by a new legion of volunteer amateurs who ask no more than a little gas money and now and then a bit of peanut butter to spread on their crackers.

Until that legion does its work, we advise walkers not to throw out their *Footsores.* We implore librarians not to junk old editions. Move them to the History Shelf. The changes in lands and waters reflected in the editions since 1977 of the four volumes, and since 1969 of good old *Footloose,* are a uniquely valuable record.

> *This is the song that doesn't end,*
> *Yes, it goes on and on, my friend.*
> *Some people started singing it,*
> *Not knowing what it was,*
> *And they'll continue singing it forever just because*
> *This is the song that doesn't end ...*

> —Shari Lewis and Lamb Chop

"In Wildness Is the Preservation of the World"

The Wilderness Act of 1964 defines a *national wilderness* as a place where "the earth and its community of life are untrammeled by man, where man himself is a visitor who does not remain." This, in the main, is the subject of our *100 Hikes* series, the lands where the technology, the exploitation, the trammeling of civilization have not been permitted. They lie beyond the frontier line—they are "the wildness without."

The subject here is "the wildness within" that frontier line, the enclaves civilization has swept around but not swallowed up. The *regional wilderness* is of sufficient size and proper topography to block out or obscure or screen sights and to mute sounds of surrounding civilization and, if trammeled, has the capacity to obliterate or soften the evidences in time; the type example in our area is the Cougar Mountain Regional Wildland Park. Equally contributing to the role noted by Wallace Stegner

("It may be the love of wilderness that finally teaches us civilized responsibility") is the smaller *community wilderness,* buffered to a degree from
the rumble-bang-honk-yowl of the city and reserved for passive, quiet,
low-impact re-creations. Nor can be forgotten the *neighborhood wilderness,* once upon a time exemplified by the vacant lot down the block and
nowadays by the unbuildable greenbelt on a bluff or in a swamp, or the
pocket park where a person can sit under a tree and hear the birds.

A wise man has said, "A city operates at high pressure in close quar-
ters—it's the hot steam of the boiler room that blasts out the great ideas
that *are* civilization. However, too much heat boils the brains. Only by
providing getaway space for a quick and easy cooling off can a city keep
on cooking."

Yet if wildness is, in Thoreau's judgment, the preservation of the world,
it is not, in itself, nor can or should it be, the whole of the world. The
walks in these pages sample railroad tracks, working waterfronts, logging roads, skid roads, farms. Views of ships and tugs and boats and
ferries. Where man lives. Works. Fools around. Trammels. Where man
has grown into the landscape to become as belonging as the aplodontia
(mountain beaver), another creature notorious for its engineering yet tolerable within the ecosystem, except perhaps when you step in one of its
mine holes and break your leg.

Trails Are the Preservation of the Wildness Within

"Trail" once embraced every sort of travel route from those serving the
most primitive means of locomotion (feet) to the most technologically advanced (the mule-drawn wagon). Because of its roots in time, the term
continues to have connotations more agreeable than, say, "gridlockway."
However, the denotation has to be cleaned up to retain the word's viabil-
ity in the era of machinery run amok. We have yet to hear NASA speak of
astronauts taking the "Mars Trail," but the National Park Service's "mo-
tor nature trail," the Geological Survey's "jeep trail," and the musclebutts'
"motorcycle trail" are egregiously oxymoronic.

Which is not to say the priests of "multiple use" (*there* is a no-brainer
they would not wish applied to their sweethearts) use the phrase out of
stupidity. Far from it. The sugar coating is intended to get you to swallow
the pill irretrievably before you retch. Even more duplicitous is "bicycle
trail," the favorite of pension-protecting parks officials who realize the
world is changing in ways it probably shouldn't but pretend everything is
just dandy if we all put on happy faces.

"Multi-use trail" appeared in the beginning to be a bright idea. The
Burke-Gilman Trail, first publicly promoted in *Footloose* before it even
existed and hailed by *Footsore* as one of America's greatest urban trails,
has cleared the scales from our eyes and stripped the reality down to the
ugly bones. It was on the Burke-Gilman that this elder surveyor awoke
from euphoria, took a look around, and saw that the King County Trails

Beaver house on McLane Creek Nature Trail (Page 230)

Plan so enthusiastically praised in his past writing was a *Bikeways* Plan. Not the same thing at all.

The *multi-use corridor* is quite possible and even wise when the proper conditions are met. One sort, typified by logging roads and out-in-the-country powerline corridors, has a sufficient width for travelers to meet and pass without jostling, has sightlines long enough for encounters to be seen well in advance, and has light traffic and thus only occasional encounters. The other sort is suited to urban-suburban areas where space is at a premium and must be shared by travelers in different modes at different speeds. There the modes must be separated, their speeds being the determinant, walkers and wheelchairs in one lane, horses in another, bicycles and rollerskates and skateboards and joggers and runners in a third. The lanes must be physically well separated by barriers to discourage crossovers and the corridor well policed to ensure that each mode stays in its assigned lane. Examples of such corridors exist across America, but the sole jurisdiction in our area which has adopted the concept, the Issaquah Parks Department, has been sneered at and scorned by the mainstream trail panjandrums who subscribe to the Establishment policy, which is to dump all the cats in the same gunnysack and instruct them to purr.

That the multi-use trail is a fraud is evident to any walker who has traveled (except on a rainy Tuesday morning in February) the Burke-Gilman or Sammamish River or any other "trail"-become-bikeway. Speeds of 1–4 miles per hour (foot) and 3–5 miles per hour (reined-in horse) can coexist with each other, but not with the family-style bicycles at 6–12 miles per hour, much less the racer on an endorphine high doing 20–30 miles per hour and devil take the walker, horse, or family-style biker who gets in the way. Pedestrians hold these facts to be self-evident. Bureaucrats at their desks opening their mouths to let out the moths and checking off on their calendars the days to retirement deny the evidences of the senses of people who *have* sense.

Foot travel is the least-impactful use of a wildland—next to sitting on a log, which is, of course, bettered by not being in the wildland at all. There should be plentiful provision for outdoor gymnasium exercises, such as riding bikes. But not in wilderness, no more than basketball should be played in museums. The in-city and near-city open spaces must be fairly apportioned between the active and the passive, the heavy impact and the low impact.

We do not sanctify the foot. Trail-running is only less objectionable than trail-biking. The runner who hollers out "RUNNER TO YOUR REAR!" in back of a walker is expressing the conviction that fast is superior to slow and has the right-of-way. The reverse is true. The runner encountering a walker should become a walker until well past the "obstruction." Jogging on trails is tolerable only in such times and places as the jogger will not offend the refined sensibilities of walkers who accept that in a time when open space is steadily being shrunk by overpopulation and overspeeding, the civilized person accepts the wisdom of "to make the world larger, go slower."

Finally, we are sentimental but not fanatic Luddites. The 4x4 mud-runner, the motorcycle brush-buster, the fat-tire bomber all may be allotted places in the recreation scheme of things. But they must, each of them, know their places and accept them. Their place is *not* on the trails developed over many generations by and for the foot and the horse. These modes of the past not only have vested historical rights but make such thrifty use of the dwindling continuum of space–time that they have the highest priority for the future. Newer modes, whether motorized or "muscle-powered" (a term employed by hypocritical merchants to salve their consciences, averting eyes from the laws of physics which make the fat-tire bike the most fun when gravity-powered), must establish and pay for their own places, not raid those already owned.

Caution, all! "The wildness within" does not have room for every new use, nor an unlimited amount of every old use. Man is not alone. Wildlife has rights, which must not be infringed. So, too, wild flora. While a justice of the U.S. Supreme Court, William O. Douglas argued that trees should have standing in the courts. In the early 1980s, the Washington Environmental Council filed suit against the state in *Plaintiff Trees;* the trees won a settlement.

To close the circle by repetition, recreation is outranked by re-creation, and both by preservation.

Trails. *True* trails.

Afoot on the Trail

Foot travel includes "walks," short excursions on easy paths in forgiving terrain, requiring no special clothing or equipment and no experience or training, and "hikes," longer and/or rougher, potentially dangerous, demanding stout shoes or boots, clothing for cold and wet weather, gear for routefinding and emergencies, rucksack to carry it all in, and best done in the company of experienced companions or eased into gradually.

Herein are described short walks suitable for a leisurely afternoon or even a spring-summer evening as well as long walks that may keep a person hopping all day. For any walk, equipment demands no more than a passing thought; as for technique, the rule is just to pick 'em up and lay 'em down and look both ways before crossing the street.

Hikes are another matter, and the novice must take care when choosing a trip to be aware of the difference and to make appropriate preparations. The novice should review a general hiking manual, such as *Backpacking: One Step at a Time* (New York: Vintage Books, 1986). On every hike where a shout for help might not bring quick assistance to the lost or injured or ill, each person should carry the Ten Essentials:

1. Extra clothing—enough so that if a sunny-warm morning yields to a rainy-windy afternoon, or if an accident keeps the party out overnight, hypothermia ("exposure" or "freezing to death") will not be a threat.
2. Extra food—enough so something is left over at the planned end of the trip, in case the actual end is the next day.
3. Sunglasses—if travel on snow for more than a few minutes may be involved.
4. Knife—for first aid and emergency firebuilding (making kindling).
5. Firestarter—a candle or chemical fuel for starting a fire with wet wood.
6. First-aid kit.
7. Matches—in a waterproof container.
8. Flashlight—with extra bulb and batteries.
9. Map.
10. Compass.

Managers of the Wildness Within

In the 1950s it became apparent that despite all the pure hearts and good intentions in such federal bureaus as the U.S. Forest Service, a bad apple could corrupt a whole barrel. In 1964 the Congress adopted the Wilderness Act to constrain the freedom of action of the managers of lands designated as National Wilderness. In 1986 the Washington legislature, on the motion of the state Department of Natural Resources, adopted a measure giving very similar protection to those DNR holdings designated as Natural Resources Conservation Areas. King County, having pioneered by creating the Cougar Mountain Regional Wildland Park in 1985 and in 1994 affirming by ordinance its wilderness character, is now being lobbied to adopt a "King County Wilderness Act," or whatever it might be called.

Constraints are essential to prevent a bad apple from obtaining the power of a management position and on her/his personal whim rotting a previously pristine barrel. They also are essential to stiffen the spines of managers and provide them with legal weaponry that they may protect good apples against being rotted from outside the barrel by tunnel-vision citizen groups and the elected officials sufficiently ignorant, stupid, cowardly, or cynical that they couldn't care less. A natural area—the wildness within—must perpetually be defended against soccer fields, bicycle runways, model airplane flyways, skateboard arenas, and (of course) golf courses. These active uses are decent and proper and necessary, but if society is to retain its passive green open spaces, it must reserve them from debates that recur with every new legislative session, every new election. To be sure, legislation never can and never should lock up lands and throw away the key; legislation always is subject to amendment and repeal. However, when a place has been carefully studied and deemed worthy of preserved pristinity, once a legislative body has put the protection in writing any move to open the door to trammeling requires that the citizen-defenders have a solid platform from which to speak.

Cities

A paper written by Benella Caminiti (to whom is dedicated a companion book to this) in 1973 addresses the problems of Seattle Parks. We quote excerpts here as a capsulization of "Generic City." Seattle had in 1973, and has in 1994, excellent people in its Parks Department and on its City Council. But lacking the defense of a Seattle Wilderness Act (or Green and Quiet Place Act?), these fine people will ever have to spend energies fending off very worthy causes which are ever proposed to invade the Green and Quiet. Says Caminiti:

> *City parks are a casualty of our times. Not long ago they were a municipal status symbol, the touch of elegance and beauty that graced a city and softened its stark commercialism ... gave relief from the alienating environment that was too full of people and cement artifice....*
>
> *Dedicated park land is continually eroded to other uses. Park boards and departments are forgetful of the unique value of open spaces to the mental and physical health of people.... Special inter-*

est lobbies view open space in the public domain as freely available for building. Sports enthusiasts obtain it for their exclusive needs.... Cultural lobbies have no compunctions about using it.... Highway departments incline to the view that park land was uniquely preserved as roadbeds ... for those fleeing a degraded city....

Land needs for recreation, education and cultural interests can be met, but this must no longer be at the expense of parks. A city without greenspace and trees is a utilitarian antheap, undeserving of the pride and loyalty of its citizens which is the bond of civilization....

Dedicated park land is and has been expropriated to other uses, subject almost daily to erosion for sewage treatment plants, highway rights-of-way, police pistol ranges, park department utility works and buildings, art museums, aquaria, zoo expansions.... Parks are of many kinds, from playlots to large urban wooded areas, and it is the latter type that is in the most hazard.... It is obvious that park land need not be the site of many special facilities. Art museums, swimming pools, theaters, etc., can and must be on other land, especially as their purpose is primarily an indoor activity.

An "arboretum" can only be an outdoor facility. Ideally every park should be an arboretum, a place where trees can grow to maturity, where visual beauty is a concern of the responsible Park Department....

Counties

In 1973, while revising the introduction to the fourth edition of Janice's *Footloose,* I wrote the manager of King County Parks to enquire about trails planned for "the wildness within." No answer. Perhaps because he was busy dealing with press allegations that Parks personnel were mowing his lawn and weeding his garden. In 1976 I dialed the Parks number to find what was new, doubting anything was. Upon uttering "trails" I was instantly switchboarded to "the trails person," who still is that in 1994, and no longer the anomaly he used to be amid playgrounders and picnic-tablers.

The horizons of the agency, extended by the voters' approval of the Forward Thrust bond issue, have continued to be enlarged. Granted, the visions are not always entirely clear and in some cases what a citizen sees prove to be mirages. The King County Trails Plan that so thrilled me in the 1970s threw off its mask in the 1980s and revealed itself as a Bikeways Plan. A splendid plan for a very worthy means of non-polluting transportation. So sexy it has captured the public heart, and what passes for the public mind (the press, that is). The pedestrian, however, is chagrined to be forward-thrusted off the Burke-Gilman "Trail." He mourns the peace and quiet in the tranquil days of the locomotives. While never wavering in his support of the "Rails to Trails" campaign he resents being deluded, tricked, bamboozled.

The transition from a narrow old focus on bawfields and privies has been symbolized and expressed by Cougar Mountain. Randy Revelle was elected King County Executive on a platform featuring a regional park there, a citizens committee endorsed boundaries as proposed by the Issaquah Alps Trails Club, the King County Council adopted the plan—but with an amendment to run a freeway through the wildland! Revelle's veto opened negotiations that culminated in an imperfect but acceptable ordinance. The King County Council and Executive joined in celebrating the wildland. But not the "old jockstrap" cabal in Parks. Their opinion was bluntly stated by the senior staffer who brayed that he never would set foot in "that g.d. pile of brush." The King County Parks manager of the time was browbeaten to put bicycles on the trails, tried to do so, was prevented, and resigned "to seek other employment opportunities." His successor used funds budgeted for trails to convert a trail to a truck road nobody wanted, except the jockeys eager to flex their bulldozers, and responded to complaints by declaring that her top aides had unanimously agreed "the Cougar Mountain Regional Wildland Park is not a wildland." She, too, resigned to seek other opportunities.

The soul of King County Parks seems to have been born again, as evidenced by its vigorous and successful defense of the Cougar Mountain "wildness within." However, as a public agency it cannot be neglected, lest it relapse to old sinning ways. That's precisely why the many excellent folk there (and the less excellent, too) urgently need the King County Council to devise legislation to protect them from doing wrong and to guide them to the right.

The same is true in other counties.

State Parks

Testifying before a legislative committee in 1993 in support of a bill to require Washington State Parks to be subjected to close legislative oversight, I cited a number of gross errors by the agency in recent years. The field staff were, in my experience, good to superb. Yet much had gone wrong. Too much.

After the committee hearing, the new director, Cleve Pinnix, who had attended to testify in opposition to the bill, waylaid me in the corridor to convey the hope I would judge State Parks not on the past but the future. In a December 1993 letter, speaking of State Parks and the pedestrian, he looked ahead to the future for trail-walking he had in mind.

If you asked most hikers to tell you about their favorite trail, my guess is you would generally have descriptions of some of the spectacular destination trails we are fortunate to have here in the Pacific Northwest ... most of the trails in the State Parks system probably would not show up on many of those lists of superlatives. The state parks, by their nature, are smaller protected areas generally located closer to population centers and on a scale that lends itself to walking and short hikes, not extended backpacking opportunities.

That proximity to people and easy accessibility during all seasons, however, makes state parks trails a wonderful opportunity for introducing people of all ages to an appreciation of the natural world.

My guess is that most of us who count ourselves as hikers were introduced to the pleasures of the trail at a young age. We learned something on those early outings about the wonder of the natural world, about the opportunities of discovery around every bend of a new path not yet taken, and about the satisfaction of ending the day tired and a bit footsore, but satisfied that a new trail had been explored. Those early experiences, I believe, are important to stimulate the interest that later leads us to become avid hikers or backpackers or even mountaineers. With that affinity for the walking trail in place, the opportunities for trails to challenge our bodies and stimulate our minds are practically unlimited....

The great value I see in our state parks walking trails is their variety and accessibility to people throughout the state. Our state parks are windows to the natural world located close to home and waiting for us to discover. The walking trails in state parks are chances to study botany, to bird watch, to appreciate geology, and to discover the vast array of subjects that the natural world encompasses.

The trails in the state parks are, for the most part, walking more than hiking trails. They represent an opportunity for young and old to experience the natural world close at hand, to slow down from the frenetic pace of an increasingly urban culture, and to trade the complexity of modern life for the simple joy of a walk in the forest. They are a gateway to the larger natural world that awaits all walkers and hikers.... What best characterizes these state parks trails in just the Puget Sound vicinity is their diversity. The trails offer a wide variety of experiences and landscape forms for the walker to appreciate. Best of all, they represent nearby and easily accessible opportunities to slow down, to reconnect with the natural world, and to appreciate the simple joy that even a short walk on an easy trail can bring.

In the wide spectrum that trail-related recreation experiences cover, State Parks' particular contribution can be a place where the walker can experience the natural world not far from home....

Pinnix spreaks well. The proof of the pudding, of course, is in the eating. The 1993 bill was defeated. Gross abuses committed since the bad past gave way to his good future have made painfully evident, at this writing, in 1994, that past malpractice is deeply entrenched in State Parks. When *will* the future be born?

Department of Natural Resources

As manager of lands granted the new state from the federal domain in 1889, and those taken by counties for non-payment of taxes, and others obtained by purchase or exchange, the Department of Natural Resources has enormous potential for nourishing biocentric kindness. Until 1980, however, though always having among its staff as firm friends of the land as could be wanted, it was on balance as ugly a servant of kinetic egotism, as wicked an anthropocentric enemy of Nature, as could be conjured up in a nightmare. The 1980 election brought a complete reversal. Under a new sort of leadership confirmed by the voters in three subsequent elections, holdover personnel have displayed unsuspected qualities repressed by previous department policy. New recruits have met the new standards. The DNR has been transformed from the worst into what is in much opinion the best manager going of "the wildness within."

This volume submits in evidence the Tiger Mountain State Forest and its subunit, the West Tiger Mountain Natural Resources Conservation Area.

To be sure, sins of the past by no means have been fully redeemed. By 1980 the decades of laissez faire mismanagement had vested abuses so deeply in the agency fabric that three-and-a-half terms of two State Land Commissioners have not been enough to sweep clean these Augean stables. The Capitol State Forest and Tahuya State Forest are two Tiger Mountain State Forests waiting to happen. But so far haven't. In this volume we have whittled their space allotments to little more than mentions, fingers tightly holding nostrils shut against the stench.

Cheerfully to report, in 1993 State Land Commissioner Jennifer M. Belcher was provoked by the "escalation of illegal activity on state-owned lands, a symptom of population growth," into issuing a "declaration of war." At her request, the legislature passed a measure to collect up to triple damages from anyone who knowingly trespasses, damages, or wastes state-owned lands and funded the hiring of investigators to control abuses of state-owned resources.

Private

Another oxymoron: "private forests." There can be no such thing, not on the scale of the corporate tree "farms." Gifford Pinchot, founder of the U.S. Forest Service, insisted that Nature's woodland bounty was the business not of bottom-line free enterprise but the "long run" of the nation. The Barbecuer Congress vetoed.

As this century ends, the Privatizers are under attack from an older strategy than Pinchot's. The Public Trust Doctrine, a tenet of the common law dating to the Magna Carta and the Code of Justinian and beyond in the dim past, says that where lands or waters are important to the whole human community, it is the responsibility and duty of public officials to look after the public interests in *all* lands and waters, public *and* "private." Corporate-scale forests can no more be "private" than can rivers and seashores, wetlands and wildlife, the sky. Two 1987 decisions by the Washington State Supreme Court acknowledged the Public Trust Doctrine as the law of Washington State, exceptionally powerful law because it is not legislative but quasi-constitutional. The PTD presently is being rescued from obscurity to a prominence that frightens the Privatizers

Mount Rainier from the shoulder of Three Sisters. Pitcher Mountain at right (Page 173)

as badly as a policeman does a robber coming out the door of a bank with a sackful of cash. The issues on which it currently centers are those of rivers, beaches, and wetlands. We predict that in the coming half-century it will be firmly established in the forests, receiving strong support in the public mind by broader knowledge of the Northern Pacific Land Grant and other Barbecuer thefts, explaining how the forests became "private" in the first place, and how recently, within the memory of the grandfathers of the current heirs of the loot. When the camera of history catches the robber with gun in hand, scooping up the cash, look out robber! Make a run for it, Privatizer!

Maps to Tie the Land Together

The aim of our guidebooks is to teach a person how to tie the land together with his/her feet and eyes. Maps are valuable aids.

For each section the contour maps are noted. The U.S. Geological Survey (USGS) maps are the basics. Better for the hiker, where available, are the Green Trails maps; the private publisher puts green overprints on USGS base maps to show current roads and trails, the data updated every other year. Look for the Green Trails key map displayed in any map shop.

Robert Kinzebach publishes *Pic-Tour Guide Maps,* aerial photos and USGS sheets with the findings of his personal explorations overprinted.

For broad orientation, pictorial landform maps are superb. *Puget Sound Region, Washington,* by Dee Molenaar, was designed and produced specifically at the request of this surveyor to cover the area from the Olympics to the Cascades, Canada to Chehalis, permitting the hiker to be related at all times to all horizons. Particularly helpful is a condensed textbook on the flip side, a history of the geologic structures and the Pleistocene glaciers; the pictorial map of the maximum extent of the Puget Lobe of the Cordilleran Ice Sheet explains innumerable terrain features that baffle the uninformed eye.

Richard Pargeter has two similar maps of somewhat different coverage. *The Puget Sound Country: A View from the Northwest* and *Washington's Northwest Passage: A View from the Southwest* cover most of the trail country in this book.

Litter and Garbage and Sanitation

If you can carry it in full, you can carry it out empty. Take back to the car every can, foilwrap, and orange peel.

Never bury garbage. If fresh, animals will dig it up and scatter the remnants. Burning before burying is no answer either. Tin cans take as long as 40 years to disintegrate completely; aluminum and glass last for centuries. Further, digging pits to bury junk disturbs the ground cover, and iron eventually leaches from buried cans and "rusts" springs and creeks.

Keep the water pure. Don't wash dishes in streams or lakes, loosing food particles and detergent. Haul buckets of water off to the woods or rocks and wash and rinse there.

Eliminate body wastes in places well removed from watercourses; first dig a shallow hole in the "biological disposer layer," then touch a match to the toilet paper (but not in forests in fire season!)—better, use leaves—and finally cover the evidence. So managed, the wastes are consumed in a matter of days. Where privies are provided, use them. On more and more trails, the rule is to carry a double bag and transport your solid wastes out of the wildlands. Distasteful? In crowded wildlands lacking privies, view the alternative.

Water

A word to the wise: For a day hike, fill your canteens at home and give the matter no further thought.

In the late 1970s began a great epidemic of giardiasis, caused by a vicious little parasite that spends part of its life cycle swimming free in water and part in the intestinal tract of beavers and other wildlife, dogs, and people. Actually, the "epidemic" was solely in the press; *Giardia* were first identified in the eighteenth century and are present in the public water systems of many cities of the world and many towns in America—including some in the foothills of the Cascades. Long before the "outbreak" of "beaver fever," there was the well-known malady, the "Boy Scout trots," which in the era of foreign travel became the "Aztec two-step" and "the revenge of the Pharaohs." This is not to make light of the disease; though most humans feel no ill effects (but become carriers), others have symptoms that include devastating diarrhea; the treatment is nearly as unpleasant. The reason giardiasis has become "epidemic" is that there are more people in the backcountry—more people drinking water contaminated by animals—more people contaminating the water.

Whenever in doubt, boil the water 10 minutes. Keep in mind that *Giardia* can survive in water at or near freezing for weeks or months—a snow pond is not necessarily safe. Boiling is 100 percent effective against not only *Giardia* but the myriad other filthy little blighters that may upset your digestion or—as with some forms of hepatitis—destroy your liver. *If you cannot boil* (as who can or wants to on a day hike), use one of the several iodine treatments (chlorine compounds have been found untrustworthy in wildland circumstances), such as Potable Aqua or the more complicated method that employs iodine crystals. Rumor to the contrary, iodine treatments pose no threat to the health. Be very wary of the filters sold in backpacking shops: don't bet your liver on a manufacturer's "guarantees."

Theft

Equipment has become so fancy and expensive, and hikers so numerous, that theft is a growing trailhead industry. Not even backcountry camps are entirely safe, but the professionals concentrate on cars. Rangers have the following recommendations.

Don't make crime profitable. If the pros break into a hundred cars and get nothing but moldy boots and tattered T-shirts they'll go straight. The best bet is to arrive in a beat-up 1960 car with doors and windows that don't close and leave in it nothing of value. If you insist on driving a nice new car, at least don't have mag wheels, tape deck, and radio, and keep it empty of gear. Don't think locks help—pros can open your car door and trunk as fast with a picklock as you can with your key. Don't imagine you can hide anything from them—they know all the hiding spots.

Be suspicious of anyone loitering at a trailhead. One of the tricks of the trade is to sit there with a pack as if waiting for a ride, watching new arrivals unpack—and hide their valuables—and maybe even striking up a conversation to determine how long the marks will be away.

The ultimate solution, of course, is for hikers to become as poor as they were in the olden days. No criminal would consider trailheads profitable if the loot consisted solely of shabby khaki war surplus.

About This Book

The order of presentation of trips in this book is based on Seattle as ground zero. First, the city itself and then the overlake suburbs-citylets.

Next, the Issaquah Alps, which offer more close-to-city wildland pedestrianism than any other piece of Washington geography. The text then moves south, organized by rivers from Cedar to Nisqually, concluding with a quick glance at the southern frontier of Whulge Country. Rewinding back to Seattle, another quick glance is taken west to the Kitsap and Olympic Peninsulas. Finally, the rivers north from Skykomish to Skagit. As noted elsewhere in this Introduction, the density of trips directly reflects the density of population. It also reflects the distance from ground zero; we have much to say about Bellevue, little about Bellingham, nothing about Tenino. The local patriot may take umbrage at the short shrift given such major population centers as Seattle and Tacoma; we refer you, dear patriot, to the companion guidebook to beaches, where lie most of the great walking to be found in the shore cities.

Facts and figures that allow the reader to choose the hike suiting his/her needs and desires of the moment are not, in this book, separated out from the text, but slipped into the trip description, where they are easy to find, and/or spelled out in the trip heading. The "hikable" season is almost in every case the year around. The "high point" and "elevation gain" are usually of minor significance; where not, we are careful to give them, and also to suggest "hiking time" and "round trip," where those affect the choice. The trips in this book are very largely *walks,* dealing not in thousands of feet and many many hours (and backpacking so rarely that even where legal we don't feature the possibility) that the data would be a super-abundance of minutiae.

The driving directions vary from the space-saving short form, expecting the reader to be able to read, and to own, a highway map, to the very detailed (and guaranteed accurate at time of surveying) guidance to obscure, unsigned trailheads. The maps in this book are often extremely helpful supplements to the text.

Buses. Public transit. There is—there *must* be—the future of pedestrian re-creation, or much of it, in urban-suburban areas. But the future is not yet. To be sure, "wilderness on the Metro 210" is more than a slogan, it is a reality, and a main reason the Issaquah Alps will remain popular—and gain fame—as the heart of wildland pedestrianism for four counties even after gridlock has made highway travel as punishing and undependable as I-5, I-90, and I-405 at commute time on a dark and stormy night. The surveyors have delighted in taking one-way walks from Gasworks Park to Bothell, Issaquah to Snoqualmie, and Green Lake to Seward Park, whisked back to square one by bus. Such ingenuities will multiply and flourish.

However, the traveler who trusts this guidebook for precise bus information is going to be sorry, then angry (at us). Where bus service presently exists, the option is promoted by citing a route number. But do not rely for such information on a book that is revised only every several years. The bus situation is too fluid. Routes are added and revised annually. To catch a bus, call your local bus company for up-to-date routes and times of service. Which company do you call? Well, if in King County, Metro. Tacoma, Everett ... we assume nobody in, say, Bellingham will try to catch a Kitsap County bus down the street from his/her house. In these pages we don't note the applicable company because in any community the service is a monopoly and the sole provider is listed in the local phone book. No book of this sort can get into the matter without being so overspecific as to be fake-definitive. We discovered that harsh reality long ago, when we carefully consulted the Metro expert, published a book, and hot off our guidebook press came hot off their schedule press new numbers and hours which did naught for our readers but infuriate them, our book being so wrong, so wrong, so wrong.

By all means, check out the buses. Get your facts straight from the horse's mouth. Here we can do little more than point you in that direction.

Harvey Manning

Harvey Manning
(Elder Surveyor)
June 1994

A Note About Safety

Safety is an important concern in all outdoor activities. No guidebook can alert you to every hazard or anticipate the limitations of every reader. Therefore, the descriptions of roads, trails, routes, and natural features in this book are not representations that a particular place or excursion will be safe for your party. When you follow any of the routes described in this book, you assume responsibility for your own safety. Under normal conditions, such excursions require the usual attention to traffic, road and trail conditions, weather, terrain, the capabilities of your party, and other factors. Because many of the lands in this book are subject to development and/or change of ownership, conditions may have changed since this book was written that make your use of some of these routes unwise. Always check for current conditions, obey posted private property signs, and avoid confrontations with property owners or managers. Keeping informed on current conditions and exercising common sense are the keys to a safe, enjoyable outing.

The Mountaineers

Madison Park and Lake Washington

THE WESTERN MORAINE: SEATTLE

In 1884 the Seattle park system was founded upon a donation of 5 acres by David and Louise Denny. "Park" then, and for years after, meant lawns and gardens for strolling, benches for sitting, always dressed in Sunday best. There wasn't much call for "walking," not in an era when everybody got enough of *that* on the way to catch the streetcar or steamer, nor for preserves of "wilderness," when plenty of *that* lay at the ends of streetcar lines and handy to steamer docks across the water.

"Trolley car parks" became popular for picnic socials of schools, Swedes, and refugees from North Dakota. "Electric parks" dated from the Midway at the 1893 Chicago World's Fair and by World War I drew throngs of fun-seekers to be dazzled and thrilled. Luna Park was near Alki Point and White City Amusement Park adjoined Madrona Park, which with Leschi Park was owned by the Seattle Electric Company until Seattle acquired the streetcars and with them the parks.

In the 1890s the bicycle craze swept across America; Seattle's street engineer, George Cotterill, responded with a system of bike paths. Whether the machine was built for two or one, Daisy did indeed look sweet upon the seat. Every fine Sunday was a Bicycle Sunday for young and old. Starting from Cotterill's system, in 1903 John and Frederick Olmsted, sons of the Frederick Law Olmsted who designed New York's Central Park, proposed a network of scenic boulevards, "emerald necklaces strung with play-grounds and parks" within a half-mile of every residence in the city. "An ideal system," they told the City Council, "would involve taking all the borders of the different bodies of water, except such as are needed for commerce, and (enlarging) these fringes ... so as to include considerable bodies of woodland as well as some fairly level land, which can be cleared and covered with grass for field sports and for the enjoyment of meadow scenery." In the Olmsted philosophy, "Civilization can't thrive in the absence of fresh air and green, open spaces" that preserve the "good and wholesome" environment of the country within the city. Far from being frivolities and luxuries, urban parks are essential to keep cities civil and humane, to keep them livable.

Extension of city trolley lines created the "interurbans" and, with them, the distant recreation sites of "trolley car tourism." But then, as the adolescent city grew toward an adulthood of green ganglia threading through a flesh of residential and commercial wood and brick and concrete, there slithered into incipient Eden the serpent—or better say, bounced and honked and backfired, disguised as the Tin Lizzie, the Merry Oldsmobile, the Buick and Plymouth and Chevy. The "tin can tourists" converted wagon roads to highways. The Sunday walk in the park and bike along the boulevard yielded to the drive in the country. Picnics shifted to Lake Wilderness and Lake Serene, Flaming Geyser and Green River Gorge, Snoqualmie Falls and Maloney's Grove, and—incredibly to those who in less than a decade lived from Model T to Model A to V-8—Paradise Valley.

A glorious party it was, it was, a stupendous half-century binge. Then Seattle awoke. With a terrible hangover. The jug of cheap gas was empty. The nearby countryside had been filled overnight by new cities. The farther countryside was receding behind freeways clogged by mobs of cars, the emerging nightmare of gridlock. For quick and easy getaways, Seattle of 1970 had to stay home—in a park system admirably suited to 1910.

In the 1960s a civic realization dawned that R. H. Thomson, revered as "Seattle's Engineer," was the Great Beast who had stolen Seattle's soul. In 1968 a Great Awakening of born-again Olmsteders approved King County's Forward Thrust, a bond issue to provide funds for parks. In 1972 the Army, short of ready cash to fight the war in Southeast Asia, dumped surplus land which was snapped up to become Discovery Park. In 1977 the Navy similarly unloaded what became Sand Point Park. Also in the 1970s, Burlington-Northern abandoned a rail line which became one of the most-used urban trails in the nation, the Burke-Gilman.

All in all, it was a decade that pious Greens cherish as the Second Coming of the Olmsteds. To a chorus of praising and clapping, in 1977 an Urban Greenbelt Plan was adopted by the Seattle City Council. But there then sprang up from a lurking in dark slimes of the human spirit the Serpent God, and it was déjà vu all over again.

Not quite. Some civic leaders had learned a lesson and taken it to heart. When in 1979 the original proposal was made for what became the Cougar Mountain Regional Wildland Park, "wilderness on the Metro 210," the first government official to publicly express support was the Mayor of Seattle.

USGS maps: Edmonds East, Seattle North, Kirkland, Shilshole Bay, Seattle South, Mercer Island

Olmsted Way

To New York City, "Olmsted" means Central Park, and to the nation, the National Park Act, and to Seattle, the Lake Washington Boulevard, the grand entrance to the Alaska-Yukon-Pacific Exposition staged in 1909 on the University of Washington campus. The 1916 lowering by 10 feet of Lake Washington, preparatory to the next year's opening of the Lake Washington Ship Canal, added a strip of new lakeshore land, as had the 1911 lowering of Green Lake for no good reason except to make new land.

The Seattle citizen who wishes to know his/her city in the intimate way never possible atop or within a machine ought at least once to do the whole 18½ Olmsted miles at a single go. Thus the eyes feel through the feet the connectedness of kempt lawns, wild marsh, an arboretum of native and exotic plants, a forest, and three lakes.

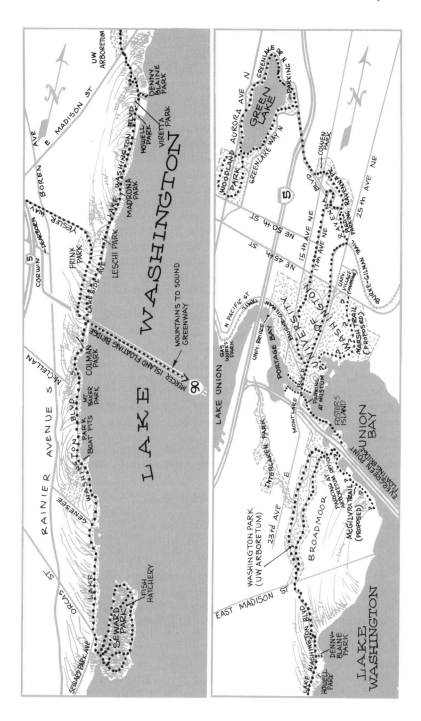

Leave the car at East Green Lake. Ride three buses, one at a time, to Seward Park. Walk back to Green Lake, sustained in rain or blisters by knowing that ever close by to abbreviate the 18½ miles is Metro.

Seward Park, round trips 4½ miles

Bus: 39

Park at the entrance, just off the boulevard at Juneau.

The Olmsted Way, done scrupulously, begins by looping around Bailey Peninsula, formerly an island. Fish hatchery, fishing piers, bathing beaches, and views to Rainier.

Lake Washington's trough was gouged by the Canadian glacier which on the most recent of several visits arrived hereabouts some 15,000 years ago and left 13,500 years ago, at the Seattle-area maximum heaping 4000 feet thick. The lake's greatest depth is 205–210 feet. The water level ranges between 20.00 and 21.85 feet above the mean low tide of the saltwater. Primevally, the lake's sole major tributary was the Sammamish River, though in flood time some of the Cedar River spilled in through the marshes. The outlet was the Black River, which joined the Cedar River in the Renton vicinity to enter the Green River, the union of waters changing name to Duwamish River for the final stretch to Elliott Bay. To keep floodwaters of the Cedar from drowning cows in Allentown and Georgetown, the stream was diverted into Lake Washington, becoming its second major tributary and its only source of pure high-Cascades water, worth billions of dollars in the values thus preserved of lakeshore real estate. Metro's good deed of shunting sewage from the lake deserves only half the credit for keeping the shore suitable for trophy homes; forgotten when the medals are issued are the cow-milkers of Allentown and clean waters of the Cedar.

The lakeshore is the number-two attraction of 278-acre Seward Park. Number one is the path through Seattle's largest ancient forest, close to 1 mile in length and averaging ¼ mile wide.

Washington Park Arboretum, round trip 1 mile or 4

Bus: 4, 11, 48

Park at Madison Playground, along the boulevard or Upper Road, or at the north Broadmoor entrance.

The 7-odd miles north from Seward Park connect a string of parks. Madison, Leschi, and Madrona were emplaced in the early 1890s to stimulate purchase of adjoining lots platted by street-railway companies. The Olmsted Plan added Mt. Baker, Colman, and Frink. But what's in so many names? They're all one. Leschi was, prior to the semi–Floating Bridge, the landing for ferries to Mercer Island and Bellevue, close by the terminus of the cablecar over the hill from Yesler Way. Trails climb the wildwoods past mysterious bulks of ancient concrete. A springtime glory of rhododendron blooms in a plantation long since gone wild, and very nicely so.

The Mountain-to-Sound Greenway crosses the Big Water via I-90. The Olmsted proceeds through Howell, Viretta, and Denny-Blaine Parks to the University of Washington Arboretum in 200-acre Washington Park, thousands of trees and shrubs from the world over, artful landscaping of ridges and valleys, marshes and ponds and creeks. The Arboretum needs to be visited plant by plant, one end to the other, along Lake Washington Boulevard, Arboretum Drive (Upper Road) on the ridge east of the valley, and valley-bottom Azalea Way. When these tours are finished it's another season and the whole job has to be done over.

Foster's Island–Waterfront Trail–Montlake Bridge, one way 1½ miles

Park at the north Broadmoor entrance or the Museum of History and Industry.

The Evergreen Point (Albert D. Rosellini) Floating (for now) Bridge and its plotted connections to a chimerical R. H. Thomson Expressway ripped off a fifth of the Arboretum-that-used-to-be, brutalized Foster's Island, drearied the marshes of Union Bay. The havoc would have been worse had not the Save the

Canoeing in an Arboretum waterway

Arboretum campaign of the early 1960s driven a stake through the heart of Seattle's Quintessential Engineer, a man high on the dishonor rolls of the city's Hall of Shame for flushing Denny Hill into Elliott Bay and ramming a sewer through Magnolia Bluff to West Point.

From the north Broadmoor parking lot the path crosses a slough to Foster's Island. Groves of water-loving trees. Sails on Union Bay. The Cascade horizon. From the island the Waterfront Trail crosses a marsh that is not primeval, formed as it was after the lake was lowered. "Never mind," says the wildlife, "It *feels* primeval." Cottonwoods and willows, cattails and horsetails and bulrushes. Mammals from mice to muskrats. Beavers with a tooth out for tender young saplings. An estimated 100,000 birds a year, visiting or nesting or miscegenating. Partly a floating walkway, partly a spongy lane of cedar chips atop floating mats of peat, the route weaves out through head-high thickets of hardhack to what would be open water were it not for lily pads, passes observation platforms and benches for sitting and reflecting. Jogging is banned; the posted speed limit is 1 mile per hour. The Waterfront Trail ends at the Museum of History and Industry, to which the city sacrificed a delicious little park in precisely a spot that cried out most pitiably for a delicious little park.

The walking continues without a break on the Lake Washington Ship Canal Waterside Trail, which rounds the corner to Montlake Cut, connecting Union Bay of Lake Washington to Portage Bay of Lake Union. Before climbing steps to picturesque Montlake Bridge, built in 1925 and doing a nice job even now in humbling hasty hordes of automobiles, sidetrip ¼ mile west to a parklet at the end of the cut. Fine view over the Seattle Yacht Club to Lake Union. The lake's maximum depth is 50 feet. Due to filling and building, its area is only half the primeval, and half of that is covered with boats and houseboats and other Privatizers of the Public domain.

University of Washington Campus, round trip 4 years

Bus: many

Fee parking on campus.

Pause while crossing the Montlake Bridge to muse. Primevally, the marshes of Union Bay seeped water to Portage Bay. In 1861 Mr. Harvey I. Pike set to work with pick, shovel, and wheelbarrow to dig a ditch joining the lakes. There wasn't much call for it at the time. However, in 1883 Messrs. Denny, Burke, & Company hired Chinese laborers to deepen the channel to float sawmill-bound logs through the marsh to a flume emptying into Portage Bay. In 1899 a band of farmers dynamited the canal, hoping to lower Lake Washington in a "whoosh!" and save their pastures from spring floods of the Black and Cedar. In 1916 the U.S. Army completed the task begun by Pike, though the Montlake Cut wasn't tidied up until 1921.

Before proceeding to the central campus, sidetrip from the bridge along the waterside path, an extension of the Arboretum Trail designed to give close but respectful views of wildlife. When Lake Washington was lowered, 610 acres of Union Bay became marsh. For decades Seattle dumped and burned household garbage here, the University complacently expecting to ultimately gain a new East Campus. The 1960s discovery that the garbage and underlying peat would be generating methane gas for many centuries to come, making any structure a potential bomb, forced the former lake/marsh to be permanently dedicated to parking lots. An outer 55 acres, though, was preserved from blacktop as the Center for Urban Horticulture. About 20 acres are gardens, research plots, and (well-ventilated) greenhouses and classrooms. The rest is a pond-studded grassland fringed by marsh, a permanent refuge for travelers on foot or wing.

The central campus is worth a few hours or years. Time lacking, the quickest way to Ravenna Park is 1½ miles on the Burke-Gilman Trail (*sic*) to Ravenna Playground.

Ravenna Park, one way 1 mile

Bus: 7, 8

Park on streets or at Ravenna Playground.

Cars cross the bridge and never know the park is in the gulch beneath. A walker in the gulch, beside the creek under the big firs and maples, scarcely is aware of the tumult above. In the late 1880s Reverend and Mrs. William W. Beck bought the ravine and nurtured a park named for the town in Italy which was the final home of Dante. Ravenna Creek then was a large stream, full of trout, flowing in the open from Green Lake to Lake Washington. The Becks built paths, waterfalls, a music pavilion. In 1902 the 25-cent admission fee was gladly paid by 10,000 visitors. The Becks named ancient Douglas firs in honor of Paderewski and assorted local politicians. The tallest, some 400 feet, was Robert E. Lee. The one with the largest girth was Teddy Roosevelt, who on a visit affirmed it was, indeed, a "big stick."

In 1911 Seattle acquired the park by condemnation in order to condemn Ravenna Creek to the nether regions of Thomson's North Trunk Sewer. Clarence Bagley's 1929 history described the park as a "dark, dank, dismal hole in the ground." In the 1930s the city logged the park. The site of the Roosevelt Tree is now a tennis court.

Even so, the trees not mill-worthy in the timber-glutted 1930s are now 60 years closer to ancience and the ravine has quite a virgin-forest look. The Ravenna Creek Alliance proposes to daylight the creek, resurrecting it from the depths to again flow in the open to Lake Washington. Why not? Birds don't fly through sewers.

Green Lake, circuit 3 miles

Bus: many

Park anywhere around the shore, except on sunny Sundays.

At the urging of W. D. Wood, a settler-promoter who in the 1890s had joined two companions in building the Green Lake Circle Railroad loop around the lake and up from the Fremont streetcar line, in 1911 Seattle purchased Green Lake and lowered it 7 feet to expose hundreds of acres for use as park, streets, and sundry civic purposes. More of the lake was destroyed by filling, the last of the dirt coming in 1932 from the big ditch dug for Aurora Avenue through Woodland Park. Now a mere 260 acres, the lake has a maximum depth of 29 feet and is in so advanced a state of eutrophication that at any season after early summer and before the fall rains, swimmers routinely contract the "Green Lake crud." Seattle City Water used to help keep the lake clean by flushing in surplus drinking water; nowadays, though, there isn't much surplus. Walkers are safe so long as they don't touch the water.

The attractions of Green Lake (lawns and trees, views of surrounding ridges and Rainier, mobs of resident and migratory waterfowl, who have their own sanctuary, Swan or Duck Island) need little praise. On a single

Green Lake's multiple-use trail

summer day as many as 10,000 people visit the park and as many as 1000 an hour take to the paths—the 2.8-mile interior path (10 feet wide) near the shore and the 3.2-mile outer path near the streets. Some 29 percent walk, 26 percent rollerskate, 46 percent bicycle or jog or run. There also are skateboards and baby strollers, and, as fast as they burst from the fevered imaginations of diseased chimpanzees, every other wheeled device that serves as an argument for nuclear winter.

Fewer pedestrians come to walk the trail than to sit in a safe refuge and, as at a hockey game, enjoy the Sabbath violence. One is reminded of New York's Central Park, which until assignment of police reinforcements was a charming springtime spot to watch the young lovers mugging the old lovers. The time for serenity at Green Lake is in a misty dawn, alone.

Woodland Park, perimeter loop 2 miles

Bus: many

Parking all along Phinney Avenue.

Adjacency to parks sold building lots. Thus, in 1891, developer Guy Carleton Phinney built a hotel, dance pavilion, boathouse (on Green Lake), shooting lodge, and woodland trails affordable by folks unable to go on safari with The Mountaineers—"wilderness on the trolley line"—the Green Lake Electric Railway (the Olmsteds hated it).

In 1899 Seattle bought the park and civilized it with rose gardens, a zoo, playfields, picnic tables, and, eventually and temporarily, a campground for tin-can tourists. In 1932 a swath of ancient forest, then Seattle's largest, was clearcut and a ditch dug for "The Great Aurora Highway," so named perhaps because its ultimate goal was not Everett but the Aurora Borealis. As still another argument for the coming dominion of the sludgeworms, on May 14, 1933, the masses turned out with flags and orations and whistles to cheer the grand opening. What did commuters gain in addition to saving 1000 feet of driving the park-skirting alternative proposed by the Olmsteds? Editorialized the *Seattle Times,* "A reminder at least twice a day that you sacrificed Woodland Park."

The bifurcated remnant teaches us that the evil done by engineers lives after them. Yet at certain hours of certain days of certain seasons the park, among Seattle's largest, can give miles of lonesome strolling. The elder surveyor's favorite used to be the middle of a heavily snowing night.

Burke-Gilman Once and Future Trail

Bus: 17 and 43 at Chittenden Locks; 15, 17, 18, and 43 in Ballard; 26 and 28 at Fremont; a dozen lines in the University District; 30 in Laurelhurst; 8 and 41 on Sand Point Way; 25 on 37 Avenue NE; 307 on Bothell Way; many lines in Bothell

A coalition of walkers and bikers, the Seattle and King County Parks Departments, and the University of Washington created one of America's great urban trails, traversing scenes industrial, marine, commercial, academic, residential, and natural, in views over Salmon Bay and Lake Union to downtown Seattle, over Lake Washington to the Cascades. The 19-mile (ultimate) length is intended as the central artery of the non-motorized transportation system of Puget Sound City, linking the Whulge Trail, Olmsted Trail, Tolt Pipeline Trail, Sammamish River Trail, and sidetrails. Sadly, history teaches that two goods do not necessarily make a better, indeed may make a bad. The elder surveyor of this guidebook regularly walked the route on his way from a room in an old millworkers' lodging house to University classrooms, on the way home picking up spilled coal for his cookstove. Trains and hoboes amicably shared the railroad with students. Years later he supported the trail coalition, most importantly by stimulating Janice Krenmayr to walk the ties for her *Footloose Around Puget Sound.* When Janice moved on to other enterprises, bequeathing her legacy to the surveyor, he walked out the full length himself and publicly pronounced it an inspiration for the nation.

And so it was, and so it can be again, but at this writing it doesn't deserve space in a walker's book except as a warning. Gresham's Law: "Bad money drives good out of the market." The Burke-Gilman Law: "Wheels drive out feet." The trail must be reclaimed by separating the footway from the bikeway, policing the footway to exclude all wheels of whatever sort, the bikeway to enforce a speed limit that prevents testosterone-poisoned racers from bullying the easy riders, the peaceable families.

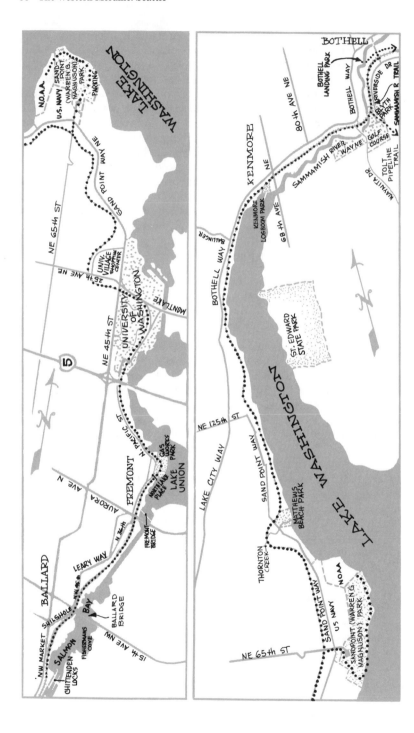

In the interim, those pedestrians refusing to bow to tyranny are advised to equip themselves with a Colin Fletcher–style staff, 6 feet long and 1 inch or more in diameter, and when in traffic to carry it in a horizontal, cross-body position. Known of old as a quarterstaff, poor man's substitute for a sword, the implement served Little John and Friar Tuck well during altercations with surly wretches serving the Sheriff of Nottingham.

When Judge Thomas Burke and Daniel Gilman and fellow town-boomers set out in 1885 to build the Seattle, Lake Shore & Eastern Railroad, their scheme was to outwit the Eastern robber barons who controlled the American transcontinental railway lines by an end run to the East via the Canadian transcontinental. After appropriate chicanery on both sides, the locals and the Easterners struck a deal by which they both got rich(er) and the public got hornswoggled (again). In the 1970s the transportation business became too much bother for the "railroad" companies which were logging, mining, and subdividing their land-grant swag; the Burlington-Northern, mergerized hybrid of a century of Wall Street bamboozles, abandoned the Burke-Gilman line. The hiker-biker coalition succeeded in wresting it from the talons of wanna-be Privatizers. A dour historian would cite the aftermath as an illustration of the maxim that a war never brings peace, only a new war. But be of good cheer. This, too, will pass. Walkers and relaxed bikers will win because their hearts are pure.

Buses permit ingenuities. For example, the car can be parked at Gasworks Park and the walk ended in Bothell. The bus, with one transfer, whisks the body 15 miles back to square one.

Chittenden Locks to Gasworks Park, one way 3¾ miles

The best walking on the Burke-Gilman is here where it doesn't yet exist as such. The unused tracks still partly in place, scenes of honest industrial grime make this Seattle's most entertaining working waterfront.

While watching vessels in Chittenden Locks, find idle amusement by mentally preparing the Environmental Impact Statement for a project bragged up of yore as one of the Seven Wonders of Seattle. Consider, for example, the impact if the closure system failed totally, as it has partly on more than one occasion. A wall of water up to 12 feet high, depending on the stage of the tide, would burst from Lake Washington to Shilshole Bay. Lake Washington would drop, in an estimated 80 hours, to the level of Puget Sound. The tides during the estimated 8 months required for repairs would forbid use of the floating bridges, assuming they did not collapse, as is likely. Barges stuck in the mud. Play boats stranded in marinas. The front yards of software tycoons stinking something dreadful.

The 1¼ miles from the locks to Ballard Bridge feature houseboats, fishing boats, and the little freighters which serve the North—*Pribiloff, Silver Clipper, Polar Merchant.* Across the tracks is Old Ballard, restored and revived and full of red bricks and lutefisk. Climb the stairway to the bridge for views west out Salmon Bay to the locks and east to the Fremont Cut.

The 1¾ miles to Fremont Bridge start with more ships (*Trident, North Sea, Orion*) and views to Queen Anne Hill. After a dull inland mile the tracks return to the water at Canal Street and pass Fremont Canal Park. Where a creek used to flow from Lake Union to Salmon Bay is the Fremont Cut, paths and poplars on both banks, ships and boats and canoes and ducks passing to and fro. On Friday the 13th, March 1914, a dam at this point, erected to exempt Lake Union from tidal flow, burst, sending a deluge to Ballard and beyond. Industry preempts the shore the final scant mile to the Fremont Bridge.

Tour the Fremont District, site of a mill founded in 1888 by four speculators, two from Fremont, Nebraska. A successor, Burke Millwork, was still operating in 1946, when the elder surveyor worked as helper on a planer and in that pre-earplugs era learned a rudimentary sign language while getting well along toward becoming deaf as a shingleweaver. The reason for a town at this point was the outlet creek of Lake Union, which permitted easy bridging in 1887 by the Seattle, Lakeshore & Eastern, 6 years before Jim Hill brought his Great Northern rails in from the north. By 1890 electric trolleys were speeding to and from Ballard along a timber trestle at 20 miles per hour; a couple of decades later the elder surveyor's grandfather, fresh in from the Old Country (North Dakota), hired on as a conductor. In 1891 the town of Fremont was annexed by Seattle and in 1917 was termed its "geographical center."

The Fremont Bridge, successor to the timber span over "the creek," opened in 1917 to serve the Lake Washington Ship Canal. The handsome bascule structure is said to be the nation's most-opening bridge, about every 10 minutes on a summer day, or 1600 times a year, or an estimated half-million times in its first 60 years (twice as many as the Ballard Bridge, also dating from 1917), letting through 100,000 vessels a year.

When Seattle learned funk, it painted the bridge blue and orange to befit the Fremont District, which had fallen into shabby decline after the 1932 opening of the Aurora Bridge on the brandnew Aurora Highway. During the history revival of the 1960s, the derelict storefronts were swabbed out and psychedelicly brightened as Fat City Tavern, Red Door Ale, Deluxe Junk, Ah Nuts Junk, The Tin Man, Fremont Recycling, Glamorama Clothing and Wedding Chapel, Dusty Springs, Guess Where, Daily Planet Antiques, Futon Frames, Happy Trails, Across the Street Cafe, Simply Desserts, Costas Opas Greek Restaurant, Pizza Art. A 48-foot-long rocket embellished with the Republic of Fremont coat of arms has been mounted atop Ah Nuts Junk to serve as broadcasting studios of Radio Free Mont. The key tourist attraction is Richard Beyer's sculpture, *Waiting for the Interurban,* a group of life-size figures whose neighbors garb them with sweaters in chill weather, put flowers in their hair in springtime, and set out bowls of dogfood for their best friend. At the base of the Aurora Bridge another artist-community cement sculpture depicts an enormous troll emerging from the cement in the act of devouring a real (but cemented over) VW Bug, said by reliable sources to be from California.

Gasworks Park

The 1½ miles from 3rd NW to Gasworks Park are a (paved) bikeway, on rainswept weekday dawns comfortably walkable past marinas, sailboats, fishing boats, and rusty old buckets kin to the one abandoned by Lord Jim.

Gasworks Park to Matthews Beach Park, one way 7¼ miles

Walkers wanting a quiet day safe from arrogant wheels stay within the confines of Gasworks Park. Inspect machinery of the plant which for 50 years, starting in 1906, generated gas from coal dug in the Issaquah Alps and along the Green River. For its opening as a park in 1975, the buildings and metalwork were made children-safe and painted gay colors. Walk the ¼ mile of frontage path on Lake Union. Tugboats, sailboats, police boats. Climb the grassy knoll for a view of downtown Seattle. Gulls, ducks, coots, crows, pigeons.

The University of Washington campus? A book in itself. For this one, gaze out Rainier Vista to The Mountain and over Lake Washington to the Cascades. Then carry on past the largest natural area of the campus, the Bob Pyle Wilderness, named for the world-famous butterfly man who as a student led the resistance against another heap of bricks. Under the

45th Street Viaduct the route leaves the campus to curve around a former bay, now University Village, returning to lake views at Sand Point.

Sand Point (Warren G. Magnuson) Park, round-trip sidetrip 3 miles

Bus: 41

Walk (or drive) east on NE 65 Street to the parking area.

Future generations will stroll the former U.S. Navy airfield in shadows of stately trees, and a shore restored to a natural relationship with the lake and the birds, and honor this 196-acre park as a jewel of the city. It's not too bad now.

The walking is on old roads closed to motorized travel and paths mowed or boot-beaten through tall grass. Sidepaths wend off through scotch-broom, hellberry, and willows to nooks on the shore for looking out to sailboards, the north and south of Lake Washington, the Issaquah Alps, and the Cascades.

At 1 long mile from the south fence is the NOAA boundary, where the Great White Fleet of scientists sets out to voyage the salt seas. Resented for muscling in on what could have been a much larger park, the Rover Boys have sought to ameliorate by providing 2000 feet of waterfront walking featuring basalt chairs and tables, pedestrian bridges inscribed with texts from *Moby Dick,* and a "sand garden" constructed of pipes.

Returned from the sidetrip, back on the Burke-Gilman: At Thornton Creek, the city's largest watershed and one of its three significant streams (the others Pipers Creek in Carkeek Park and Longfellow Creek in West Seattle) not banished to a Thomson sewer pipe, a path ascends past a Metro pumping station to a lake panorama. A wildwood greenery is under reconstruction by citizen volunteers of the Thornton Creek Alliance.

Another surcease from speeding wheels is Matthews Beach Park. Stroll in peace up the forest knoll and down the lawns in views over the waters to sails and mountains.

Matthews Beach Park to Blyth Park, one way 8 miles

Local folks may be seen afoot on dark and stormy nights and dawn constitutionals, but few visitors come from afar to walk the 3 miles of residential neighborhoods to the city limits, then 2½ miles by lakeside homes of Sheridan Beach and Lake Forest Park.

However, Logboom Park is a good-in-itself, reached via 61 Avenue NE off Bothell Way. Groves of cottonwood, willow, maple, and alder are isles of cool peace on summer days. The shore, mostly marsh-natural, is habitat for mallards, domestic white ducks, exotics originally from Asia, and weird hybrids. The concrete pier, located where rail cars once dumped logs from a timber dock to be "boomed up" in rafts for towing to the mills, gives views down Lake Washington and across a marina to the mouth of the Sammamish River.

In 1993 the Burke-Gilman was completed the 2½ miles through industrial Kenmore and by pastoral greenery of the river, which is crossed on a refurbished rail bridge to Blyth Park, 19 miles from Chittenden Locks. Here the Burke-Gilman ends, the Tolt Pipeline and Sammamish River Way begin.

Other Trips

Beacon Ridge. A 200-foot-wide, broad-view powerline swath, horses grazing, roosters crowing. Country in city much of the 5 miles from Jefferson Park to Skyway Park.

Greenbelts. In 1977 an Urban Greenbelt Plan proposed 14 areas for preservation. A Beacon Hill Greenbelt Trail has been roughly pioneered from Dr. Jose P. Rizal Park to 13 Avenue S, a one-way distance of 1¼ miles to near the start of the Beacon Hill powerline lawn. Citizens are planning ecosystem restoration and interpretive paths for St. Mark's Greenbelt. In various stages, hampered by shortage of

Burke-Gilman Trail

funds and an excess of greedhead speculators, are Southwest Queen Anne, Northeast Queen Anne, Duwamish Head, East Duwamish, East Duwamish–South Beacon Hill, and West Duwamish Greenbelts.

A greenbelt doesn't have to "do" anything. It serves by simply lying there making no noise (but soaking up a lot), polluting no air or water (but always cleaning), being looked at ("part of the urban fabric"), and being lived in (not by thee and me but by squirrels, rabbits, weasels, muskrats, raccoons, and beavers, and by red-tailed hawks, great blue herons, gulls, nighthawks, horned owls, screech owls, geese, jaegers, ducks, and grebes, and by moles, voles, mice, and rats, and by pigeons, wrens, and warblers, and by those sly old coyotes that everybody in the neighborhoods assumes are just plain dogs).

THE EASTERN MORAINES: OVERLAKE

In melting away from the Seattle vicinity some 13,500 years ago, the Canadian ice left three north–south highlands of morainal debris trisected by two long troughs. The troughs soon were pretty well systemized by Lake Washington and Lake Sammamish. The highlands, however, remained, when European settlers arrived, in the unorganized stage the geomorphologists call "infancy." Where had been respectable streams from the glacier front now were lakes, marshes, swamps, and bogs connected by dribbles and seepage. Messy. Under the generalship of the R. H. Thomsons, the landscape was tidied up, the water gotten out of sight, wetlands civilized to become real estate. After a century the westernmost moraine (Seattle) had just three significant streams flowing on the surface, only the most major of lakes, and no bogs at all. The highland had been hastened to an artificial "maturity," the water mainly in sewers or flowing underground from basement to basement.

The forced maturing was well advanced on the Bellevue-Kirkland moraine when a momentous word burst on the public consciousness like a new star rising: ecology. The populace always had been fond of nonhuman creatures, as witness Woodland Park Zoo, circuses, and national park chipmunks, but had been led to believe by engineers that when living space was concreted the displaced wildlife would simply move in with relatives. Now the citizenry was taught that every nook of Nature is full up with relatives, no empty rooms for cousins; destruction of habitat is destruction of critters. Also learned: If a tract of land is half dry, half wet, 90 percent of the wildlife will be found in the wet half. Wet is wild. Wet *is* wildness.

Thus it was that before the middle of the three moraines could be totally dried up, Seattle style, public opinion swung dramatically away from All Power to Private Property toward Keep Bellevue Boggy. Imprisoned creeks were set free and signs installed naming them so they no longer could be dismissed by developers as "ditchwater." What does this revolution mean to the trail-walker? Scarcely a trip described in following pages is not given its central interest by the wet—lakes, creeks, marshes, swamps, bogs.

The easternmost of the morainal highlands, East Sammamish Plateau–Grand Ridge, 25 miles in length from I-90 to the Snohomish River, entered the 1980s very nearly in a state of Nature, resembling what a traveler

Luther Burbank Park

between Seattle and Everett would have observed early in the twentieth century, and between Bellevue and Bothell before World War II. By the 1990s, however, the Private Greed Doctrine, formidable as the glacier from Canada, had come down like a wolf on the fold, biting and scratching for jawsful of gold. To be a pedestrian or equestrian on this dark and bloody ground is not necessarily to be an environmental activist through genetic inheritance. Traveling there does it. To mix in another and very elaborate metaphor, imagine an iceberg being forcibly pushed beneath the surface of the sea by a band of ice-hating pirates. They may manage to get it under the water momentarily. But buoyancy will prevail. *The Public Trust Doctrine must prevail*. To quote a great American of that other Revolution, "If this be treason, make the most of it!"

As for the recreational future of the combat zone, planners long have envisioned a system of regional trails hitching the Issaquah Alps to the Tolt Pipeline and Snohomish County, the Sammamish trough to the Snoqualmie valley. Good. However, the visions have been clouded by the miasma of "multi-use" trail. Walkers may well need quarterstaffs for a while, until there are true trails on the easternmost moraine, solely for hooves/feet, with *separated* bikeways provided for wheels.

USGS maps: Mercer Island, Bothell, Malty, Kirkland, Redmond, Issaquah, Fall City

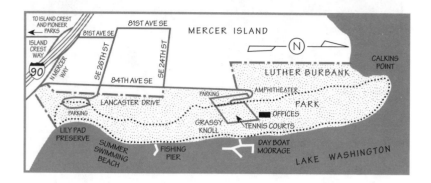

Luther Burbank Park

Bus: 202, 210, 226, 235

Go off I-90 on Exit 7, Island Crest Way, turn onto 84 Avenue SE, and from it at SE 24 Street enter the park.

The City of Mercer Island has 50½ miles of "trails." Yes, most are what in Seattle are called "sidewalks," but some 15 miles are separated from roads. Yes, of course, mostly bikeways. A pamphlet giving descriptions and maps is free at the City Hall, 9611 SE 36 Street, Mercer Island 98040.

The only walking worth a journey from afar is in the 77-acre King County park, 3000 feet of lakefront, on the north shore of the island. Walk north from the headquarters building past a froggy cattail marsh to Calkins Point and views of the University District. Follow the shore south to views of the East Channel and Cougar Mountain, to the fishing pier, through madrona–Indian plum woods to the swimming beach and the marsh at the park border. Complete a 1½-mile loop inland through meadows, up and down the Grassy Knoll.

Mercer Slough Nature Park

The hand of man, wielding a shovel, lowered Lake Washington by 9 (10?) feet in 1916 (1917?), converting Mercer Bay to a slough and bog, and dug ditches to dry things up enough to grow garden truck. After opening of the Bellevue Shopping Square, the business and industry which love flat land because it builds up fast and cheap, began running short of the dry variety and invaded the wet. However, in order to free developers from foreign (Seattle) meddling, a city was incorporated. That entailed a parks department, and Bellevue chanced to hire a person who was not the picnic table-privy-and-bawfield specialist then typical of parks departments but a friend of the wet. Parks Director Lee Springgate recalls, "I remember getting a constant barrage of criticism for throwing money in a swamp. It feels good, after all these years, to see that people recognize the importance of wetlands." In the era when Bellevue was a stopover on the migration route of Cadillacs from Orange County to Dallas,

Bellefields Nature Park

civic shame was felt over being so soggy, so inferior to dried-up (bogs filled in, creeks condemned to sewers) Seattle. But when residents stop looking at land as merely real estate, they tend to get hooked on swamps, be bored by golf courses and other fertilizer-and-weedkiller–drenched lawns fraudently lauded as "open space."

Thanks to the dogged persistence of Bellevue Parks, there now is a 326-acre Mercer Slough Nature Park, the largest urban wetland in the region, the largest wetland park in King County and the western United States. Sited within an hour's drive of 2,000,000 people and an easy bus ride of near that many, it is more than a Bellevue amenity, it is a regional treasure, a freshwater equivalent to the Seattle Aquarium. The sedges and rushes, willows and dogwoods, shelter 168 of the 212 species of animals found in wetlands of the state, 104 species of birds.

Some 6 miles of nature trails (foot-only) and a 5.3-mile periphery bikeway ultimately will hitch together an interpretive center, a farmers market selling produce grown on 50 acres of city-owned-and-preserved-as-such farmland, a viewing tower and shielded viewpoints for watching beaver, herons, waterfowl, and whatever else swims, flies, creeps, scurries, or burrows, and new ponds and waterways to replace wildlife habitat lost to development.

Paddle-only craft are permitted on the 2 miles of slough. Canoes and kayaks can be rented weekends, noon to 6:00 P.M., through the summer into fall. Call (206) 455-6887.

South Trailhead. Bus: 220, 240, 340. Go off I-90 on Bellevue Way SE 0.2 mile to South Bellevue Park & Ride, and on the south side find a short entry path to the trail. Just adjoining to the south, a parking lot is planned for the future interpretive center.

North Trailhead. Bus: 220, 240, 340. Continue north 0.2 mile on Bellevue Way (or drive south from SE 8 Street via 112 Avenue SE) past the Winters House to SE 24th and turn off to the Farmers Market at Overlake Blueberry Farm.

East Trailhead. Drive 118 Avenue SE ½ mile south of SE 8 Street to Bellefields Nature Park.

North is the way to go from the Park & Ride/interpretive center, but note must be made of south. The bikeway. Worth walking the short bit to the T where the right heads for Enetai Beach Park and the left parallels the massive concretery and hurtling roar of I-90, surrealistic so cheek-by-jowl with cattails and flitting-swimming birds. The bridge arching gracefully over Mercer Slough is the pedestrian's proper turnaround after a look south to the gray geometry of freeway and down to the tea-colored water of the slough and north along the tantalizing alleyway hemmed in tight by impenetrable (not to critters) willow jungle. In ½ mile the path reaches the east side of the valley and 118 Avenue SE (Lake Washington Boulevard, it used to be). Less than 1 mile south is Coal Creek delta, the south part preserved in Newcastle Beach Park. The bikeway turns north, never more than inches from the highway, to a (current) deadend just short of Bellefields Nature Park. The blacktop lane is dullsville but useful as apartheid to segregate from nature-trailers the bikers and runners who don't care where they are so long as they're going fast enough. A walker lusting for distance will be happier taking any of a number of accesses to the railroad. Turn south for Newcastle Beach and Renton, north for Woodinville.

At the future interpretive center site, the north calls. Adjoining but well screened from the Park & Ride, the Center site is beside a reconstructed slough replanted with native trees, shrubs, and whatnot plants. Boardwalk-trail turns east from the valley wall, far out over what was, until 1917, the bottom of Lake Washington, now a wetland of willow jungle, cattail marsh, sphagnum bog, and squishy meadow. The tumult of I-90 is lost in that of I-405. Above the reeds as distant as a vision loom the towers of downtown Bellevue. Here is vividly "the wildness within."

At a Y a gravel path turns left to the Farmers Market at Overlake Blueberry Farm, a scant ½ mile from the interpretive center site. Picnic tables. Paths into the blueberry farm for U-Pick. Parking for some twenty cars; on sunny weekends the Park & Ride is the better hike beginning.

From the Farmers Market Y, the right fork soon becomes a long ramp through willow swamp and hardhack jungle to a view platform on banks of Mercer Slough. A photogenic bridge crosses to the Bellefields Nature Park.

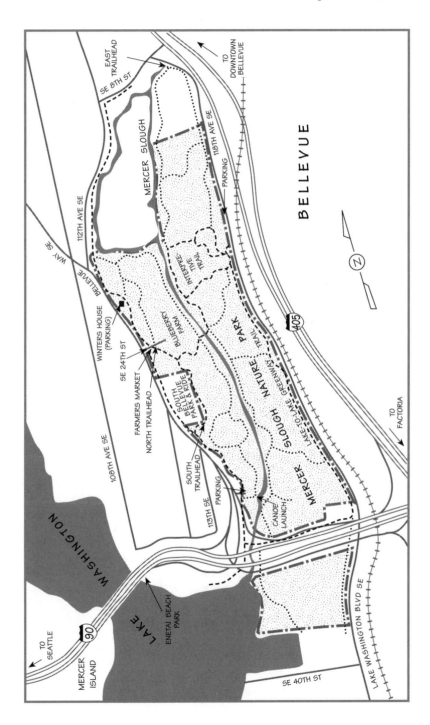

Ah yes. The Bridge. Coming from north or south or east, many walkers are content to lunch here and turn around.

To describe the route from the east, a ten-car parking lot beside 118th is the start of a 1-mile loop trail. The sign "Bellefields Nature Park 1966" identifies it as the birthplace of the Bellevue Parks reclamation project. The path descends a bank to what was, until 1917, the shore of Lake Washington and enters a wildland only three-quarters of a century old (before that, it was wild water), but wilderness that is Paradise enow for a lover of "the wild and the wet." To do the loop counterclockwise, at a series of ys take always the right (one of these is a sideloop that returns to the lakebed loop). Wood-chip path alternates with boardwalk through willow-swamp jungle where the wild things are. The mood is briefly shattered at the bank of Mercer Slough, where can be seen above the thickets a monstrous squatting office building of the nefarious Bellefields Office Non-Park which was blessed by the complacent Bellevue City Council of the 1970s, though the scene was intended by the Parks Department and God to be part of the Nature Park.

Let the bitterness pass. Turn south along the slough. Pass stubs to the tea water where, as a reader board says, "bufflehead, goldeneye, wigeon, gadwall, merganser, and ruddy duck" pause for food and rest during migration and the year-rounders include "Canada geese, mallard, and great blue heron." The way leaves the slough for a mowed meadow, where stands a big old white-barked paper birch (native) as well as a big old lonesome blueberry bush (alien). (Free eats in season.) The wood-chip path ts with the ramp to The Bridge. Loop left back to 118th through lawn corridors and poplar groves. A reader board tells the sequence on a line at this place from west valley wall to east: shrub/scrub wetland, Overlake Blueberry Farm, Mercer Slough, meadow, forest, forest wetland, 118th.

Lake-to-Lake Greenway Trail

Defensive incorporations by residential communities a-feared of Shopping Square entrepreneurs forced Bellevue to resign itself to be the "city between the lakes" rather than the "city on the lakes." Not to mind. Open water isn't the only good wetness. Students of wildlife actually prefer a stew of muck, murk, and weedery. An earlier version of this guidebook contrasted the names "Seattle Lakes Trail" and "Bellevue Bogs Trail," and by no means to the disfavor of the latter. Still, civic pride felt hurt, and Parks having acquired, at enormous cost, slit windows on the Big Water to the west and the Little Water to the east, the route was officially christened the Lake-to-Lake Greenway. Very sexy.

The 7 miles of the Greenway Trail, hitched to some 15 miles of other walkways, connect a necklace of small-to-middling parks deserving of more or less attention by feet. To get inside the (wet) skin of the city, a connoisseur of geography ought at least once to do it all in a single journey, looping back via one of several variant routes or catching a bus.

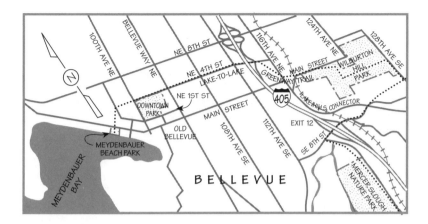

Before setting out on this or any other Bellevue exploration, stop by City Hall or the Lake Hills Ranger Station for the large *Bellevue Park Guide* map and the delightful booklet, *Nature Trail Guide*.

Meydenbauer Beach Park

Bus: 226, 235

Drive west from Bellevue Way NE on Main Street through "Old Bellevue" to 100 Avenue NE. Turn right to NE 1st, then left, following park signs.

The interest in this western terminus, other than as an alley to look out on Lake Washington, is that it was the site of the last American whaling station. (The whalers just wintered here; the whales were in the ocean, of course.) The trail (well, sure, it's a sidewalk in this stretch) goes east to Downtown Park, crosses over Mercer Slough and under I-405 to Main Street, and proceeds to Wilburton Hill Park.

Wilburton Hill Park/Bellevue Botanical Gardens

Bus: 208 on 1st, walk to park

Go off I-405 on Exit 12, turn east on SE 8 Street, and turn left at the stoplight onto Lake Hills Connector, which bends north to become 116 Avenue NE. Turn east on SE 1 Street, over the railroad tracks. Turn right on Main Street to the Botanical Gardens parking lot and then the Wilburton Hill parking lot.

The marvel is that a 103-acre chunk of country survived the construction all around it of the All-American Shopping Square City. That this largest of the city's upland parks was snatched from the jaws of the blacktoppers in 1988 was a triumph of the new, grown-up Bellevue. But then came a second civil war, between the contemplatives who treasured the hilltop, 230 feet, for its high and long views and no sounds louder than the wind, and the daddies and mommies in club sweaters who lusted to cheer the shrieks of their kinetic offspring as they kicked a baw and each other around a field of bloodied grass.

The bawfields won. At times (dawn) the contemplative can hear birds. The 2 miles of woodland paths are an amenity for neighbors, not worth a journey from very far. As for the Lake-to-Lake Trail, the 1 mile from the east edge of the Botanical Gardens down through alders to 128 Avenue NE goes quickly, and a short bit on SE 4th brings the feet to Kelsey Creek Park.

But hold on! Don't leave the scene without walking the railroad tracks from SE 1st south to the Wilburton Trestle, a timberwork 948 feet long and 100 feet high at the center, built in 1904, and latterly provided a safe walkway. The rails still see the occasional train, running 22 miles from Black River Junction in Renton to Woodinville, a better walk than the Burke-Gilman because the iron wheels disturb the peace far less than some others.

Finally, the contemplative walker can do very well, thank you, without Wilburton Hill and even the trestle, but must spend many hours through the changing seasons in the 36 acres of the Bellevue Botanical Gardens. The beginning was in 1947, when Harriet and Cal Shorts commenced converting their patch of wildwoods to a "sample of paradise." When it was donated to the city, the Bellevue Botanical Garden Society had an even grander vision and under the leadership of Iris Jewett saw the dream realized. The society and Bellevue Parks now maintain and display plant collections for horticultural demonstration, education, and passive recreation. Stroll the Perennial Border, the Ground Cover Garden, the Waterwise Garden, the Fuchsia Display, the Eastern Gardens. Explore the botanical library. Browse in the Garden Shop.

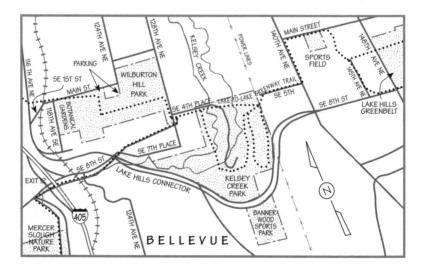

Kelsey Creek Park

Bus: 220, 273, 274, 920 (Lake Hills Connector at SE 8th)

Go off I-405 on Exit 12, turn east on SE 8 Street, cross Lake Hills Connector at a stoplight onto SE 7 Place, and drive via 128 Place SE and SE 4 Place into the park.

That the agricultural past be not forgotten, and that children may know other animals than dogs and cats, this former farm has been revived, barns and pastures, cows, pigs, horses, burros, goats, and sheep. Another attraction of the 80-acre park is the Fraser House, a cabin of squared-off logs built nearby in 1888 and moved here to be preserved. There also are undeveloped natural areas, valley marshes, and hillside forests.

A figure-8 route looping around the edge of the bowl-shaped wetland, the creek's floodplain, combines the Farm Loop and the Hillside Loop for a 2½-mile total.

The Lake-to-Lake Trail follows a path under hillside powerlines to the street-end of SE 5th. Walk 2 blocks to 140th and turn left ⅓ mile to Main Street. Trail resumes on Main, goes behind Sammamish High School through marshes to 148 Avenue NE, at 1¼ miles from Kelsey Creek Park hitching to the Lake Hills Greenbelt.

Barns and farm fields at Kelsey Creek Park

Lake Hills Greenbelt Park

Bus: 221, 227

To start from the south, park in lots on 156 Avenue SE at Phantom Lake or SE 16th. From the north, park on 148 Avenue SE or in the lot of the Farmers Market at SE 8th.

The Original Inhabitants rendezvoused here to pick the fall crop of native blueberries and cranberries in the bogs and marshes bordering "Lake Primeval," draining northward to Kelsey Creek. The Originals having been departed, a homesteader dug a ditch to drain the waters to Lake Sammamish. The old lake shrank to two remnants, Phantom and Larsen. Ove and Mary Larsen came from Denmark in 1852, homesteaded at "Blueberry Lake" in 1889, combining farming (they sold wild cranberries and blueberries in Seattle) with his job in the Newcastle mines. Other immigrants, from Japan, began farming hereabouts in the early 1900s. In 1918 the Larsens sold 80 acres to the four Aries brothers, who ran the area's largest farm, shipping carrots, celery, peas, lettuce, cauliflower, potatoes, cabbage, and parsnips to Montana, Minnesota, and the Yukon. In 1947 Louis Weinzirl planted domesticated blueberries. In 1960, K-Mart rolled out the blacktop. (Thus we have been taught by Bellevue's great historian, the late Lucile McDonald.)

Of the 8-mile wetland once continuous from Lake Washington to Eastgate, the middle 2½ miles between Kelsey Creek Park and Larsen Lake went the age-old anthropocentric way of drying-up and building-up. But the preservation instincts of Bellevue Parks gained a powerful supporter, the Storm and Surface Water Department, which had learned the cheapest way to get its assigned task done is to let Nature do it. The Urban Wildlife Enhancement Project converts monotonous monoculture of hardhack spirea to diverse habitat of pond, wetland, dry land, woodland, and vegetation which provides food, water, shelter, and living space for wildlife. Duckweed, soft rush, yellow iris, reed, canary grass, salmonberry, and forest filter stormwater runoff, protecting water quality. Other cooperators are State Fish and Wildlife and Ecology Departments. Though it fails to enrich developers, the Lake Hills Greenbelt not only entertains the taxpayer but saves him/her money.

Of the Greenbelt Park's 154 acres of land and 17 acres of lake (one of the city's two largest parks), only 2 percent will be developed, keeping 78 acres as woodland and wetland, 22 acres in blueberry bushes, and 20 acres as community vegetable garden plots leased to individuals growing for family tables. It is a "sensitive" park sensitive to the needs of wild creatures, who have large preserves left strictly to them with no human entry, and sensitive to the needs of neighbors for peace and quiet and sensitive to the needs of visitors who want to listen to birds.

At the south end is 75-acre Phantom Lake, elevation 250 feet. A sidewalk along 156 Avenue SE connects south ½ mile to the trail linking Cabot, Cabot, & Forbes Business "Park" (formerly the Bellevue Airfield) and Robinswood Park. The lake is a designated "quiet zone," no motorboats, no loud radios, no whooping and hollering. The public access is at the south end of the Greenbelt Park. Pond lilies bloom yellow on the waters (these being the native species, not the alien which blooms white on Lake Washington).

Muskrats ramble through the willow swamps. Great blue herons fish. Bald eagles perch in snags. A viewing platform permits a stroll out from shore to watch little birds chasing big birds away from nests, and littler birds chasing ...

The 1½ miles of the Greenbelt Park from Phantom Lake to Larsen Lake are the most popular natural-area walk for many miles around. From adjacent homes and by car and bus the people come. One wonders, where did they walk before? Many probably didn't. Give folks a place to put their feet and they take the hint.

Start from anywhere. The elder surveyor's favorite is from the south end. First, a walk out over Phantom Lake on the viewing dock. Immerse the spirit in the isolation under the big sky mirrored in serene water. The sounds of distant traffic are as from another planet. The cattail and willow shore, and even the far shore ringed by homes (set respectfully back from the water, quietly amid the trees), preserve the peace. One speculates about the exact route of the Original Inhabitants' trail shown on the 1895 USGS map.

The way north is between 156th SE (hedged by a band of shrubbery) and a working farm (note the rich, black, peaty soil, the lush green crops). In ½ mile is a stoplight crossing of SE 16th to a sizable parking lot. Just uphill is the ranger station; ask about guided interpretive tours. Supplied with the pamphlet, tour the Butterfly Garden, its dozens of plants appealing to a dozen and more species, from Cabbage White and Brown Elfin to Faunus Angelwing and Painted Lady. A path enters the Community Garden; sign up in winter for a patch of earth which will in season

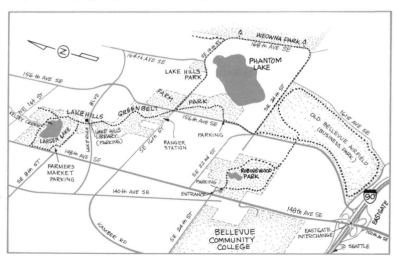

reward the delver with the nigh-forgotten taste of fresh vegetables. In season the commercial crops may be purchased virtually as soon as they come from the ground at the little farmers market.

Farms on the right, willow woods and cedar woods and new-made sloughs (to replace the vanished old sloughs) on the left, through marsh grasses and plantations of native shrubs and flowers set out to replace the alien weedery, by signs explaining the history, the ecology, and the habitats of osprey and red-tailed hawk and kingfisher, the river otter and coyote. In ½ mile the paved trail (few bicycles, and those mainly of kids and easy riders, friends of the land and the pedestrians) crosses Lake Hills Boulevard and passes the Lake Hills Library to a T.

The left goes ½ mile through woods and Larsen Lake Blueberry Farm to 148 Avenue SE at SE 16th. A sidewalk connects north ¼ mile to a tiny parking area at the north end of the Larsen Lake trail. A quieter way, separated from traffic, follows a wood-chip path from the thirty-car parking lot and farmers market just north of 16th through the blueberries. Watch for coyotes. Beware the truculent, nest-defending redwing blackbird.

Right from the library-near T the trail lies between untamed marsh of a "wildlife enhancement area" and tamed blueberries, fenced off lest ye be tempted, to lakeshore woods and rounds Larsen Lake in hardhack and willow. Frogs splash and ducks paddle and fish swim. Pond lilies spread green pads and erupt yellow flowers. A pier thrusts out for views. Murky waters of Kelsey Creek are crossed. At ¾ mile from the T is 148th, facilitating a loop.

From near the lake a sidepath north goes ¼ mile to the end of the Greenbelt Park on 151 Place SE bordering the asphalt jungle of the farm-and-wetland-murdering K-Mart Center. Watch carefully in the woods for a scattering of the uncommon (hereabouts) aspen and beech.

Weowna Park

Bus: 252 to SE 16th and 148th, walk 1 mile to park; 225 on SE 24 Street; 229 on 156th

Drive to 168 Avenue SE. Park on SE 19th and other sidestreets.
Virgin forest, a strip 1 mile long and ¼ mile wide, in the heart of the

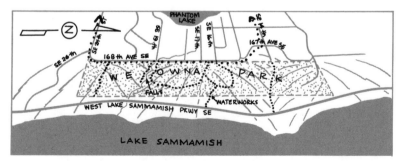

Overlake Borough of Puget Sound City? The heck you say! The hiker accustomed to lowland second-growth gets giddy confronted by Douglas firs up to 6 feet in diameter.

The ravines! The creeks! Situated on the "breaks" from Lake Hills to Lake Sammamish, the park is deeply incised by streams. The outstanding one is not from springs but Phantom Lake, flowing in the 5-foot-deep trench hand-dug in glacial till a century ago to make dry pasture. The raw newness of Phantom Creek is evidenced by its pretty falls over till and blue glacial clay and its canyon sliced in drift, the more picturesque for the location among some of the most venerable trees.

That the virgin forest has been preserved is the unlikely concatenation of four circumstances: (1) the precipice would have been hard to log; (2) the owner, a retired logger, was nostalgic for the deep woods he had spent his life daylighting; (3) a subdivision scheme (don't try to puzzle out an Original Inhabitants' name—it's "we own a park") failed; and (4) a Forward Thrust purchase. There has been no development by King County and will be none when Bellevue assumes ownership; it is and must remain wildland, little done to it except someday to systemize the trails.

Parking is next to impossible on West Lake Sammamish Parkway SE, elevation 100 feet, and most of the old trails there have been blocked off by brandnew houses. The wise plan is to walk from the top, elevation 275 feet.

The Lake-to-Lake Trail uses the Phantom Lake Loop Trail to reach Weowna. Walkways follow both SE 16th and SE 24th for ¾ mile (each) from Lake Hills Greenbelt to 168 Avenue SE, where walkway runs 1 mile along the park's upper boundary. The paths beaten out over the years by local folks are readily spotted. A walker poking about on them, up and down and sideways, can total some 4 miles, though the Lake-to-Lake through-route is only about ½ mile.

At SE 19th, the bus stop, Phantom Creek emerges from a culvert under 168th. Paths lead down both sides to the big trees and awesome chasm and deadends.

Just where SE 14th bends into 168th, search for the Trillium Trail,

Weowna Park

as it was signed in the 1970s. Come in early April for a name-deserving display. Near Lake Sammamish Parkway are a spring and old springhouse.

For the fullest tour, better than a mile, up down and sideways, follow the walkway south beside 168th; a barricade prevents access to the wildwood until just short of 24th, where a major trail descends to an ultimate end in a backyard, as do several sidetrails. Walk until blocked, retreat, take another. The firs run to 4 feet in diameter. Good views of Till Falls and its fearsome plunge basin. One of the sidetrails loops back up to 168th at the Phantom Creek culvert.

Weowna Beach Park

The breaks baffled the developer, the Lake Sammamish shores were snapped up for summer cabins which were patched up for year-round living or replaced by trophy homes, walling off the water, but in 1994 the Lake-to-Lake won through to a window on the Little Water by purchase of 0.8 acres, 126 feet of shore. No development, no boat-launch, no swimming beach, next to no parking. So, do it by walking down the hill from Weowna Park, crossing West Lake Sammamish Parkway, peek-a-booing the lake, and climbing back up the breaks.

Lake-to-Lake Variants

There's more than one way to get from here to there on the Bellevue trail system. The Meydenbauer-Weowna line employs some 7 of the city's 70 miles of off-street walkways. Other ways to go:

- From Enetai Beach Park walk north through Mercer Slough Nature Park, by sidewalk to SE 8 Street, and hook up with the mainline at Kelsey Creek Park.
- From Kelsey Creek Park walk south through Bannerwood Park to the greenbelt (saved in the nick from street engineers) of Bellevue Community College, and turn east to Robinswood Park and the former Bellevue Airfield (Cabot, Cabot, & Cabot Business "Park") and north to the Phantom Lake Walkway.

Kirkland Watershed Park

Bus: 234, 255, 258, 275

Go off I-405 on Exit 17 and turn west on SE 70 Place, which bends south as NE 68 Street. Turn south on 108 Avenue NE to a two-car parking space at the main park entrance, 110 Avenue NE at NE 45 Street. Elevation, 400 feet.

How much good stuff can be crammed into 60 acres? The forest grown since turn-of-the-century logging—large Douglas fir, huge maples dripping licorice fern, groves of madrona, fine big cedars, alder, and hemlock, the occasional gigantic cottonwood, mysterious plantations of two-needle (lodgepole?) pine. Thickets of yellowberries, white lawns of candyflower. Canyons carved in glacial drift, creeks trickling through horsetail bot-

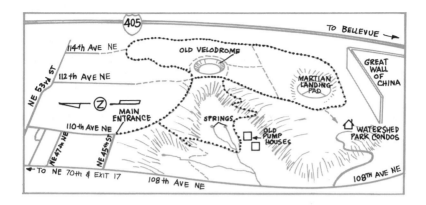

toms. Mysterious artifacts of a vanished civilization. And sampling it all, a roundabout, up-and-down-and-up loop trail of some 2 miles.

To do the loop in the recommended clockwise direction, set off up the main trail (old service road, abandoned). Pass a major trail descending to the right; this is the return leg. The path skirts the edge of a precipice plunging to a green canyon on the right and ascends to the plateau top at 425 feet. An entry trail from 112th joins on the left (signed "No Horses— No Motorcycles" but tracked by fat-tire bikes) just before the first of the artifacts, hypothesized by David Quimby, who introduced the elder surveyor to the watershed, to be an Old Velodrome.

For the loop, keep north through fine woods. But hark! What is that roar? One had forgotten there are freeways. The trail bends around to head south, passing an entry from 114th, and emerges from forest at the huge bowl Quimby identifies as the Martian Landing Pad. What is that emptiness above, where formerly was a green roof? It is the sky! With swallows in it! Keep straight ahead to the Great Wall of China at the far side of the Pad. Pass an entry trail used by the people who live behind the Great Wall. Turn west along the Pad to its west end. Pass an entry from Watershed Park Condos. Look out to towers of downtown Bellevue, to heights of the Issaquah Alps. Reenter forest, the canyon gaping on the left, and proceed north to a Y a few steps short of the Old Velodrome.

Now for the nicest part of the walk, though the trail is thin and steep and slippery. Take the left fork and switchback down the precipice, deeper and deeper into the green. Pause to rest on hillside benches. Look through the treetops, down to the birds, out to glimpses of Lake Washington. But what has happened to one's hearing? The roaring has stopped! When the ears dropped off the brink the freeway dematerialized, was shipped to Mars. Birdsongs submerge the generalized hum-rumble of the distant city.

At the bottom of the canyon the springs seep out of aquifers, through horsetails, joining to form a creek. The path crosses, climbs to the narrow crest of a ridge to a T. The right climbs to complete the loop.

Kirkland Waterfront

Bellevue is the "city between the lakes." Kirkland, dating from an earlier time of fewer shoreline-hugging plutocrats, is the "city on the lake." The goal of its Parks Department is a continuous walkway beside or near the water the 5 miles from Juanita Bay to Yarrow Bay. Partly in open marsh, partly on beach, partly through lanes of marinas and condos and eateries and shoppes, it is such a route as cannot be matched by Seattle or any other city that comes to mind. (Well, Tacoma, but that's in another guidebook.)

The imaginative way is to do the whole thing at a single go, loitering as lazily as may be wished, counting on the Metro bus to whisk the bones back to the start.

Juanita Beach Park, loop ¾ mile

Park the car or get off the bus (234, 258) at the King County park on NE Juanita Drive. Walk the ⅓-mile promenade that encloses the swimming beach. Views past Juanita and Nelson Points across the lake to Sand Point and the tip of the Space Needle, down the lake to Hunts Point and the Evergreen Point Bridge. Beware of the ducks and geese and crows sighting in on your lunch.

Juanita Bay Park, thorough walkabout 1¾ miles

Bus: 234, 255, 258, 275, 931

Park along Juanita Drive in a dozen-car lot where 98 Avenue NE rises from the swamps.

This "largest jewel in Kirkland's tiara of waterfront parks" is also the

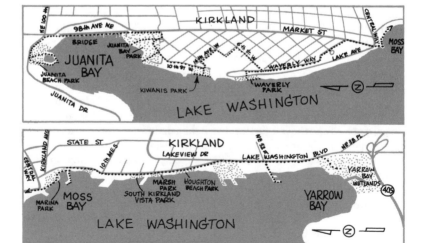

Kirkland waterfront

city's largest park, 103-odd acres, 2100 feet of shoreline. It became possible when a golf course, converted from a French-run frog-legs farm in 1932, closed in 1975, and the citizenry voted funds to fend off a millionaires' row of glitzy exhibitions of wealth.

No bawfields here, no kinetics, no boat-launch. Rather, "an alternative to our structured everyday lives." The Southern Meadow, upland, is mowed, irrigated, manicured, and provided with play area, picnic shelter, benches, and a paved trail through groves of weeping willow and birch, Douglas fir and maple. The Wetland Meadow is left for Nature to manage, supervised by bossy blackbirds. Two deadend boardwalks permit dry-foot, non-destructive walking out through the buttercups and yellow flag and cattails to views of marsh and lake. The highest priority is wildlife habitat.

The abandonment of a stretch of highway converted a causeway built in 1935 to a path crossing ½ mile of bayshore and Forbes Creek wetlands. The structure was replaced in the 1990s by a new-built promenade bridge. Muskrat and raccoon and opossum and beaver and skunk live here, and more than 70 species of birds; in winter, as many as 1600 birds have been counted at a time: osprey, barn owls, bald eagles, herons, downy or hairy woodpeckers. Salmon spawn in Forbes Creek.

Kiwanis Park–Waverly Park–David Brink Park, one way 2 miles

The walkway is on quiet residential streets; follow your nose.

Where 10 Street W bends to become 14 Avenue W, find an obscure path down the bluff to Kiwanis Park, 2.5 acres of wild shore and huge cottonwoods.

Near the northern dead-end of Waverly Way, descend the park entry road through forest to the beach of Waverly ("Skinnydipper") Park. Walk out on the fishing pier for views south to Moss Bay.

The 9-acre site of Waverly School, become David Brink Park honoring the longtime director of Kirkland Parks, opens to blufftop views north past Champaign Point and across the lake to Sand Point and the tips of Seattle's towers. Paths and sidewalks connect to Marina Park at the foot of Market Street.

Shoreline Trail, one way 2 miles

Bus: 230, 251, 254

When Kirkland resolved to be "a lakeside town rather than a town near a lake" (nothing personal there, Bellevue), it was the first city in the state to complete—in 1974—a shoreline master program pursuant to the state Shoreline Management Act of 1971. It is the only city to envision a trail all the way along its portion of Lake Washington. Since 1973 it has required developers to provide public walkways across private property on the shore. Single-family homes are exempt. The seven condos built over the water before 1973 (a practice now forbidden) will continue to wall off the water until comes, as it must to all condos, time for rehabilitation. Then, zap. Since new condos likely ultimately will replace single-family homes, it is not an impossible dream that one day there will be an unbroken waterside walkway from Juanita Bay to Yarrow Bay. As of 1993, half that distance is open. From Market Street south the fraction is larger than that. Though the walkway is interrupted by (temporary) deadends, requiring retreats to detour via the sidewalk, the pedestrian is by and with the lake the entire 2 miles from Marina Park to Yarrow Bay Marina.

The start is Marina Park, built in 1970 exactly where Market Street used to run out to a ferry dock; until the end of War II a person could walk on the boat, debark 4 miles later at Madison Park, and catch the bus to downtown Seattle. That cannot be done anymore, another example of entropy. However, there is a public dock for rich people arriving in Kirkland by boat; poor folks are permitted vicarious enjoyment. The 2.6 acres of walkway, beach, and lawn give fine views of lake and people and "so many ducks that swimming would be hazardous to the health."

The walking route returns (presently) via Kirkland Avenue to Lake Street and proceeds south to the Port of Moss Bay Marina. Coffee shops, art galleries, bistros, pizza parlors, florists, pawnshops, restaurants (at least 150), antiques, jazz joints. The way beyond is partly sidewalk, partly shore walkways through the post-Enlightenment condos, pleasured by a series of parklets. The first is .02-acre Street End Park, providing a view of Harbor Lights Condominium, protruding 250 feet into the lake (modern laws would forbid this) and boasting the city's only over-the-water swimming pool. South Kirkland Park is the next opening in the wall of buildings. Then comes Marsh Park, "Muscle Beach," where adolescents take off their clothes to perform mating rituals, and finally Houghton Beach, where families huddle under the benign eye of a lifeguard who doubles as guardian of public morals. Along the way to here, at the old boundary of Kirkland–Houghton, Lake Street becomes Lake Washington Boulevard. The southern dead-end is at One Carillon Point, a complex of luxury condos that overpowered the city council and refused to let public feet by.

However, feet can continue on sidewalk to Yarrow Bay Marina, a nice sidetrip to observe the toys of rich condo people. The city has two shore easements to the south but cannot hook them together without more easements—that is, more condo building, fewer condo lawyers.

Carillon Point (Shipyard)

In 1946 the Lake Washington Shipyard, which built ferries, War I wooden freighters, postwar steel freighters, and, in War II, destroyer escorts and seaplane tenders, closed. The Skinner Corporation leased parts of the land to other industrial uses and to a professional football team from Seattle. Then it put forth a plan for "Shipyard Park," a 100-room hotel, a 461-slip marina, 40,000 square feet of space for eating, boozing, and shopping, 467,000 square feet of office space, a 24-unit condo, 125 apartments, and 1746 parking stalls. Promising, in addition, a path along the entire ¼ mile of shore, a rebuilt stream freed from its culvert and stocked with salmon, and two small beach parklets. Skinner declared this would be "the pendant on the necklace of Kirkland waterfront parks."

After the customary smiling by the band of DSTs (Designated Sweet Talkers), blustering by the legion of lawyers, suing by the citizenry, developer reneging on promises, and public officials caving in, 1989 saw the "grand opening" (*sic*) of Carillon Point, $120 million of red brick hotel and dollar-devouring shoppes and pads on "31 acres along a breathtaking section of the south Kirkland waterfront."

Yarrow Bay Wetlands

Since the 1950s one grandiose scheme after another has been proposed to dry up the third-largest marsh on Lake Washington. Since the 1950s one schemer after another has slunk away with his battered lawyers and his crumpled architects' pretty pictures, defeated by the citizens of Yarrow Bay. In 1986 a developer got around them, obtaining permission from Kirkland to build The Plaza at Yarrow Bay in exchange for giving the city 66 acres of cattails, blackbirds, muskrats, and woodpeckers. Hardhack and willow-tangle and hellberries forbid human entry. The place serves people by storing floodwaters and cleaning polluted runoff.

Mainly, however, it serves as habitat for salmon, bass, pheasant, hawks, bullfrogs, and water rats. It never will be a major people park; at most there may be a path to a viewpoint.

St. Edward State Park

Bus: 260

Drive Juanita Drive NE north from Kirkland or south from Kenmore to the obscure park entrance at NE 145th. Turn west to a Y and keep right to the parking at the main St. Edward building, elevation 350 feet.

In 1977 Puget Sound City obtained—half a century after any realist would have judged the last chances long gone—a wildland park on Lake Washington. The necessary fortuities were: a property owner (the Archdiocese of Seattle) with soul, and an anomalously alert group of state and federal legislators and officials.

No raw wasteland was this, such as was obtained from the U.S. Navy

St. Edward State Park

the same year, at Sand Point, but instant wildland park, the forests already installed. Most of the 316 acres—all the steep bluff and the several superb ravines and the 3000 feet of waterfront—will remain as they were under stewardship of the Church—green and quiet. They will, that is, once State Parks gets the gumption to evict the fat-tire bikes whose joy is bombing down to the shore, screaming at little children to get out of the way.

Where to walk? Where the seminary students did for years and the deer and coyote still do, tramping out a trail system of a dozen-odd miles. For a sampler, do a figure-8 loop of some 4½ miles.

From the main building descend the Beach Trail, losing 338 feet in ⅔ mile, through a forest of maple, alder, dogwood, hazelnut, cedar, Douglas fir, and madrona. Views into shadowed vales give the feeling of touring the great halls of a forest mansion. Sidetrails invite left and right.

For the first loop follow the shore trail ¼ mile along the waterside terrace (underwater until the lake was lowered) to the south boundary. Retrace steps to the picnic lawns at the foot of the Beach Trail. Watch mallard hens convoy flotillas of ducklings, gaze to boats on the water, to Kenmore up the lake and Sand Point down. Then, just to the south, take a prominent path up a ravine to a skinny ridge crowned by a cathedral forest, and at ⅔ mile from the shore leave trees for lawns of the St. Thomas enclave and follow roads and grass paths north ½ mile to the start.

For the second loop, again descend the Beach Trail—or one of those mentally noted sidepaths. Turn north on the shore through a succession of monster cottonwoods, two with caves that invite kids to crawl in. In ½ mile the park ends. Retreat a few hundred steps to the only major up-trail. The way climbs steeply through glorious fir forest, then sidehills a jungle gorge where devils club grows tall as trees. At the Y the left fork drops to the creek and climbs to suburbia; take the right a final bit up to the plateau and at ⅔ mile from the lake return to the parking lot.

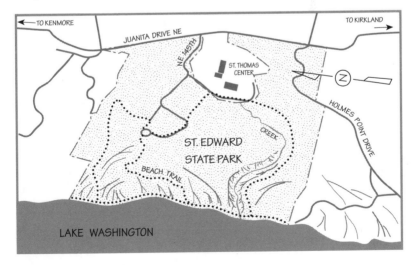

Sammamish River Once and Future Trail

Bus: 307 to Bothell; 251, 253, 254 to Redmond

In 1977, before the Save the Sammamish Trail Association won its famous victory, the elder surveyor walked the 10 miles from Redmond to Bothell, and the 10 miles back from Bothell to Redmond, and in all the long day met nobody but cows drugged out on cuds and lonesome horses wanting a hug. Murky waters floated ducks and coots. Tweetybirds flitted in reeds, clouds of gulls circled, hawks patroled. Pastures and cornfields sprawled table-flat east and west to forested valley walls, muting the faraway highways. Accustomed to skulking in dark woods, the surveyor was dizzied by the size of the sky.

On a fine spring Sunday of 1981 he found the new-built trail united in one big smile. Bicycles by the family (rentals in Bothell and Redmond), rollerskaters by the platoon, horses rejoicing in the companionship of riders, joggers, walkers, and, on the parallel water trail, kayaks and canoes and rubber rafts. Tiny children were staggering-toddling or being carried on parents' backs, in kiddyseats, on bikes, in strollers pushed by fathers on rollerskates. The age-challenged were enjoying the sunshine on a flat, paved, no-obstacle path (beside it, a gravel horse path). Everyone yielded to wheelchairs. It was a scene to start tears of joy, to prove the innate goodness of humanity, the providence of the "multi-use trail."

Nor was this the last of the good news. Since 1989, more than 700 volunteers of the Friends of the Sammamish River have been revegetating the riverbanks, and in 1994 King County Parks joined in. The King County Farmlands Preservation Program was funded by the voters and through 1985 had bought development rights to 70 percent of the valley's agricultural lands, nearly 1000 acres in total. To be sure, far more acres than that were being held by fortune-hungry speculators and much of the agricultural produce now was instant lawns for houses of instant cities.

There seemed no end of good. King County Parks consolidated ownership and easements along the west bank of the river for a second and parallel trail. A campaign was making head to undo some of the evil wreaked by the farmers who in the 1930s–1940s channelized the river to claim Nature's wetness for man's croplands, the holocaust completed by the U.S. Army Corps of Engineers in 1965, when it shortened up the meanders, cleaned out shore jungles and slough swamps, mowed the banks to prevent an infestation of nesting birds and rambling muskrats, and made 30 miles of wildlife habitat into 14 miles of ditch.

Then arrived the kinetics. Government sat on its bottom in the classic pension-protecting posture of see no evil, hear no evil, speak no evil. As these words are typed, the Sammamish River used-to-be Trail is mocking the concept of multi-use, shaming the name of democracy. Bicycles, in-line skates, and skateboards rule, and only the fastest and rudest of these thrive.

It cannot be accepted. The Sammamish is too good to give up. Walkers

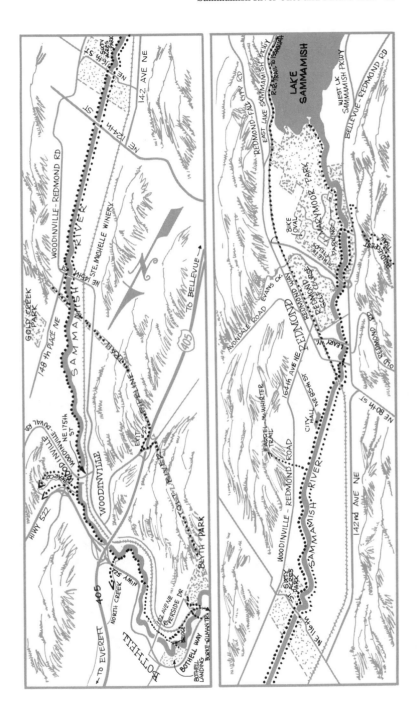

of the world, unite! You have nothing to lose but a pain in the neck. You have a smile to regain. Take up your quarterstaffs, ye band of merry men and women!

Blyth Park, Bothell's biggest at 36 acres, is the junction of the Burke-Gilman and Sammamish River Trails-That-Were and the Tolt Pipeline. From Main Street in Bothell drive the 102 Avenue bridge over the river and turn right on Riverside Drive to the park, elevation 25 feet.

The trail turns upstream, through cottonwood-alder-willow forest, beside cattails and reeds raucous with blackbirds. At ½ mile from Blyth Park is the Park at Bothell Landing.

When Bothell turned its back on its beginnings as a stop for the steamers coming up from Lake Washington and—in high enough water—proceeding to Lake Sammamish, it became just another hick village selling gas and groceries and the occasional hamburger. Briefly, after 1912, it could boast of lying on the Pacific Highway from Seattle to Everett. However, this soon became "the old Everett Highway" and the hamlet moldered. When it once again turned its face to the river it got Soul. The shops on the mall of Bothell Landing offer ice cream cones, books, and T-shirts. The Park at Bothell Landing is a dandy spot to watch ducks and canoes, to picnic, to swim. Of historic interest are the buildings: the 1885 Beckstrom Log House; the 1896 Lytle House, now the Senior Center; and

Blyth Park

the 1893 William Hannan Home, now the Bothell Historical Museum (Sundays, 1:00–4:00 P.M.).

Landing Park, elevation 20 feet, lies just off Bothell Way. At ¼ mile from its graceful wooden bridge arching over the river is 102 Avenue NE. At ¾ mile from the bridge (1¼ miles from Blyth), the trail crosses the river to another popular parking-starting place just off Highway 522. For a short bit the way is a sidewalk along the old Bothell-Woodinville Road, which now deadends at the river. A bridge over North Creek leads to a forest of concrete pillars whose foliage is concrete ramps—the interchanges of I-405 and Highway 522 and whatnot.

At 2¾ miles from Blyth Park the trail crosses Bear Creek and goes under NE 175 Street in Woodinville (parking). The scene changes. To this point there have been river and greenery but also trailer courts, apartment houses, assorted urbia, and concrete. Now begins ruralia as the broad trail and companion river strike out into the center of the plain. At 4¼ miles is the junction with the Tolt Pipeline and at 4¾ miles the underpass crossing of NE 145 Street (parking and a sidetrip to Ste. Michelle Winery, ¼ mile away, to buy cheese and crackers for lunch—the winery has 90 manicured acres for strolling).

Shortly beyond the underpass crossing of NE 124 Street (parking), at 7¼ miles is NE 116 Street and the county's Sixty Acres Park—stay out unless you're wearing team togs and kicking a soccer baw. At 8 miles is the junction with Redmond's Farrel-McWhirter Trail.

At 8½ miles the scene again changes at Redmond City Hall, beside the river at the deadend of NE 85 Street (parking). Watch for the Levine sculpture, *Sitting Woman,* who is doing it without a chair and badly needs attentions of the sort the folks give *Waiting for the Interurban* in the Fremont District.

Quitting farms, the trail follows the river through the city, passing under the railroad to Issaquah and lofty masses of highway concrete. At 8¾ miles it crosses Leary Way (parking) next to "downtown" Redmond. Across the river lies the abandoned golf course which some want to become a shopping center and some a park. Guess who'll win? At 10 miles from Blyth Park is the entrance to Marymoor Park.

Tolt Pipeline

When the Seattle Water Department built the pipeline in 1963 from its new Tolt River Reservoir 30 miles to the city, it acquired for the purpose a strip of land some 100 feet wide. Cooperation with King County Parks led to establishment of a 12-mile route for foot, horses, and bicycles, up hill and down dale, from city's edge through suburbia, from Bothell to the Snoqualmie River valley.

The trail may be walked straight through if return transportation can be arranged. Most hikers, of course, start at one end or somewhere in the middle and walk this way or that as far as inclination leads. Parking

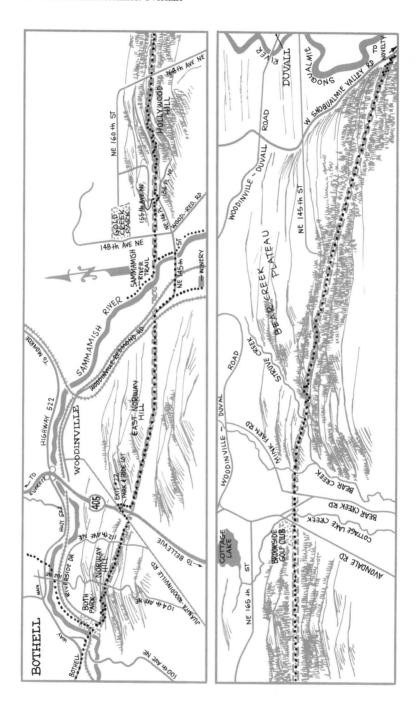

availability is a consideration. Some accesses have room for one or two cars, others for a half-dozen, others for none. Buses are more by the year.

Blyth Park to Norway Hill, ¾ mile, elevation gain 450 feet

Drive to Blyth (or get off bus 931 in Bothell) via the bridge over the Sammamish River and Riverside Drive.

The junction of Burke-Gilman, Sammamish River, and Tolt Pipeline routes will make Bothell famous (or infamous, perhaps). Officially the Tolt Pipeline is not open to feet up the wooded slopes from Blyth Park, though a ¾-mile path winds south from the Burke-Gilman/Sammamish River junction to the pipeline.

Norway Hill to I-405, 1 mile, elevation gain 50 feet

To drive to the official trail start, from Bothell cross the Sammamish River and turn left. In 0.5 mile turn right on 108 Avenue NE. In 0.5 mile pass a road to the right, NE 164 Street, to the trailhead, signed "Tolt Pipeline Park Trail," parking for three to four cars. Come near on bus 931.

The way descends by houses, through woods, a long ½ mile to 112th (parking) and ¼ mile more to I-405. To cross, turn left up a farm road to a freeway access and follow footpaths marked on the pavement. Pass a Pool It Parking Lot; get here on bus 257 or, by car, by taking Exit 22 from I-405 and crossing the freeway on NE 160th to the lot on the west side. Beyond the freeway the route turns right to rejoin the pipeline, all this crossing business taking about ⅓ mile.

I-405 to Sammamish River, scant 2 miles, elevation gain 125 feet

Backyards. A good rest stop in tall firs of East Norway Hill County Park. Climb to cross busy 124th (some parking). A nursery marsh-field left, houses right.

Ascend to 400-foot top of East Norway Hill. Fields. Acreage estates. Horses. Broad view east to Cascades. Descend to Sammamish valley. At bottom, cross railroad tracks to limited parking by Woodinville-Redmond Road.

The short stretch of trail to the Sammamish River is not officially open. And there's no bridge. So, to continue onward a detour is necessary.

Sammamish River to Bear Creek Valley, 4 miles, elevation gain 650 feet

Detour south to NE 145th. For compensation, at that point take a sidetrip into park-like grounds of Chateau Ste. Michelle Winery. Walk the trails. See the duck ponds.

Cross the river and turn north on the riverbank path (see Sammamish River Once and Future Trail). Alternately, if driving, go north on 148th NE to the swath and good parking. From the riverbank to 148th NE the trail is in county park; nice fields, marsh grasses, river, waterfowl. Total distance of this detour is 1 mile.

Ascend steeply from 148th NE to a 350-foot crest. Horse ranches. Nice

Fog-filled Snoqualmie Valley from the Tolt Pipeline

woods. Views back down to the Sammamish and over to East Norway Hill.

Where the pipeline makes an air crossing of the deep gulch of 155 Avenue NE, find a path to the right down in woods. On the far side of the gulch climb steeply to a subtop hill at 350 feet. Big stable here. Horse estates.

Drop to a tangled ravine, then begin a steady uphill in big-fir forest. Pass a pleasant vale to left pastures, barn, horses, sheep. Climb to the 545-foot summit of Hollywood Hill and a road, 168 Avenue NE; parking for three to four cars. Grand views west to downtown Seattle, Puget Sound, Olympics. Continue through pastures, cows, horses, old barns. Then into forest. At the east edge of the high plateau, views of Pilchuck, Sultan, Index, Phelps.

Descend in wildland to remote quiet. Continue on the flat, by pastures, marshes, to the green valley bottom of Bear Creek and Brookside Golf Course. Here at Avondale Road is good parking and bus 251.

Note that all along this Hollywood Hill stretch are paths taking off this way and that. What marvels lie hidden in these woods? In 1977 the question might well have been asked. In 1994 the answer, for the most part, is "new houses—bushels of new houses—googols of new houses— miles of new fences."

Bear Creek Valley to Snoqualmie Valley, 4 miles, elevation gain 350 feet

Cross the splendid flat bottom of Bear Creek Valley, which actually has three creeks and tributaries, plus marshes, pastures, woods. In succession cross Avondale Road (parking), Cottage Lake Creek, Bear Creek Road (parking), Mink Farm Road (parking), Bear Creek, and Struve Creek. Passing houses secluded in woods, start upward in wildwoods, climbing to the summit of Bear Creek Plateau at 525 feet.

Stay high nearly 2 miles, largely in woods, much still wild, though the developers have in mind building several New Redmonds up here by the end of the century. Until that happens, trails will continue to take off every which way over the plateau, many not posted "Private Keep Out" and thus open to exploration.

The pipeline gives views out to the Cascades, down to Snoqualmie pastures. At last it descends on a switchbacking service road to the West Snoqualmie Valley Road at 50 feet, close to the Snoqualmie River. Very cramped parking here.

To continue, turn south ½ mile, then east on Novelty Hill Road (NE 124th, bus 311) 1 mile across the river and valley to join the Snoqualmie River Trail at Novelty.

To pick up the Tolt Pipeline and follow it east to the Cascade front, see *Hiking the Mountains-to-Sound Greenway* (Seattle: The Mountaineers, 1994).

Other Trips

Pioneer Park. A deep green ravine, a year-round stream, the wild gem of the City of Mercer Island. No golf course, not yet.

Marymoor Park and Bridlecrest Trail. A path and wooden walkway traverse birdy marshes to the outlet of the Sammamish River. A 2-mile trail ascends forest and pastures to Bridle Trails State Park.

Bridle Trails State Park. A 481.5-acre forest nearly a century along toward ancience. The ranger warns newcomers setting out to explore the 28 miles of wheelfree trails, "You could get lost in there." A consummation, says the wildlander, devoutly to be wished.

Lake Sammamish Railroad. As long as the iron horse runs, there'll be no other wheels and no Privatizer fences the 9 miles from Marymoor Park to Lake Sammamish State Park.

O. O. Denny–Big Finn Hill Park. From a ¼-mile strip of Lake Washington public beach a path ascends Big Finn Creek to the snag of a Douglas fir which was nigh on to 600 years old when the top blew out in a big wind. Was 26.3 feet in circumference. And still is.

Farrel-McWhirter Park and Trail. The 200-acre pasture and for-

600-year-old Douglas fir in O. O. Denny Park

est, formerly a working farm, has been hailed as "the jewel of Redmond's park system." The 2 miles of in-park trails and the 3-mile trail to the Sammamish River Trail were conceived to be the heart of the north King County horse country. But the fat-tire bicycle cometh.

Redmond Watershed Reserve. The 806 acres were envisioned in 1986 as an "urban wildland park" on the model of the Cougar Mountain Regional Wildland Park, but in 1994 the city of Redmond finds itself struggling to come to terms with the self-bestowed title of "bicycle capital of the Solar System."

Renton-to-Bellevue-to-Woodinville Railroad. Still used by trains, the 7 miles along Lake Washington from Coulon Park to Bellefields Park are far more appealing to walkers than the parallel bikeway. South and east from Coulon is the rail way to Elliott Bay, north is the way to Kirkland and the Sammamish River and Issaquah, glory be.

ISSAQUAH ALPS

At night, having clandestinely clambered to the rooftop of Parrington Hall, a University of Washington student would find his eyes drawn east over the darkness beyond Lake Washington to winking beacons lighting the airway for the Sons of Lindy, who a mere 16 years before had soloed the Atlantic. The farthest east the student could see was well into the mountains, atop McClellan's Butte. Next west, close to the Cascade edge, was Rattlesnake Mountain. Nearest to campus was the wink of a peak shown by the Geological Survey map to be the same elevation as Snoqualmie Pass, yet—incredibly—rising virtually from the very shores of Lake Washington. A building-clamberer grown up on the glacier-homogenized landscape north of Seattle, his Boy Scout heart ever roaming ridges of Olympics and Cascades, could not but be mesmerized by such highlands on the city's doorstep.

Laymen suppose these near-Seattle loftinesses are "foothills of the Cascades." Geologists in the campus time of that sometime geology student considered them to be remnants of a range which once had extended from Cape Flattery to Yakima, the "Old Mountains." In 1976 the building-clamberer, having become a politically active hillwalker and seeking to give the anomaly a politically viable unity, christened them the "Issaquah Alps." *Not* foothills of the Cascades. Rather say, Seattle is built on foothills of the Alps.

When Puget Sound City began its sprawl eastward, developers lusting for the quickest profits advanced across the lower and flatter lands like the creeping crud on a baby's skin. Their bottom-line vision never sharp, the thrust of highlands 20 miles out from the Cascade front was invisible in the myopia of greed.

The eyes of those who early in life had taken vows of poverty, wittingly or not, were clear enough to see the chance of "wildness within" the a-building megalopolis.

The trail system of the Issaquah Alps (in these pages no more than introduced, and that by a light sampling) has the major share of the vehicle-free, wildland walking *within* Puget Sound City, 200 miles or more from trailheads accessible by automobile in a half hour or so from any home in King County (and northern Pierce and southern Snohomish Counties and—not counting ferry time—eastern Kitsap County). Many trailheads, and more planned, lie on public transit lines; when the group which soon was to found the Issaquah Alps Trails Club staged its first publicity stunt, in 1977, drawing more than a hundred walkers from near and far, it pointed toward the future by advertising, as the theme of the stunt, "Wilderness on the Metro 210." Startled by the mysterious mass movement from their city's downtown toward Tiger Mountain, Issaquah folk summoned children into the house, locked the doors and barred the windows, turned the dogs loose, and called the police. A decade later the elder surveyor of this volume, having publicized the trails in 1977's *Footsore 1* and narrowly avoided arrest and trial for building unauthorized trails on public land, was honored as Grand Marshal of the Great Big Salmon Days Parade. The City Council, Chamber of Commerce, and the press were hailing "Issaquah: the Trailhead City," providing the Trails Club free housing in a city-owned building and helping fund a full-time coordinator of city, county, and state trail plans.

Westernmost of the Issaquah Alps is Cougar Mountain, leaping from Lake Washington to a summit of 1595 feet, as tall as three and a half Queen Anne Hills one atop the other. Here, in 1985, was formally dedicated the Cougar Mountain Regional Wildland Park, expected to grow ultimately to 4000–5000 acres.

Next east is Squak Mountain State Park, topping out on a summit of

Mine shaft near Newcastle railroad terminus

2000 feet. Beginning as a Bullitt family gift of 590 acres, by the early 1990s county and state funding had nearly quadrupled the size.

Tiger Mountain is a range of peaks, reaching from West Tiger, hanging in the sky over Issaquah and I-90, to Middle Tiger, to South Tiger above Highway 18, and culminating in East Tiger, 3004 feet.

Citizen activism was basic to the successes of the Issaquah Alps in the 1980s, but no less crucial were two political fortuities. Randy Revelle was the darkest of horses in the race against the incumbent King County Executive, the developers' handyman. He campaigned on a platform featuring Cougar Mountain, held a press conference on the summit attended by the elder surveyor and hardly any press, and threw the developer crowd into panic with his 1981 victory. By vetoing a flawed ordinance passed by the County Council and jawboning to obtain a satisfactory one, he presided over dedication of the Cougar Mountain Wildland Park in 1985, months before going down to defeat at the hands of an itinerant baseball entrepreneur from California who terrified the sportswriters and the fans by threatening to take his major-league toys and play in some other yard.

Similarly, nobody ever had heard of Brian Boyle before 1980, when he came out of nowhere to win the primary and in the finals toppled the incumbent State Land Commissioner, who had held office since state government was housed in trogs at the margin of the Canadian glacier. Days after election, Boyle took a hike on Tiger Mountain, soon afterward engineered the land exchange that got Weyerhaeuser out of Issaquah Alps' hair, in 1981 established the 13,500-acre Tiger Mountain State Forest, and in 1989 shepherded through the legislature a new land designation, within the state forest, a West Tiger Mountain Natural Resources Conservation Area.

East of Tiger, beyond the Raging River, is the connector to the Cascades, Rattlesnake Mountain, treated in a companion volume to this. South of Tiger, beyond Highway 18, is Taylor Mountain, the connector to the enormous wildlife reservoir of the Cedar River Watershed, closed to hunting and all other recreations that might infringe on the right to life of wildlife.

North of Tiger, beyond I-90, are Grand Ridge and the East Sammamish Plateau, where skirmishes presently in progress are a prelude to the final battle (Armageddon?) to take back into the public domain the Northern Pacific Land Grant corruptly given away to the robber barons of the Gilded Age and handed down through the decades from one greedhead to another. Interestingly enough, in 1994 a de facto partial revestment of the land grant was in progress. An heir of the Big Steal sought to build an instant new city on Grand Ridge. Activists of the Issaquah Alps Trails Club were in the forefront of outraged citizen protest. King County government having joined the lynch mob, the Big Thief at last yielded up for public park purposes hundreds of acres of the booty. Meanwhile, King County had purchased for park purposes the "Section 36 property," 636 acres on the East Sammamish Plateau where developers were salivating like Yellowstone geysers. So, there will be woodland trails, among other park amenities, but not in such form as can be guidebooked until near century's end. At this writing the melee is so fierce that the surveyor wouldn't know where to tell a walker to go without risk of having his brain scrubbed and blown dry by a developer's DST (Designated Sweet Talker).

USGS maps: Mercer Island, Issaquah, Maple Valley, Hobart, Fall City, Snoqualmie

Cougar Mountain Regional Wildland Park

In 1983 the King County Council and Executive adopted by ordinance the plan proposed in 1980 by the Issaquah Alps Trails Club for a "great big green and quiet place" on Cougar Mountain. Acquisitions began in 1984 and continue from time to time; by formal dedication in 1985 it already was far and away King County's largest park and, as well, America's largest urban wildland (confirmed by 1994 master plan ordinance) dedicated to *low-impact, non-mechanized* recreation.

The park boundaries are "opportunistic," which is to say flexible, ready to take advantage of opportunities as they may arise or be created. The core park eventually may total some 4000 acres or more, not counting the contiguous Coal Creek Park and the close-by trail-connected May Creek Park. In addition there are, and will be more, "ray trails" from the core to homes and Metro bus stops. Greenbelt walking corridors have been obtained by developers' dedications along Far Country Creek on the south, De Leo Wall and China Creek on the west, and Lewis Creek and AA Creek on the north. Bellevue Parks, Issaquah Parks, and Renton Parks have connecting trail systems. The Mountains-to-Sound Greenway passes by, to Seattle west and Snoqualmie Pass east.

The trails here are an introductory sampling. Free maps provided by King County Parks at trailheads suffice to follow the entire system of maintained trails, which are well signed. A larger, more comprehensive map published by the Issaquah Alps Trails Club covers not only the park but its adjoining area, including Coal Creek Park and May Creek Park.

Newcastle Historic District

Go off I-90 at Exit 11 or Exit 13 to Newport Way. Turn east from the first or west from the other, to SE 164th. Turn south on this arterial, which changes name to Lakemont Boulevard and in 3 miles bends sharply to cross Coal Creek. A sideroad off the bend leads to the Coal Creek Townsite ("Red Town") trailhead, elevation 600 feet.

Seattle & Walla Walla Railroad (Coal Creek Regional Wildland Park), round trip to The Farm 2¾ miles

The peaks of Cougar Mountain (originally the Newcastle Hills, until a coal-hating property owner of the 1950s invented a name he found less

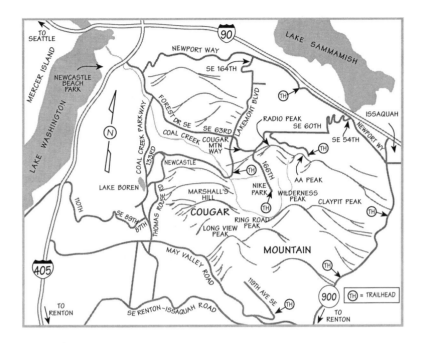

offensive to his nostrils) wrap in a horseshoe around the basin of Coal Creek. Seattle's first railroad never got to Walla Walla nor even the Cascades but in 1878 did reach a profitable deadend at the Newcastle mines, then King County's largest industry. In 1933, with the "company mine" already 3 years defunct, the railroad gave up the ghost—the 55 years of ghosts who nowadays walk the woods in company of coyote and deer and bear (and cougar). A great notion has been floated to place the 22-mile route from Newcastle through Renton to Elliott Bay and the site of the King Street coal docks on the National Historic Register.

Why not? The excitement up north is memorialized by a Klondike National Park, one segment located on Seattle's Skid Road. But the distant gold was no more than a flash in the pan, quick fortunes for a handful of Puget Sound merchandisers and a taste of big-time show biz for frontier journalists. The local coal steadily if pedestrianly fueled the Puget Sound economy from the 1860s into the twentieth century. Mining didn't quit at Newcastle until 1963 and a few miles to the south continues to this day. (See *Coals of Newcastle,* by Lucile and Dick McDonald, published by the Issaquah Alps Trails Club, 1990.) Annually on the first Sunday in June, a gala festival, "Return to Newcastle," is presented by King County Parks in association with the Trails Club and the Newcastle and Renton Historical Societies.

From the trailhead parking area cross the county road to a field, pass a remnant of concrete foundation from the hotel, and at the field edge find the Coal Creek trail (Elizabeth's Trail), descending the ravine dug for a tram which brought supplies up from the railroad to the hotel and company store. The path passes the awesome hole of an airshaft for a mine abandoned in 1886 and then splits. The left fork crosses the creek on a pretty bridge to the old rail grade, the route wide and level except for a detour around a slope of waste rock dumped from the "gypo" mines which operated after the company mine and railroad quit. Another pretty bridge recrosses the creek to unite the two forks. The united way soon comes to a third bridge, back across the creek to the rail grade.

The energy expenditure for the 2¾-mile round trip is not great, but don't expect to do it in an easy hour. An easy morning or afternoon, yes. But there's too much to see, to muse on, to permit speed. Innumerable spur paths give delightful looks down to the creek as it steadily incises into a deep gorge. Benches allow comfortable admirations of the falls of the north fork of Coal Creek; above here the main fork goes dry in summer, the water seeping into the mines. The history is thick, though most is incomprehensible without first having read *Coals of Newcastle* or taken a guided walk during the "Return."

The informed and perceptive walker will spot bits and pieces of the past and conjure up that half-century bustle of railroading and mining: chunks of coal, brick, rusty iron; concrete foundations of a power plant and of the locomotive turntable; climbing roses blooming high in trees, the gaiety of apple-blossom time. Sites are passed of the railroad ticket office-waiting room and the coal bunkers, the takeoff of the spur line of

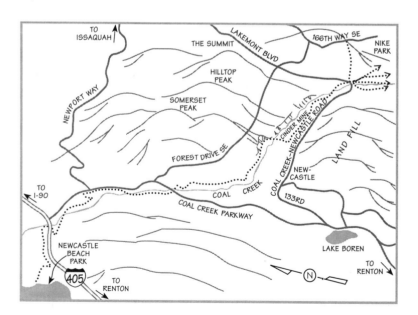

the Washington Lumber and Spar logging railroad, which from 1920 to 1925 extended 13 miles of lines through the high basins. A sidetrail climbs from the valley to the site of the Newcastle School (1914–1969).

The history is near-submerged in the "new wilderness" rebuilt by nature in the past half-century; the tall, steep walls and lush forest of the gorge block out sights of civilization and soak up the noise, making room for the babble of creek and chirping of birds. In season, spawning salmon are fed upon by bald eagles, great blue heron, kingfishers, bears, coyotes, raccoons, and weasels; Coal Creek serves as a major link in the wildlife travel corridor between Lake Washington and the Cascades.

At a long 1 mile the grade is obliterated by the Cinder Mine, where waste rock dumped from the company mines was cooked by the spontaneous combustion of coal into pink and yellow clinkers. Until 1984 these were mined for processing into cinder blocks and running tracks. Beyond the pit the grade resumes and at a scant 1½ miles from the trailhead enters The Farm, as it was until 1977. Roaming the fields where the cows so recently grazed adds a pastoral element to the historical picture.

Coal Creek Regional Wildland (and/or Wildlife) Park (to give the full, just name) continues downstream to I-405, and there is no good reason the Coal Creek Trail cannot ultimately extend to Newcastle Beach Park on the Lake Washington delta of Coal Creek. The route can be—and is— walked now. However, to paraphrase the dictum of Conrad Kain, noted mountain guide, "Walkers can go where the brush does grow—but they must be sturdy walkers." Shortly before The Farm, the Primrose Trail takes off from the rail grade down an old farm lane and passes an artificial pond (cattails, frogs, ducks) and a petite Grand Canyon where the creek cuts a wall of tawny sandstone and tumbles over tawny blocks ("Sandstone Falls"). The tributary Scalzo Creek enters, flowing from Tony Scalzo's mine in the Primrose Seam. In ¾ mile from the rail grade is a resumption of Coal Creek Trail, which in a scant 1 mile reaches Coal Creek Parkway. Beyond here the explorer will be increasingly challenged though never necessarily defeated. As for the Seattle & Walla Walla, at The Farm it leaves Coal Creek and takes aim (or did) on Renton, and from there Seattle.

Coal Creek Townsite, loop trip 1 mile

Newcastle was a floating sort of town. The initial main settlement, "Old Newcastle" or "Old Town," was at a site now lying off the Coal Creek– Newcastle Road on 72nd. The final center was the town of Coal Creek, or "New Town," referred to here as Coal Creek Townsite.

This short loop takes little effort and gives great pleasure: the creek, the forest mixture of native maple and cottonwood and exotic poplar, the intermingling of wildflower blossoms with garden escapes gone wild. The deeper appreciation, of course, is to look beneath the half-century of greening to the decades of industrial grime and noise, of human work and play, happiness and tragedy. "But where," asks the visitor, hearing

Seattle skyline and the Olympic Mountains from Cougar Mountain

the story of the town, "did it all go?" Some of it rotted into the ground and was grown over by the green. Most of it was hauled away piece by piece, salvaged and scavenged and recycled, as was America's way in the Great Depression.

As a prelude to the loop, take the short path into the gulch of Red Town Creek. Pass the Military Road (trail, now) which went over the mountain and down to Issaquah. Spot in the creek an exposure of the No. 4 Seam; at an exposure like this, downstream, the riches of Coal Creek were discovered in 1863.

Begin the loop at the wheels-barring gate, officially called "Red Town Trailhead." Hill Street, the return leg of a counterclockwise loop, climbs steeply left. Go straight ahead on the Wildside Trail. The path follows the grade of a road once used to haul logs to a sawmill and, after that, by the gypo miners who took over the area when the Pacific Coast Coal Company quit in 1930. The Bagley Seam lies beneath the trail as it passes the Bagley Seam Trail, climbing left, and crosses Coal Creek at the site of the

82

Wash House, whose foundations lie buried under a heap of waste rock dumped by the gypos. The company miners coming off shift went directly to the Wash House and then home, where they were cleaner than their wives—who in the era of suffragette agitation eventually were granted a weekly Ladies Day. The way intersects the Rainbow Town Trail. Turn left on it to the concrete arch of the Ford Slope, which from 1910 to 1926 was the center of company mining, embodying the newest technology. It went down the Muldoon Seam at a 42-degree angle for 1740 feet (850 vertical feet, to 250 feet below sea level). Eleven electric locomotives worked underground on a number of levels in the Muldoon and adjoining seams. The coal was lifted to the surface by a steam hoist, the mine cars hauled down Coal Creek by the electrics for dumping in the top of the bunkers, which loaded rail cars for transport to Seattle.

Continue on the road-trail uphill from the Ford Slope, passing a sidetrail, right, to a concrete dam in Coal Creek. The reservoir supplied water to the mining operation and doubled as a sawmill pond. It tripled as the ol' swimmin' hole, where on alternate days in summer the girls swam and boys hid out in the woods, and the boys swam and girls hid out, neither sex owning any swimming garb not issued by Mother Nature.

The road climbs to a T, 750 feet, with the Indian Trail (here called Red Town Trail), used by the Original Inhabitants for overland travel between Coal Creek and May Creek, and later by farmers and miners. Turn left through Red Town, a principal neighborhood of Coal Creek, eighty houses on four streets. The name (invented and mainly used by children) came from the color the houses were painted by the company, which owned them. Other neighborhoods were White Town, Rainbow Town, Finn Town, and Greek Village. The trail crosses the 1000-foot-wide band in which the coal seams of the Newcastle Anticline intersect the surface: from south to north, the Jones, Dolly Varden, Ragtime, Shoo Fly, Muldoon, May Creek, Bagley, No. 3, and No. 4; off by itself to the north, dating from a later geological age, is the Primrose Seam.

Pass a sidepath left, the Bagley Seam Trail, descending a ravine formed by the collapse of an entry tunnel; the Cave Hole Trail right; and the site, on the right, of the palatial Superintendent's House. Turn left and descend Hill Street, passing the sites of the Hospital, the Doctor's House, and the Saloon.

De Leo Wall via the Wildside Trail, round trip 4 miles

The De Leo family homesteaded at the base of 1125-foot Marshall's Hill a century and more ago. The steep slopes rising from May Valley culminate in a super-steepness several hundred feet tall. Views are over pastures and houses of May Valley to highlands concealing the Cedar River, to the eminence of Echo Mountain, and, most eminent of all, Rainier, and over the Big Valley of Renton-Southcenter-Kent-Auburn to the Sea-Tac Airport, the pulpmill plum of Tacoma, and where St. Helens used to be.

From Coal Creek Townsite trailhead walk past the gate and straight ahead on the Wildside Trail, over Coal Creek, past the Wash House site, and across the Rainbow Town Trail to a split. The right fork is the main Wildside way, but for a splendid short sideloop take the left, the Steam Hoist Trail, to the massive concrete footings from whose anchoring a 2000-foot-long cable lifted five loaded mine cars at a time from depths of the Ford Slope. At a second split the right climbs from the valley floor to join the main-way Wildside. (But before doing that, take the left to the Mill-pond Dam, where a conduit built in 1916 carried Coal Creek 885 feet from the ol' swimmin' hole underneath the mineyards.)

The Curious Valley, trenched by a stream from the glacier front and vastly oversized for the amount of modern water, is shown on the maps as akin to Paul Bunyan's Round River in that it drains both ways at once, which is Curious indeed. The north end of the wetland, up to ⅛ mile wide, occupied by the impenetrable tulgeywood of the Long Marsh (actually, mostly Swamp, a little bit bog), empties to Coal Creek, the south end over Far Country Falls and down to May Creek. Along the east side of the valley runs the Red Town Trail, which on the way to the Far Country changes name to the Indian Trail. The west slopes haven't seen wheels in years; it is the wild side.

Trail signs guide the feet unerringly to De Leo Wall, but to many other destinations as well. Going off right, the Lazy Porcupine Trail climbs to China Summit and proceeds through headwaters of China Creek; the Marshall's Hill Trail leads to the summit and a loop to De Leo Wall. Going off left are the other end of the Steam Hoist Trail, the Marshall's Hill Trail to the Indian Trail at the Ball Park, the Wildside Connector Trail to the Indian Trail at the Quarry, and the Wildside itself to the Indian Trail at the entry to the Far Country. So loop yourself silly.

Or don't. The straight and narrow Wildside goes up a little, down a little, sidehill a lot, at the final junction, 700 feet, changing name to De Leo Wall Trail (originally, Dave's Trail, because he pioneered the route). The maples become majestic because the firewood cutters of the 1980s never got this far, and the alders and cottonwood bigger because the pulp-wood loggers of the 1970s also quit, and the firs because no lumber-loggers have been here since the Coal Creek mill closed up shop in the 1920s.

Rounding a spur of Marshall's Hill, the way enters the haunting glen of Dave's Creek, a cold trickle in lushly moist shadows of respectably sizable Douglas fir. What is that sound? Silence! The buzz of bees can be heard! For a while, until a few more steps bring in earshot the never-ceasing, region-pervading rumble-drone of Sea-Tac Airport.

But now, at 950 feet, 2 miles from the trailhead, are the promised views, from a buttress of andesite plucked steep by that old glacier. Bring out the corned beef sandwiches and apple pie. If you could care less about the distant view, try the close one. The grassy bald is edged by madrona, serviceberry, *Ceanothus sanguineus,* and, not far off, Oregon white oak. If lucky (*not*) you may find poison oak. In spring the lunchroom is brightened by paintbrush and blue-eyed Mary and strawberry, honeysuckle and vetch and baldhip rose, Easter lily and chocolate lily, a garden growing to one side of the sky.

Ready for a loop? Return home via the trail over the top of Marshall's Hill and down to China Summit.

Coal Creek Falls, round trip 2½ miles

After heavy rains a suspicion lurked in the ears of pedestrians hearing thunder in the brush that something interesting was happening down there. But the brush was enough to make an ape quail. Then a neat sequence of ancient logging roads was found; the secret was revealed to human eyes and instantly became one of the best-loved short hikes.

From Coal Creek Townsite trailhead walk by the gate and turn left up Hill Street, which on the flat of Red Town, 750 feet, bends right as the Red Town Trail, prelude to the Indian Trail. Just past the site of the Superintendent's House turn left, uphill, on the Cave Hole Trail. Until establishment of the Regional Park this route was driven by trucks of firewood loggers; earlier in the century, it was the horse-and-wagon access to the Klondike Reservoir and various coal prospects. The Pacific Coast Coal Company, builder of the road, took care not to undermine it by digging too close to the surface, but the latter-day gypos mined to the grass roots, causing the subsequent slumps of the ground surface known as "cave holes." The trail ascends to the Clay Pit Road at 1200 feet, 1½ miles from Coal Creek Townsite trailhead.

The ascent from Red Town zigs left across an open-pit mine in the No. 3 Seam and zags right to recross the No. 3, then the Bagley Seam; at the zag corner, a sidetrail goes off left to Red Town Creek dam and the Military Road. At ⅔ mile, 950 feet, the Coal Creek Falls Trail goes right off the Cave Hole Trail. The way crosses the Bagley and Muldoon Seams, contours along slopes high above the Curious Valley, passes the Coal Creek Falls Connector dropping to the Indian Trail, and turns sharp left into the cleft of Coal Creek, and to the falls, 950 feet.

In winter the falls do indeed often thunder, boiling up gales of spray to fill the gorge. But often they fall dead silent, a crystal palace of icicles. In summer they also are quiet, a drip-drip-drip down the 30-foot slab, enough on the hottest of days to cool the shadows under the big hemlocks and maples. Granite erratics dropped by the glacier litter the potholes swirled out in the tawny bedrock sandstone. Coal Creek here is flowing over sedimentary structures; a stone's throw to the south the bedrock is volcanic, an andesite breccia.

The High Country

For the Nike Park trailhead, drive SE 164th–Lakemont Boulevard 2.3 miles south from Newport Way or 0.8 mile north from Coal Creek Townsite. Turn east and up on SE Cougar Mountain Way. In 0.6 mile, where it turns sharp northeast to become 168th, go off south on 166 Way SE. In

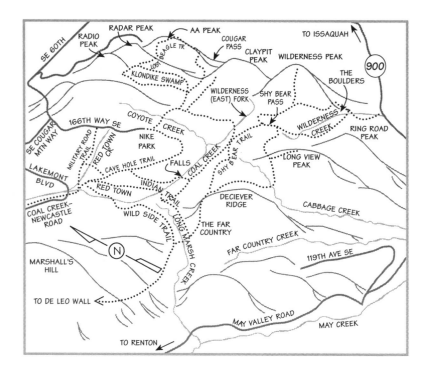

0.7 mile is Nike Park, planned to be the point where public vehicles stop. (As of 1994, a gate stops them sooner.) The Army had Nike missiles here in underground silos. Elevation, 1200 feet.

For the Radar Park trailhead, from the turnoff to 166th continue on 168th, which turns sharp right to become SE 60th. At 0.6 mile from 166th, turn steeply uphill right on Cougar Mountain Drive. At 0.8 mile from SE 60th is the outer gate, closed at dusk. Elevation, 1350 feet. When the outer gate is open, drive 0.3 mile more to the inner gate at the entry to Radar Park, enclosing the summit of Anti-Aircraft Peak. This is where the Army had its command radar for the Nikes. The trailhead is at the outside of the inner gate. Elevation, 1400 feet.

Here is the sky country of Cougar Mountain, the high basins where Coal Creek pulls itself together from the seepages of Klondike Swamp, Coyote Swamp, and the East Fork, and where—across the low divide of Cougar Pass—West Fork Tibbetts Creek has its source in Lame Bear Swamp. This is wind country, where living gales roar through the trees, and cloud country, where storm-driven mists extinguish exterior reality. Finally, it's snow country, often white for weeks at a time and subject to blizzarding from October through April. Above the basins, ringing them to exclude too-vivid reminders of Puget Sound City, are three of Cougar's summits.

Anti-Aircraft Peak–Clay Pit Peak, loop trip 5½ miles

For the longest and widest and most views, this is the favorite, traversing slopes or summits of two peaks, passing two of Cougar's largest swamps and what will be, one day, a large lake/marsh sure to be adopted as regional nesting headquarters of the great blue heron.

From the Nike Park trailhead, the walk starts on the Clay Pit Road, where trucks roll a few weeks a year and never on weekends. The lease to the Newcastle Brick Plant predates the regional park and has some years to run. Ultimately the road will dwindle to a foot-and-horse trail. Except for the clay trucks and King County Parks work vehicles, that's what it is now. No public wheels.

Pass the Coyote Creek Trail on the left and the Cave Hole Trail on the right. At a long ¼ mile go off left on the Klondike Swamp Trail. Primevally this headwaters basin of Coal Creek held a lake a mile long and a thousand feet wide. A dam across the lower end increased storage capacity to 10 million gallons, the principal water supply for the mines. Perhaps partly due to leakage, but largely because of evaporation when the ancient forest was logged in the 1920s, the lake became the Klondike Swamp, a magnificent huge wetland certain to remain a wildlife refuge even in a future when the trails are thronged.

At ¼ mile from the Clay Pit Road, pass the Cougar Pass Trail, right; for a shorter loop hike, take this trail (see later). In a scant 1 mile from the road turn right on the Lost Beagle Trail, which ascends forest above the swamp to the army-built fence enclosing Radar Park. The trail parallels the fence, passing a stone's throw below the summit of AA Peak, and joins the AA Ridge Trail, which joins the Tibbetts Marsh Trail, which emerges from woods on the Shangri La Road-Trail a short bit from Radar Park trailhead, 1400 feet, ¾ mile from the Klondike Trail. A few steps to the left is the entry to Radar Park, now broad lawns for the children to romp about, broad views to Lake Washington and Seattle, and the blabber-towered summit knoll, 1450 feet. Come here on an icy winter day to watch the winds pile snowdrifts that would do North Dakota proud. The biggest views—the airplane-wing views—are not inside the fence but across the entry road on the grassy knoll of the Million Dollar View. Had King County not bought the spot, that's how much would have been paid for it by the plutocrat builder of a trophy home, in views from Olympics to Cascades, Seattle to Bellevue, Lake Sammamish (a swandive below) to Mt. Baker and the San Juan Islands.

Full up on views, descend Shangri La Trail ⅛ mile and turn right on Tibbetts Marsh Trail. Quickly turn right on AA Ridge Trail to a Y where Lost Beagle Trail goes right; stay left on AA Ridge Trail, first along an old railroad grade, then turning off left down AA Ridge, through alder-maple forests, fir-hemlock-cedar forests, marveling at the enormous stumps of Douglas fir, enjoying the standing trees, 60 and 100 years young. At a scant 1 mile from Shangri La is Cougar Pass, 1250 feet, the divide between Coal Creek and West Fork Tibbetts Creek. At the junction here, the right fork leads ⅛ mile to the Klondike Swamp Trail. Turn left along the edge of Lame Bear Swamp, as formidably inaccessible to humans as a wetland gets. At ⅓ mile from Cougar Pass, the Tibbetts Marsh Trail is intersected. The left descends to cross West Fork Tibbetts Creek and climb Anti-Aircraft Peak. Turn right, uphill, ¼ mile and emerge from woods to the wide-open spaces of the Clay Pit, 1375 feet.

The Clay Pit Road goes right 1 mile to Nike Park. (On the way find a short path left to a great big grate over an awesome hole in the ground.) But before leaving the pit, ascend the slopes (note black streaks—the Primrose Seam) to the top, a few yards from the wooded summit of Clay Pit Peak, 1525 feet. The views are out over the Sammamish basin and East Sammamish Plateau to the Cascades from Pilchuck and Baker to Glacier and Index and Teneriffe and Si.

When the mining ceases, as it may any year or not for some years, it is proposed that the notch cut in the impervious clay to drain the pit floor be dammed. Nature would then take care of creating a large lake-marsh, the terrain so shaped during the final days of mining to provide peninsulas and coves and wildlife-refuge islets. In no more than a decade the great blue herons would begin nesting.

Shy Bear Pass via The Boulders, round trip 2½ miles

Go off I-90 on Exit 15 and drive south on Highway 900 to the Newport Way stoplight. Continue on Highway 900 south 2.6 miles to the Wilderness Creek trailhead parking area. Elevation, 365 feet.

The name, "The Wilderness," was not given lightly. This truly is a wildland, partly railroad-logged in the 1920s and cat-logged in the 1940s, but in each case by a quick once-through, man's intrusion limited to a few days, nature then let alone to rebuild. Part never was logged at all, and the virgin forest of Douglas fir on the slopes of Wilderness Peak is as noble an assemblage of ancient snagtops and wolves as is to be found so near Seattle.

The trail bridges Wilderness Creek and ascends switchbacks along the gorge, views down to waterfalls, across to a pair of tall, arrow-straight cottonwoods, and up through interlaced billows of maple to tiny fragments of sky. The creek is recrossed to a Y. Cliffs Trail goes right, in 1 mile attaining the summit of Wilderness Peak, 1595 feet, Cougar Mountain's highest point; go left to The Boulders, house-size chunks of fern-covered volcanic rock fallen from cliffs plucked over-steep by the Pleistocene ice. Far enough for a picnic lunch in the green gloom of handsome big trees, beside the splashing creek. In summer, 20 degrees cooler than outside.

The way recrosses the creek and swings away from it in switchbacks on slopes of Ring Road Peak. At an unsigned split the left is to Ring Road; go right, through a bottom and over the creek to the fabled under-a-boulder Cougar Mountain Cave, sleeping room for three bobcats or one bear. From these Upper Boulders a long boardwalk enters the boggy flat of Big Bottom. To this point there have been a few stumps from the high-grading done by the gypos, not enough to mar the feel of pristinity. Now, on

Coal Creek

the slopes of Wilderness Peak, there are no stumps at all, an unmolested ancient forest of Douglas fir.

The ear notes to its surprise that sounds of automobiles and quarry and all-around civilized hubbub have mysteriously muted. Amid the forests which are half virgin and full virgin, the surrounding peaks have blocked out the chattering simian world. This is perhaps the quietest nook of the Cougar Mountain Regional Wildland Park. Blink your eyes, stamp your boot twice, and say, "I am in the heart of the North Cascades." And you *are.*

Beyond and above the fern-hung maples and big hemlocks of Beautiful Bottom, at 1¼ miles, is Shy Bear Pass, 1320 feet. Time to break out the pickled herring and brie? Or perhaps merely to take a swig from the water bottle and press on. Which way?

Straight ahead, the Shy Bear Trail descends Cabbage Creek, in 1½ miles reaching Far Country Lookout and then continuing to the Indian Trail; another fork leads to Fred's Railroad and multiple choices.

To the left, the Long View Peak Trail attains that summit in a scant ½ mile and proceeds via Doughty Falls and the Skunk Cabbage Farm and Malignant Deceiver Ridge to the Far Country.

To the right, the Wilderness Peak Trail ascends a scant ½ mile to the summit. Linkage to the Wilderness Cliffs Trail enables a looping return via Wildview Cliff and Big View Cliff.

There is no view from Wilderness Peak. The Douglas firs growing here were perhaps half-a-century old when the gypos came through and weren't big enough to bother with. But now they're getting on to the century mark. A few steps away is where the gypos quit and the virgin ancient forest begins. When clouds slide through, dimming the trees to Platonic essences, or snowflakes float through white-sagging branches, who needs to see Southcenter?

Squak Mountain State Park

Between 1595-foot Cougar on the west and 3000-foot Tiger on the east is 2000-foot Squak, in some opinion the noblest beast of them all. That it has fewer trails than neighbor mountains is owing not to inferior quality but a smaller floor plan. It's a "pinched" mountain—squeezed between two channels of the Canadian ice. But because of that it's the steepest of the Alps and thus, pound for pound, most challenging.

Squak forests were not extensive enough to finance logging railroads of the sort boasted by Cougar and Tiger. Squak got narrow-gauge trucks, able to cling to cliffs on skinny gouges. The gypos high-graded more forests than they clearcut and let large sections strictly alone; the mountain has more virgin timber than any patch of real estate so close to downtown Seattle.

The greatest event in the history of Squak was the purchase of most of Section 4 by the Bullitt family as a country retreat. In 1972 the family

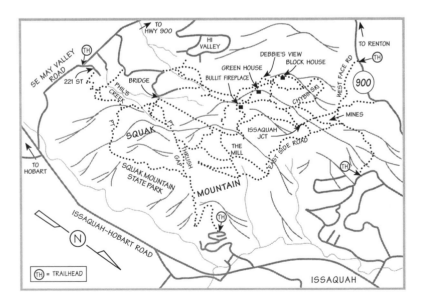

gave the land—590 acres—to Washington State Parks, stipulating that it be kept "forever wild"—no roads, no tree-cutting, no wheeled machines, not even any horses. (Note: Some trails herein are referred to as roads, such as "North Ridge Road," because that's what they used to be. They aren't anymore.)

This core ownership, though long languishing in official neglect and public obscurity, set the stage for the second greatest event, or series of events, in the history of Squak. In 1989 funds from a King County bond issue were used to purchase 400 acres of Section 5, adjoining Section 4 on the west, giving King County the steep slope down to Highway 900, a wildlife travel corridor to Cougar Mountain, and 150 acres in Section 10 (more virgin forests), 50 acres in Section 4, and 120 acres in Section 3. Funds from a state bond issue acquired for the state park 200 acres in Section 16, down to May Valley Road, 160 acres in Section 10, and 340 acres of Section 9 which a California mega-developer was plotting for millionaire mega-estate trophy homes; the remaining 280 acres of the section are intended for acquisition and are under such intense public attention they are very unlikely to host anything mega. The State Department of Natural Resources long has had and still does 120 acres in Section 10. Finally, the City of Issaquah has acreage in Section 33, on the north, planned as a trailhead utilizing easements by developers' dedications through to the park. In summary, as of 1994 the Squak Mountain State Park and contiguous King County Parks and City of Issaquah Parks are a very, very grand total of 2130 acres, expected to soon become a still grander 2430 acres.

The state, county, and city folks presently coordinating plans won't finish for a while, and necessary construction and trail-signing won't be complete until later in the decade. Thanks to stipulations by the Bullitts, management of the core park is a settled matter. Thanks to the wildness-preserving sensitivity of that core, and the fragility of the supersteep terrain ringing it around, the mountain never can become a "forest gymnasium," must self-evidently be defended as a "wildland museum." Outside Section 4, provision will be made for horses, including a hoped-for link in a riding route from Cougar to Tiger and on east to the Cascade Crest.

Once things settle down (in 1996?), the Issaquah Alps Trails Club will be publishing a detailed map of trails and trailheads to complement and enlarge upon the comprehensive map by the Interagency Trails Coalition. Trailheads at the moment are a major embarrassment. Issaquah ("Trailhead City") is planning entry access from the Trailhead Center in the city near the Metro bus stop. Another is being sought from Highway 900 through the abandoned clay pit in Section 32, and another is intended from the May Valley Road. Though hikers who know the area well are using them now, for the general public they all are futures. The most popular current trailhead, from Mountainside Drive at the edge of residential development on the north ridge, crosses private property and is used only by sufferance, which may be discontinued at any time.

A legal trailhead exists on Highway 900, but the parking is too awkward and too hazardous to serve future needs. Such as it is: From the Newport Way stoplight drive Highway 900 south 2.1 miles south. A few feet south of Milepost 19 and just north of Sunset Quarry, spot a narrow, gated woods road. Park nearby on the very narrow highway shoulder. Elevation, 425 feet. (Better, park to the north on safely spacious shoulders-turnouts and walk the powerline service road south to intersect the woods road. The latter, gated against public vehicles, is referred to herein as the West Face Road.)

Central Peak–Northeast Face, loop trip 6 miles

A classic of the Alps, on everybody's list of favorites. The whole route is in splendid forest, some of it alder-maple grown up since the 1920s, some of it big old firs and hemlocks the gypo loggers were in too much of a hurry to molest, and some of it virgin. Though no single smashing view elicits sighs and gasps, at a number of points are windows—cumulatively, to every point of the compass. Some hikers prefer times when the windows are closed by clouds, the views all inward to the forest.

From Highway 900, elevation 425 feet, ascend the West Face Road past the gate, gaining elevation at a meaningful rate but with plenty to keep the mind off hard labor. The firs and hemlocks and maples and alders are big and old, a beauty of a mixed forest. Creeklets waterfall down green gulches. The mountainside drops steeply off, opening panoramas through a sky of green leaves. Fairy bells and columbine line the way, and swordfern and lady fern and licorice fern and maidenhair fern.

At 1¼ miles, 1090 feet, the road switchbacks right, and soon left, and in a scant 1½ miles passes close by the North Ridge Road, on the left; a few steps up the latter is Issaquah Junction, 1275 feet, where the East Side Road goes off left—remember it, it's the return leg of the loop.

Continue up the West Face Road onto the North Ridge Road. For the simplest route to the summit, at 1400 feet, ¼ mile from the junction, go off left on Lower Summit Road, which curves south, in and out of forest vales, around spurs, a joy. At 1700 feet, 2¼ miles, a sideroad climbs right a short distance to the Bullitt Fireplace, all that remains of their summer home. Continue straight ahead to Central Peak, 2½ miles, 2000 feet, and a thicket of radio towers.

Views would be meager were it not for slots cut in the forest to let microwaves in and out. One gives views of May Valley, Cougar Mountain, Renton, Lake Washington, Puget Sound, Vashon Island. Another shows Lakes Sammamish and Washington, Bellevue, the Space Needle, and Mt. Baker. To the south is a screened view of the Cedar Hills Garbage Dump, Enumclaw, and Rainier.

Don't turn around just because you've bagged the peak—loop onward, the best of the trip lies ahead. Descend the service road a short bit to 1925 feet and turn left on the Summit Trail, a lovely wildland path down

Squak Mountain trail

a ravine of lush mixed forest. At a scant 3 miles from trip's start on Highway 900, in the notch between Central Peak and Southeast Peak, is Thrush Gap Junction, 1500 feet. Turn left, north, on a trail that in the 1920s barely held the primitive Mack trucks and chain-drive Reos. At little A Creek are stringers of an old bridge, fern gardens in the air. The road-trail contours, blasted from andesite cliffs, a wonderful stroll in ginger, solomon's seal, and oak fern, screened views out to Issaquah and Tiger Mountain.

At a scant 3½ miles the road-trail abruptly ends on the crest of a spur ridge, 1600 feet. Traces of grade go out on the spur a few feet to a strange clearing. Sawdust! The whole slope is sawdust, nurturing a gorgeous sprawl of twinflower. Here, high above the valley, a portable sawmill operated—a "tie mill," carted around on a truck, to square small trees for railroad ties. Another surprise: a view—not of the expected Issaquah but over Cougar Mountain to towers of downtown Seattle.

Plunge down the sawdust into woods, quickly hitting the East Side Road-Trail at 1300 feet. Turn left and contour around tips of spur ridges, into an alder-maple ravine, by windows out on the valley. At 4¾ miles the East Side Road completes the loop at Issaquah Junction.

West Peak Loops

This pair of little classics offers the same variety and intrigue as the big classic, scaled down for a shorter day.

Ascend the West Face Road from Highway 900, 425 feet, to the second switchback, at 1¼ miles, 1220 feet. Go straight off the end on the Chybinski Trail, a 1920s logging road that hasn't seen wheels since. The grade runs to the edge of a deep ravine and seems to end. Stringer logs of the old bridge span the gap, sprouting hemlocks. Admire. Then backtrack to the bypass trail down over an admirable trickle-creek and up again to the grade. Gently climb by holly and trillium, then contour the steep mountain wall in columbine, selfheal, and coltsfoot. At Choices Junction, 1¾ miles, 1525 feet, a decision must be made between two loops.

Chybinski Loop, 3 miles

Turn right, down a steep, washed-out cat track. In ¼ mile it gentles at 1070 feet. The cat track also completes a loop, but the much better option is to turn right, up the bank, onto an old grade with a few logs to cross but not so many to mar pleasure in alder, fir, and hemlock, the trickle of a creek, the windows (in winter) out on Cougar Mountain. At ⅓ mile from Choices Junction the grade obscurely joins the West Face Road at 1025 feet, a scant 1 mile from the highway.

West Summit Loop, 4 miles

From Choices Junction continue on the road as it starts south, bends north, steadily climbing. At a Y switchback right, up, to the summit plateau, 1750 feet; the lower subsummit, 1785 feet, lies to the left. Pass a short spur road to the Block House and continue to a saddle at a scant 2½ miles. To the right, no trail access and no views but much green solitude, is West Peak, 1950 feet. Stick with the road as it drops steeply to hit the North Ridge Road at 2¾ miles, 1575 feet. Proceed downhill to the West Face Road and go left to square one.

Tiger Mountain State Forest

The "tiger" may have been: the cougar, mountain lion, catamount; the tiger lily which blooms so gaudily in late spring; a Scots word, *taggart,* meaning rock; or a rocky Scot named Taggart. In Issaquah it used to be called Issaquah Mountain; in Preston, Preston Hill.

During the last third of the nineteenth century, bullteam loggers cut the giant cedars and Douglas firs of the lower slopes. Their careless fires and the blazes set by settlers to clear the land for hops and cows ran wild up the mountain. In the 1920s railroad loggers arrived, based at three mills. From the Hobart mill they built a trail of rails angling upward across the west slopes to Fifteenmile Creek and ascending its valley to the summit ridge. From the High Point mill, they engineered the famous "Wooden Pacific Railroad," a tramway that went straight up the fall line

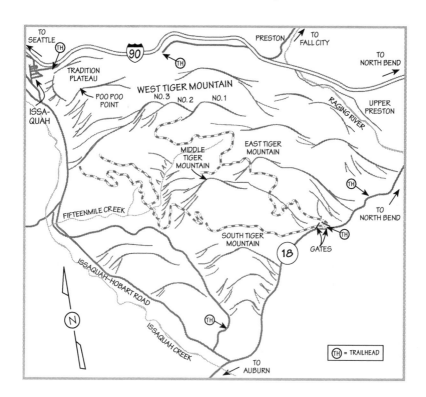

to the 1900-foot level, where a rail grade was gouged on the contour around the jut of West Tiger Mountain, through Many Creek Valley, to a deadend at Poo Poo Creek. From the Preston mill a series of switchbacks climbed to the summit ridge. (Historians are investigating whether there were, in addition, a mill and rail lines from Kerriston.)

The "lokies" began to quit the mountain in the Crash year of 1929 and by the middle 1930s had moved elsewhere, picking up their rails and ties to carry away with them. Tiger was abandoned to the new-growing forests, the wild creatures, the occasional hunter, and a scattering of moonshiners. The sole human structures on high were a state fire-lookout tower atop East Tiger and an airway beacon on West Tiger.

But there were hikers. The rail grades provided a network of routes to nearly every corner of the mountain. The boots of local folk pounded out accesses from their homes to the high country. The state trail to the fire lookout was walked by city folk who knew nothing more of the trail system; when the trail was replaced by a service road, they accepted that as equally serviceable for feet. Recreationally speaking, modern times came to Tiger—with a jolt—in 1966 when The Mountaineers put the service road in their epochal book, *100 Hikes in Western Washington*. Thousands upon thousands of urbanites learned to their delighted surprise that within minutes of their homes they could set out on a hike that would take them to a wild and alpine-like experience. The flood of hikers shared the road amicably with horses, with the few sturdy family cars ascending slowly (lest something get busted) to a picnic, and with the motorcycles of civil riders who chose that vehicle for the open-air freedom.

In the mid-1970s the idyll went sour. The family cars and the view-seeking motorcyclists were driven out by the 4x4s with roll bar and winch whose sport is "mud-running" and "snow-catting" and just plain slamming through the brush; the dirt bikes sans muffler, sans spark arrester, sans any feeling for nature except as something to mess up for ego sake, whose sport is churning soil, muddying creeks, scaring the wits out of family-car drivers and hikers; the three-wheel and four-wheel ATVs, machines so dangerous they kill more of their drivers than they do hikers.

Further, in the mid-1970s the Weyerhaeuser Company, which in 1900 had acquired better than half the mountain from the Northern Pacific Land Grant, paying James J. Hill $6 an acre, or about $500,000 for its

Big Tree Trail

entire Tiger holdings, and had banked at least 25 times that through the first-round clearcutting, returned for a second barbecue. The State Department of Natural Resources, trustee-manager of nearly half the mountain, acting for a number of public-agency trusts (the largest being King County), prepared to follow suit. As the two commenced harvesting the virgin forests left by the railroad loggers, they opened new roads which instantly were taken over by the wheel-crazies and the gun-crazies.

By 1980 Tiger Mountain resembled a war zone. Bullets flew in every direction, despite the only legal shooting being during hunting season, and that with shotguns. To walk the roads was to risk being mugged or raped or at the least hazed and menaced. The police rarely could be talked into answering reports of crimes, saying that to safely venture onto the heights required a platoon of Marines.

But in 1980 the tide turned. A

new State Land Commissioner (head of the DNR) was elected, Brian Boyle. He came to the mountain, he saw, and in due time he arranged a land exchange that got Weyerhaeuser off the mountain (except for the summit ridge of West Tiger, where it retains the lucrative tower colonies). In time, too, the DNR, under Boyle and his successor in office, managed to bring law to the mountain.

Finally, responding to a proposal by the Issaquah Alps Trails Club for an "urban tree farm," Commissioner Boyle proclaimed a Tiger Mountain State Forest, a "working forest in an urban environment," to provide a continuous flow of forest products while serving as a laboratory to experiment with new forestry techniques ("kinder, gentler") compatible with the contiguity of Puget Sound City.

As of 1994, timber sales are held every year, the harvesting observed by industry visitors from throughout the Northwest and the nation who recognize that here they are watching the evolution of the future. Balanced consideration is given all, not merely some, forest products, a term here extended to wildlife habitat, pure water for fisheries and domestic consumption, preservation of the history of the forest industry, teaching of environmental sciences in the schools, research in forest sciences, and civil recreation, both on the roads and on the near-city, quiet trails— "wilderness on the Metro 210." As of the fall of 1994, *all* management roads have been closed to unauthorized public motorized vehicles, four-wheel *and* two-wheel, to become genuine (not hogwash) "multi-use trails" for walkers, horses, and bicycles.

Serving as the point group for the environmental coalition, the Issaquah Alps Trails Club gives the DNR three cheers for seeking to preserve the forest industry from self-destruction, to develop and display on Tiger a model by which the frontier past can at last be exchanged for a civilized future.

Still, the Trails Club always has insisted that on one sector of the mountain the topography and soils are not suitable for a sustained output of wood fiber and have a much higher social value being devoted to other products of a "working forest." On West Tiger Mountain the "tree farm" must be evaluated alongside the "recreation forest," as described by Lars Kardell, professor at Sweden's University of Uppsala:

> *Recreation forests should be given an imaginative kind of care, or in the best of cases, no care at all. We have to get away from the dominant production philosophy based on rotation schedules and clear-felling. In addition, I believe it is important to let the forest remain forest, rather than to urbanize or civilize it. There is a real risk that some new technical gadgetry will inspire demands to put the consumption-focused recreation of the computer age into our forests. If this happens, the forests will become only backdrops for something foreign to their nature. Our constant hunt for new sensations should stop at the edge of the forest. Within the forest we should*

learn that there are plenty of exciting things to discover, experience, and understand.

After detailed studies of the entire mountain, in 1989 the West Tiger Mountain Natural Resources Conservation Area was established, one of twenty-one such DNR preserves in the state where gene pools take precedence over resource extraction, and *low-impact* (the phrase used in the legislation) recreation over devil-may-care kinetic razzing around. Though the language is less lofty than that of the National Wilderness Act of 1964, the result is much the same. On West Tiger and its companion NRCAs is the heart of a Washington State Wilderness System.

As of 1994 a number of large additions to the Tiger Mountain State Forest must be obtained to guarantee the integrity. Also, the boundaries of the West Tiger Mountain NRCA remain to be fixed. However, recreational goals have largely been reached. Some 52 miles of trails are freely open to feet, 14 other miles in the eastern sector of the forest accessed by Highway 18 are freely open to feet, horses, and bicycles, and 19 miles of gated management roads are freely open to feet, horses, and bicycles.

A selection of representative trails is described in these pages; for the full menu, see *Guide to Trails of Tiger Mountain State Forest,* by William K. Longwell, Jr., published by the Issaquah Alps Trails Club and revised periodically.

Trailheads

The Tradition Plateau trailhead is far and away the most popular, made so initially by its high visibility from I-90, increasingly by its wealth of short and easy family-friendly trails plus longer adventure trails. The Metro 210 bus stops just north of the High Point interchange. To come by car, go off I-90 east of Issaquah at Exit 20, and turn right on the frontage road 0.4 mile to the turnaround at the gate, elevation 450 feet. As of 1994, walk 0.6 mile past the gate to the Puget Power powerline swath and a bit beyond to the Tradition Plateau trailhead and its picnic tables and restrooms. Elevation, 500 feet.

The downtown Issaquah trailhead is superior for local residents, visitors arriving by the Metro 210 (more frequent service than at High Point), and folks with glitzy cars which invite theft and vandalism at every trailhead along I-90. Go off I-90 on Exit 17, drive south on Front Street, and turn east on Sunset Way to where it bends left to become a freeway on-ramp. Park anywhere on Sunset or adjacent residential streets. Elevation, 150 feet.

For other, lesser trailheads, see the trip descriptions that employ them and/or Longwell's Bible.

Tradition Lake Natural Resources Conservation Area

The Issaquah Watershed, it used to be, and much of it still is owned by the city, the rest by the State Department of Natural Resources, Puget Power, and several entrepreneurs who need to be bought out before they

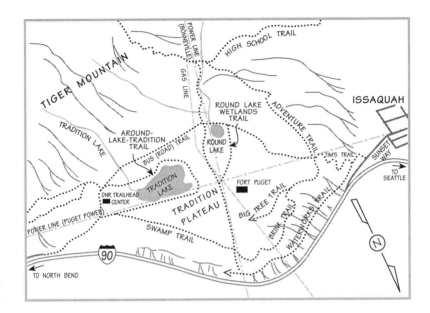

vandalize a regional treasure. As a de facto public park, the plateau survived a greed scheme of the 1970s for a New Issaquah on the plateau (log the forests, mine the gravel, "rehabilitate" Tradition Lake, build condos and their inevitable golf course, and millionaires' mansions on the view estates). That attempted raid was followed by a lesser silliness over logging the plateau. However, wisdom always lurked in the back of the civic mind, and on December 20, 1993, the Issaquah City Council designated the city property a Tradition Lake Plateau Natural Resources Conservation Area to be managed in conjunction with the DNR's West Tiger NRCA.

The plateau trails are easy to reach and easy to walk. They serve families with tots on parents' backs or toddling on their own feet, school classes studying the wild world, assorted pedestrians, and—on the powerline swaths—horses. But no wheels of any sort except on service roads. Bikes were permitted on one trail (the Bus Trail) until they had done such damage to soft tread and had been found so costly to police they had to be banned. In any event, the foot population on the trails has become so large (the most popular wildland walking in the region) there literally is no room for wheels; their bulkiness, speed, and unmaneuverability make them excessively consumptive of trail space.

Trails of the plateau most commonly are walked from the Tradition Plateau trailhead on the east or downtown Issaquah on the west. From the latter start on Sunset Way (elevation 150 feet), climb to the plateau, and continue to the Grand Junction (500 feet) at Fort Puget of east-west powerline (Puget Power) and north-south powerline (Bonneville) and natural gas line; distance from Sunset, ¾ mile. The same point is ½ mile,

and 0 elevation gain, from the Tradition Plateau trailhead. With this dif-
ferential in distance and energy expenditure to be kept in mind in the
case of each trail offshooting from the powerlines, they will be described
here in sequence from the west.

Tim's Trail, one way ¼ mile

At a turnout a bit past the easternmost homes on Sunset Way, a volunteer-built staircase ascends to the abandoned railroad grade just short of
where a long trestle used to cross the valley of East Fork Issaquah Creek.
Walk left several steps to the start of the path, built by former Issaquah
Councilman Tim O'Brian, ascending a narrow ridge beside a deep gorge.
Ancient forest! Within Issaquah city limits! The climb continues to join
the powerline at the brink of the Lower Plateau, 425 feet. The ascent
gives good access to trails and is in itself popular for the views down into
the wilderness gorge and, at the top, out across Issaquah to Lake
Sammamish.

Waterworks Trail: The Springs, round trip 2 miles

In Pleistocene time, as the Canadian glacier receded, a great lake
formed at the Cascade front where now is North Bend. At a certain period the water overtopped High Point and flowed into another lake, a
predecessor of Lake Sammamish, dammed by the glacier at a level much
higher than the lake of today. An enormous delta was built, hundreds of
feet deep, layers of sand, gravel, and clay. In the post-glacial period the
East Fork of Issaquah Creek sliced through the delta. On the north side
of I-90 the sand and gravel have been mined for many years. On the
south side the delta is intact; the Tradition Plateau is none other than
the old lakebed, as remodeled by subsequent erosion. The abundant rainfall and snowmelt from West Tiger Mountain flow to the delta. Some feeds
surface streams and the two kettle lakes (Tradition and Round). Most
sinks into an underground reservoir which was Issaquah's water supply
until construction of I-90.

The reservoir empties through an underground aquifer (or two) capped
top and bottom by impervious layers of clay-rich sediments. At the scarp
cut by the East Fork they seep out, trickle out, and gush out—one spring
after another for half a mile. The larger of them passes through concrete
filtration boxes formerly connected to the city's main water tank, now
removed. Issaquah kids with an attachment to historical roots come here
on summer-day pilgrimage to drink the waters, declaring, "You just don't
get water like that from city pipes."

From the site of the former water tank, the former service road was
destroyed by I-90 construction. Drop from the service road almost to the
shoulder of I-90 (illegal to walk *on* the shoulder) and angle upward across
the slope to a resumption of former road.

At ¾ mile from the railroad grade is the last collection box and the end
of the service road-trail. A rude animal path continues up and down a
scant ¼ mile to the gas line.

Brink Trail, one way from Puget powerline to gas line ¾ mile

Just short of the step up from the Lower Plateau, 425 feet, to the Upper (Main) Plateau, 450 feet, a sign to the left marks the start of the Brink Trail, originally built by this author as a political protest against logging ancient trees. The act of civil disobedience caused the Issaquah City Council to consider throwing him in jail, as had been done to Thoreau for protesting the Mexican War.

"To make the world larger, go slower." To your right is forest swamp. To your left is the brink of the Lower Plateau, above a series of gulches where the devils club and salmonberry are so densely interwoven, the soil so kneedeep mucky, that neither from the brink above nor the Waterworks Trail below can an explorer sanely venture. Where the wild things are. On quiet days and all the nights they also are on the brink. Returning from an afternoon's construction, the builder found his disobedient new trail ratified by seals of approval by deer, a coyote, and a bear. Listen to the loud, unseen waterfalls of The Springs issuing from the aquifer and tumbling down to East Fork Issaquah Creek. The civilized din of I-90 enhances the "wildness within."

Big Tree Trail, one way from Brink Trail to gas line ½ mile

A few steps from the powerline on the Brink Trail, the Big Tree Trail turns off right, the mucky path pioneered by the elder surveyor in the late 1970s replaced in 1994 by DNR plankwalks which protect the soils and keep the boots clean and dry. An average pace can reach the east end in less than a half hour. But an afternoon is not enough. Examine the path for tracks and sign of coyote, cougar, deer, bear, raccoon. Sit on a mossy log beside the swamp, through which water moves ever so slowly and quietly, enjoy the blossoms of lily-of-the-valley, and fill lungs with skunk cabbage. See eight species of fern and scores of mosses and lichens and liverworts. Hear the winter wren and varied thrush. The wildland arboretum has two unique features, as well. A stretch of cedar puncheon dating from the 1880s is the area's only known surviving bullteam skidroad, along which oxen dragged the "big sticks." So much time has elapsed that trees then too small to interest loggers have grown to noble dimensions, a rain-forest mix of Douglas fir, Sitka spruce, hemlock, cedar, and fern-hung maple. Some Douglas firs were too large for the bullteams—one measures 24 feet in circumference and has been found by coring to be 1100 years old.

Adventure Trail, one way from Puget powerline to High School Trail ¾ mile

Where the Brink Trail goes off the powerline left, the Adventure Trail goes right, crosses the clearcut swath (passing an alternate entry to the Round Lakes Wetland Trail, described next), enters forests, climbs and drops, up and down, through splendid tall firs near the west edge of the "plateau," which in this section actually rises to little ridges cut by little vales. Near its end this construction by the outdoor club of Pine Lake

Middle School tops a 600-foot saddle and joins an ancient roadbed descending to the (gated) service road from Issaquah High School. The trailhead off Issaquah's Second Avenue gives access to this and other trails, but a common practice is to ascend the service road the short way to the Bonneville powerline and loop on back to the Grand Junction at Fort Puget.

Round Lake Wetlands Trail, one way from Puget powerline to Bonneville powerline ¾ mile

An offshoot from the Adventure Trail is one entry to the Wetlands Trail. Atop the step to the Upper (Main) Plateau is a second. Near Fort Puget a connector trail also takes off from the Puget swath.

Deep forest. QUIET. The freeway vanishes from ken of the ears except as a distant murmur which could be a river, or wind in treetops. The forest is old. Some of it, virgin. Even the second-growth is sizable and it is not monoculture, but mixed, the reforestation done by Nature, who loves all Her children, including the vine maple whose billows fill gaps in the forest canopy, letting in an airy-green daylight. If the forest as a whole is not ancient, some of the Douglas firs truly are, or nearly. One fallen giant nurses a colonnade of hemlocks; death is an inseparable part of the life of a forest.

Round Lake

Cottonwoods announce arrival at the first of two wetlands on the route. The trail splits, the left fork emerging in ¼ mile on the Puget powerline just west of Fort Puget and the Grand Junction. The right proceeds along the edge of the swamp, whose forest is mainly deciduous, entirely different from unmixed conifers. Beyond the second wetland is Round Lake—or is, that is, before winter's rainwater seeps into the ground or evaporates. The trail divides into segments of an around-the-lake route. The left crosses an isthmus between swamp and lake and is joined by a multiplicity of paths branching from the close-by Bonneville powerline, which may be followed north to Grand Junction to close a loop. A longer, nicer return is via the Bus (Road) Trail to the Tradition Plateau Trailhead.

Swamp Trail, one way from gas line to Puget powerline ½ mile

Where the Brink Trail goes west from the natural-gas swath, the Swamp Trail goes east into forest on an old road built in the 1970s for the last (and we do mean the last, so bitter was the protest by the new Issaquah Alps Trails Club, and ultimately by the general citizenry) logging on public lands of the Tradition Plateau.

(The curious adventurer can find a path beaten out by animals and the elder surveyor of this guidebook off the edge of the plateau, down to an intact 1930s bridge of the old Sunset Highway over East Fork Issaquah Creek, under the I-90 freeway, and up the far side of the valley to the old railroad grade. Turn left along slopes of Grand Ridge, drop to another under-the-freeway creek crossing, and come out on Sunset at the east edge of Issaquah. Turn right to High Point Exit 21 and the section of old Sunset Highway renamed Preston Way. Loop yourself giddy.)

Cross the natural-gas swath to The Swamp. It used to have a magnificent wet-footed forest of big old wet-loving cedars. But Weyerhaeuser's "Tree Farm Family" man came by with a come hither look in his eye and Issaquah sold off the noble relicts for a pitiful pot of cash money. However, Nature has many lessons to teach here about both death and life. The Chief Ranger of the Issaquah Alps, Bill Longwell, built this trail to open for students pages in a textbook on swamps. The original path having been destroyed by fat-tire bicycles, the DNR has hardened the route with boardwalks and banned bikes from all Plateau trails except the service roads. The flowers of the swamp differ from those of deep dry forest. Wet-loving birds throng. Animals up to elk in size enjoy the easy access to lush browsing.

How does The Swamp get so wet? Outlet-lacking Lake Tradition's water seeps through an aquifer under the Puget powerline, emerges on the Lower Plateau into The Swamp, then passes through both north–south swaths into the forest between the Big Tree and Brink Trails, and finally seeps on down to Issaquah Creek.

The trail climbs to the Upper (Main) Plateau, traverses a stand of Douglas fir thinned to boring monoculture in the same orgy as the slaughter of cedars in The Swamp, and comes to the Puget powerline just across from the Tradition Plateau trailhead.

Around-Lake-Tradition Trail, loop trip 1½ miles

All the Tradition Plateau trails described to this point in sequence from the outskirts of Issaquah are as readily accessible by walking west from the DNR's Tradition Plateau trailhead facility—and with less sweat, starting from an elevation of 500 feet and staying mostly on the plateau flat, which in glacial times was a lakebed delta built by streams gushing from the ice. The trails combine easily and obviously in any number of loops suiting the time and ambition of any hiker/stroller, from piggy-backer and toddler up to such gimpy-legged ancients as the elder author of this guidebook. The kinetic-aerobic walker can keep feet busy all of a long, hard day. The gimpy elder repeats, "To make your world larger, go slower."

Starting from the Tradition Plateau trailhead facility entails a ½-mile walk from the gate on the powerline service road, described above in "Trailheads." The trailhead, just off the Puget powerline swath, is a sylvan and architectural delight. A path leads to picnic tables tucked individually in nooks of the fine (not ancient but getting older and better by the year) forest. An interpretive center displays a trail map and a guide to plants and animals and historical artifacts. A handsomely rustic open-sided shelter serves as rainy-day classroom for field-tripping teachers and pupils. A restroom building which blends unobtrusively into the wildwoods conspicuously does not tie to a sewer but composts on the spot—a feature viewed with shock and alarm by robot-heads unable to imagine a public facility lacking massive enough engineering to guarantee full employment for by-the-book urban Health Departments.

The Around-Lake-Tradition Trail is one of the two most popular walks from the trailhead. (The Bus (Road) Trail is the other.) Signs at all junctions lead unfailingly from the restroom/shelter area to the lake trail, which begins on a wide, wheelchair-friendly nature trail with benches, window views out to the lake, a pretty bridge over Tradition Creek, and a full assortment of trees, plants, and birds.

The Tradition Lake Shoreline Restoration Project has relocated the old trail from the lake edge, where soils and vegetation are too fragile for heavy pounding, and is replanting species long since trampled into the mud. There are tree-framed glimpses of the water, the floating ducks, the pond lily in yellow bloom. Birdsongs. Groves of old cedar, big Douglas fir, some well into their second century, halfway-ancient.

A connector trail, left, leads a short way to the Bus (Road) Trail. At 1 mile from the DNR trailhead, the lake trail emerges from forest on the Puget powerline, just short of the Grand Junction with the Bonneville line and the gas line. For the loop, follow the "Puget Trail" east, pausing for the open views of the lake and the backdrop of West Tiger Mountain. In unsettled weather, an exciting cloud show. Get out the binoculars to pry into the private lives of waterfowl. Swing the gaze through the tree-tops on the chance of a bald eagle. See if you can spot either of the two beaver lodges on the shore, exposed in late summer when the lake level drops near nothing. The lodges were abandoned in the early 1970s or thereabouts. As with human loggers, when there's nothing left to chaw the beaver got to be gittin' along.

Historical curiosity quoted from the comprehensive guidebook by the Chief Ranger: "This area was originally called 'Snake Valley.' The lake, of course, was 'Snake Lake.' The first surveyors, running section lines, found 'the ground ... almost entirely covered with various species of snakes. They were also knotted in heaps upon the fallen timber and hung dangling from the lower limbs of small trees.' Still want to visit here?"

Bus (Road) Trail, one way ¾ mile, loop trip 1¾ or 2 miles

No, it is not now and never has been on a Metro line. The name comes from an artifact that apparently served a rancher as a chicken house or the like and has been identified by Trails Club archaeologists as a vintage 1940-or-so Greyhound Scenicruiser. This curiosity is less fascinating, actually, than the area's aged apple trees (plundered in harvest time by the bears; note how they have top-pruned the branches), failed irrigation projects, and other mementoes of a hardscrabble agricultural past on a 130-acre homestead. The road-trail has seen, in a more recent past, disastrous mucking-up by wheels, which is why they now are banned from this route. As repaired by DNR trail crews, it gives the slow ambler a succession of pleasures: the bridge over Tradition Creek, which shifts to wholly underground flow by summer; the groves of maple and the stands of alder whose silvery lichens seem to light the forest from within; young conifer forest demonstrating that successional characteristic of an ecosystem, the self-thinning which reduces the number of trees to what nutrients can sustain, those which don't make it falling down to feed the little bugs and worms which feed the big bug-and-worm eaters.

From the DNR Tradition Plateau trailhead the crushed-rock, wheelchair-friendly nature trail serves as prelude to the once-road now-trail, the feet unerringly guided by a series of trail-junction signs. After years of being churned to a mudhole mudrun by wheels, first those of jeeps and motorcycles, then of fat-tire bicycles, the way has been narrowed to trail width by sidelogs, firmed by ditches, and barred to wheels of any kind, only walker's feet and horses' hooves permitted. (Why hooves and not wheels? Because the impact on tread by the former is distributed over four large points of suspension and that of the latter is concentrated in narrow linear grooves where rainwater does not puddle and evaporate but flows, trenching gullies; because the former readily can be held to a pace compatible with walkers, while the latter, even when carrying the "easy riders" with friendly smiles on faces do not on a narrow route mingle happily with pedestrians, and at the speeds essential to the joy of the "bombers" are a menace to the physical and mental well-being of visitors come not for an outdoor-gymnasium experience but a wildland-museum experience.)

The West Tiger 3 Trail is passed and the bridge over Tradition Creek crossed; note relics of the preceding bridge volunteer-built by the Chief

Ranger. The Nook Trail is passed, climbing ¾ mile to the Section Line Trail. Then see the Bus, the veritable Bus! A connector trail goes off to the Around-Tradition-Lake Trail. Leaving airy-light deciduous forest, the way enters dark forest of big cedar and fir.

At ¾ mile from the trailhead is the big sky of the gas-line swath and the adjacent Bonneville swath. Turning north, the walker passes the Round Lake Wetlands Trail and in a scant ½ mile reaches the Grand Junction of utility swaths. Turning east, the loop shortly passes the west end of the Around-Lake-Tradition Trail, which can be taken the scant 1 forest mile to complete the loop, which also can be completed by the long ½ open-sky mile of the "Puget Trail."

West Tiger Mountain Natural Resources Conservation Area

The DNR management plan for the West Tiger Mountain NRCA calls for a final size of about 4400 acres. As of 1994, only 854 acres of the 13,500-acre Tiger Mountain State Forest officially have been placed in the NRCA. The 400 acres of the companion City of Issaquah NRCA bring the total to 1254 acres. Private inholdings of 394 acres threaten the integrity of the concept; these time bombs *must* be acquired before they go off.

Tiger as a whole is the flagship of a new-style DNR philosophy of working forests within the urban-suburban zone. West Tiger is the flagship of the NRCA concept. Better say, "a" flagship, since as of 1994 it has twenty companions, but its unique location makes this most especially the pioneer in preserving "the wildness within." Wheels are *not* judged "low impact." But neither are feet considered to have *no* impact. Sitting on a log, motionless and silent, the human body has *some* impact. Set feet and mouth in motion and impact grows. Speed the feet to a jog, or put them atop spinning toys, and/or simply multiply the bodies, and the impact grows from low to medium to high to unacceptable. An NRCA cannot serve every recreation. Neither can it meet demands for unlimited amounts of any species of recreation. These matters are on the agenda of the flagship ecosystem.

During the Great Pedestrian-Equestrian Crusade to preserve trail country in the Issaquah Alps, hikers staged work parties specifically to build trails frankly "political," aiming to acquaint the public with the importance of Tiger. Having served that purpose, many of these can be abandoned for the sake of sensitive ecosystems. Other paths will be deemphasized, given little maintenance and no signing and no guidebook space. In these pages we describe only officially approved and recommended and maintained trails, and of these only a sampling.

West Tiger 3, round trip from Tradition Plateau trailhead 5 miles, from downtown Issaquah 8½ miles

The views from West Tiger are a dramatic lesson in the geography of Whulge country, spread out like an enormous relief map from Black Hills, Rainier, and the remnant of St. Helens on the south, Olympics west, San Juan Islands, Baker, and Shuksan north, and Cascades east. The saltchuck

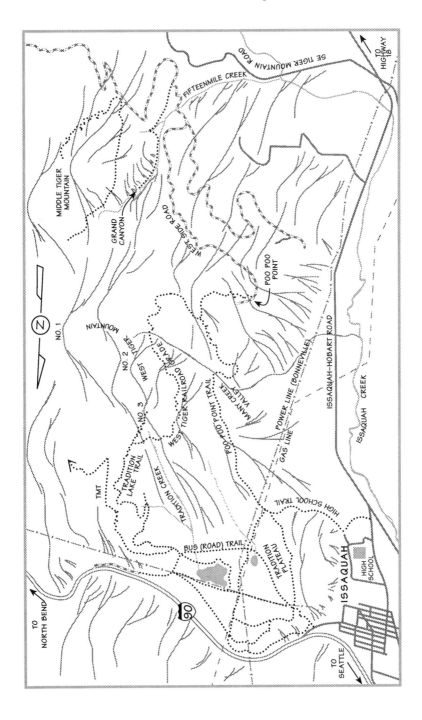

from The Narrows to Elliott Bay to Admiralty Inlet and Skagit Bay. Cities from Tacoma to Seattle to Everett.

Of the West Tiger peaks, 3 is the lowest—and the best. It juts out farthest, hanging in the sky over downtown Issaquah, a swandive from Lake Sammamish. Burned naked by fires, blasted by cold storms in winter and hot sun in summer and vicious winds the year around, the thin soil barely covers bedrock andesite. Trees grow slow, pseudo-alpine. Spring brings mountain-meadow–like color of lupine, tiger lily, ox eye daisy, and spring gold.

Though it may be said with some truth that "all trails lead to West Tiger 3," the most-used is the Tradition Trail. From the DNR Tradition Plateau trailhead, walk the Bus (Road) Trail a scant ¼ mile to a Y. Go left, soon turning steeply up from the plateau flat in mixed forest. The way winds and switchbacks, passes spurs left and right. Avoid confusion at a switchback just beyond a crossing of a creek, which trickles most of the summer; take the switchback left, recrossing the creek.

At 1370 feet, a scant 1½ miles from the Bus (Road) Trail, the old logging road ends. Constructed trail turns straight up the fall line, the angle soon easing. In a long ½ mile is West Tiger Railroad Grade, 1900 feet. (On the way, avoid the slash in the forest made by Boeing to bury its powerline to the electronic gadgetry atop West Tiger 2.)

The trail crosses the grade and continues up, emerging from forest into views over Grand Ridge and the Snoqualmie Valley to the Cascades, and then proceeding through shrubs, over andesite rubble (or when winter winds blow from the North Pole, in drifted snow) up the ridge crest, at ½ mile from the railroad grade reaching the summit, 2522 feet.

For a special treat, stay for the sunset over Puget Sound and the Olympics.

West Tiger Railroad, loop trip 10 miles

Go off I-90 on Exit 17, drive south on Front Street to Sunset Way, turn left to Second Avenue, and turn right 0.7 mile, passing Issaquah High School, to just short of Second Avenue's junction with Front Street, here become the Issaquah-Hobart Road. Park on the shoulder, somewhere on Second Avenue or a side street (not easy to do during school hours), elevation 175 feet.

Between the era of logging that employed oxen and horses as pulling power, and modern logging with trucks, for several decades the railroad dominated the industry and tracks were laid throughout lowlands and foothills. Most grades have been converted to truck roads or otherwise obliterated. The longest remaining unmolested near Seattle is the West Tiger Railroad Grade, running 4 miles—the entire distance at an elevation of 1900 feet—from the north side of West Tiger Mountain around to the west, then south, in and out of the enormous amphitheater of Many Creek Valley. Logging concluded here in 1929. When hikers arrived in large numbers in the late 1970s, they found the clearcuts grown up in handsome alder and maple or mixed conifers, interspersed with patches

Issaquah, I-90, and Lake Sammamish from Poo Poo Point

of virgin forest ignored by the loggers as too small (then) or unhandy. Except for fallen bridges the grades were just as they had been when the rails and ties were pulled up for re-use elsewhere. The West Tiger Grade is a chapter in the history of the forest industry and deserves to be designated an Historical Landmark.

The trailhead location described here is in itself a chapter in rail history, being none other than the Issaquah Switchback, where the railroad made a sweeping turn to begin gaining elevation along the slopes of Tiger in order to climb to the "high point" between Issaquah Creek and the Raging River. From the Second Avenue sidewalk, follow the curve of the grade around the football field, and go off right on a woods road (known to oldtimers as the State Road), gated to exclude public vehicles, a long 1 mile to the Bonneville powerline. Climb andesite slabs across powerline and gas line to the forest edge, 510 feet.

Two side-by-side former roads-now-trails take off from the gas line, diverging. Left is the Section Line Trail; take the right, the Poo Poo Point Trail (High School Trail), and ascend steadily into Many Creek Valley. At 1200 feet, 2½ miles, the way in quick succession crosses a not-in-summer creek, all-year Gap Creek, and the deep, richly forested ravine of West Creek. A jumble of rotted logs tells of the one-time logging-truck bridge.

Folk escape here from city turmoil on hot summer afternoons, sit beside the sparkling waters under marvelous big cedars, and eat a picnic supper in the wildness and the cool.

A bit beyond still another ooze of a creek the former road ends, at 1280 feet, and a trail sets out straight up the slope, going through a stand of ancient Douglas fir at 1500 feet. In a long ½ mile from the road-end, having gained 700 feet, the trail intersects the West Tiger Railroad Grade, 1900 feet, 3½ miles from the high school.

For a sidetrip off the loop, or a destination in itself, turn right on the grade ½ mile to its end, follow a path down to and up from Poo Poo Creek, to the end of the West Side Road, and ascend it to Poo Poo Point, 1775 feet. The airplane-wing views are straight down to green pastures of Issaquah Creek and the row of yellow schoolbuses by the high school, south to May Valley and Rainier and Renton, west over Squak and Cougar to Seattle and the Olympics, north to Issaquah, Lake Sammamish, and Baker.

The name? No, not from the vocabulary of little kids. In the winter of 1976–77 there was heard in downtown Issaquah the haunting call of the Yellow-Shafted Talkie Tooter, the "poo! poo!" and "poo-poo-poo-poo-poo" by which the choker-setter talks to the yarder. Thus was ushered in the Second Wave of clearcutting, the cleanup of patches of virgin forest ignored by the First Wave of the 1920s. The loggers boast that mowing down the ancient trees on Poo Poo Point opened one of Tiger's finest views. Well, give Weyerhaeuser (then in charge around here) *that*. But this was not merely virgin forest, it was old-growth. One observer commented, "If the company owned Seward Park, it would log that, too." Soon thereafter, the stumps of the old-growth trees mysteriously disappeared, too embarrassing to be left for ancient-forest photographers to document.

To proceed on the loop, turn left on the grade and round a spur ridge into Many Creek Valley on a steep sidehill that gentles in the squishier, creekier center of the amphitheater. Whenever the grade runs out in empty air, backtrack to find the path down and up to a resumption. Note stringers of old bridges, mostly broken-backed and fallen, a few still intact, nurse-bridges growing ferns and hemlocks and candyflower in midair. Watch for railroad ironware, logging ironware—rusting history.

Having crossed West Creek at 1 mile from the top of the High School Trail and Gap Creek in ¼ mile more—the two largest of the eight or so (many) creeks—the grade curves onto steep south slopes of West Tiger. Now for something completely different: virgin forest of nobly large and tall Douglas firs, too small to interest loggers of the 1920s but sizable enough to give today's hikers a sweet taste of what the whole mountain was like just a couple of human generations ago.

A sidetrail climbing right to West Tiger 3 and the Tiger Mountain Trail is passed, and then the Section Line Trail descending left to the Tradition Plateau and climbing right to West Tiger 3. At 2½ miles on the West Tiger Railroad is the Tradition Trail, descending 2 miles to the Bus (Road)

Trail junction. The loop is closed by 2½ miles on the Bus (Road) Trail, Bonneville powerline, and Old State Road.

The hikers who discovered the rail grade in the late 1970s were mightily puzzled by the fact it connected to nothing. At both ends, deadends. The mystery was explained by Fred Rounds, who when the weather was good used to emerge from the Newcastle mines to go logging on Tiger. He explained to us newcomers how the "Wooden Pacific Railroad" connected the lumber mill (all remains obliterated by I-90) at High Point, elevation 450 feet, to the 1900-foot rail grade. Steam donkeys lifted rails and railroad cars and locomotive and loggers up this tramway and lowered tramcars loaded with the "big sticks" whose stumps are gaped at by hikers of today.

If a loop longer than these 10 miles is desired, stay on the grade as it bends around the ridge to the

Hang glider with West Tiger Mountain in background

north side of West Tiger, in 1 mile from the Tradition Trail joining the Tiger Mountain Trail where it descends from West Tiger 2. In another ½ mile the united way crosses headwaters of High Point Creek to a split. The TMT descends left, the grade contours on to intersect a powerline swath straight up to the summit of West Tiger 1, gaining 1000 feet from the grade in less than ½ mile, an honest-to-golly mountaineering feat when under a foot of snow. A 15-mile loop is completed by descending the TMT to its north trailhead near the DNR Tradition Plateau trailhead, thence via Bus (Road) Trail and all to Second Avenue.

Tiger Mountain Trail: North End

October 13, 1979, was the official opening of the Tiger Mountain Trail, by then 7½ years in the thinking and 3½ in construction, occupying close to 300 person-days, costing a total in public funds of $0.00, and resulting in a 10½-mile route that subsequently was acclaimed by a foundation-sponsored group engaged in a tour of inspection from coast to coast as "the greatest near-city wildland trail in the nation." Subsequent relocations of the north and south trailheads have lengthened the distance to 16 miles. Along the way are broad and varied views, plant communities

ranging from virgin fir to alder-maple to pseudo-alpine andesite barrens—
a rich sampling of the good and great things of Tiger Mountain. The idea
for this masterpiece may be said to have been hatched at a Mountaineers
meeting in 1972. However, the fledgling never would have gotten out of
the nest had it not been taken under the wing of Bill Longwell, who chose
the route and led hundreds of work parties—Mountaineers, Volunteers
of Washington, Issaquah Alps Trails Club, youth groups, students at Hazen
High School—and went out himself on countless solo "parties." Says
Longwell in his definitive guidebook, "By late 1988 425 person-days, about
2000 hours, had gone into the trail. Finding a route took 40 trips. Then
came 122 work parties...." That was by summer of 1989. The work continues, under supervision of the DNR now and largely done by its trail crews.

The supreme hike of the Issaquah Alps is the TMT end-to-end from
the (working) Tiger Mountain State Forest to its (wilderness) West Tiger
NRCA, doing the entire 16 miles and 2200 feet of elevation gain (from the
south trailhead) in a day, a good bit of exercise but in ordinary conditions
(spring to fall) perhaps not overly taxing. The favorite method is a two-
car switch, placing a car at the north trailhead, then driving to the south
trailhead.

The trip is not recommended for every casual stroller to do on his/her
own. An experienced wildland navigator can find the way readily by consulting *Guide to Trails of Tiger Mountain* by (who else?) Bill Longwell,
Chief Ranger of the Issaquah Alps. The inexperienced would do best to go
on a trip guided by the Issaquah Alps Trails Club or The Mountaineers or
other group. Hikers must keep in mind that in winter the snow may pile
deep on the trail and in any season the clouds may blow wildly by. Fortunately, all along the route are escape hatches to lower and safer elevations; see the Longwell guide.

The Chief Ranger endorses the two ends of the Tiger Mountain Trail
as not only its easiest walks but unsurpassed in forest magnificence. The
south end is in the "working forest," treated later in these pages. The
north end, the subject here, is a perfectly splendid 5-mile round trip, elevation gain 1000 feet, from the Tradition Plateau trailhead.

Follow "TMT" signs from the restroom building to the Bus (Road) Trail,
turn left on the West Tiger 3 Trail, and turn quickly left again on the
TMT, signed "High Point Trail 2.4, West Tiger Railroad 4.4, Fifteenmile
Creek 8.6, Middle Tiger 10.6, West Side Road 12.3, Hobart Road 16.0."
The last of these is the south trailhead, the next to last the former trailhead
before the extension past South Tiger.

The way sets out on the plateau flat in mixed forest grown rich and
mellow since the railroad logging three-quarters of a century ago, then
turns up to sidehill-gouge slopes of West Tiger 3. A rude slash in the
wildness is crossed, the violence committed to bury the cable supplying
power to Boeing's information superfreeway tower atop West Tiger 2.
Mutter an oath and hurry on, soon to enjoy a long, sturdy, Longwell-built
bridge over a trickle-creek.

Issaquah Alps Trails Club party on West Tiger 2, above fog-filled Snoqualmie valley (Photo: Harvey Manning)

The trail climbs through alder-maple forest where post-logging regrowth has not yet brought the succession to conifers. Then, rounding a spur ridge, the alert hiker notes an absence of sawn stumps. The mood of the scene changes from deciduous light-and-airy to fir-hemlock shadowed-somber. In the main the trees are not large, obviously are young. Yet it is a *virgin* forest because a forest fire left too little to justify attention by 1920s loggers. But were it not now preserved in the Natural Resources Conservation Area, 1990s loggers would come a-running to mine out the scattering of near-ancient Douglas firs which survived the blaze with no worse damage than a bit of charcoaling of the thick bark which renders these elders virtually fireproof. From "Anschell's Allee" (ask the Chief Ranger why he gave that name) sawn stumps resume, rotting corpses of monster ancients.

The route swings off the dry-forest spur ridge into the jungle wetness of a deep, wide canyon, where a major branch of High Point Creek is bridged. The tread swings up and out of the canyon, bridges the creek's main branch in a deeper, wider canyon, and just beyond Milepost 13 intersects the High Point Trail.

The junction is far enough for a pleasant afternoon's lesson in the procession of forests from fire and/or logging to (or near) ancience. For quite a full day, see the Longwell guidebook (songbook, really) which carries on and up to the West Tiger Railroad, up more to the eyes-wide views from the slopes of West Tiger 2, and more from the highest point of the TMT,

Manning's Reach, 2600 feet. Rest on the bench built for Manning by the Chief Ranger and return to the Tradition Plateau via the TMT or any of the looping alternatives.

Tiger Mountain (Working) State Forest

The management plan adopted for the state forest in 1986 specifies a watershed-by-watershed rotation of harvests around the mountain, a steady-out sustained yield from a compact unit of land, quite different from the industry-model sustained yield in which Wisconsin is clearcut to the last bush, then Washington, then Indonesia, then Siberia, then maybe Wisconsin again. Contrary to ominous warnings that the industry would boycott Tiger Mountain State Forest as a birdwatcher-treehugger trick, every timber sale advertised has brought a flood of bids higher than the DNR valuation. Contract loggers come from throughout the Northwest to bid, wanting to get in on this laboratory experiment and help shape the future.

"Working" distinctly entails harvesting cellulose, but not—repeat not—at the expense of other forest "crops." Trail recreation is a valuable crop and will not be sacrificed, as it routinely was under the Weyerhaeuser regime. Some trails may be relocated from time to time to remain in forest cover. Others may be given permanent greenbelt protection, notably when they traverse ecosystems too sensitive to withstand logging.

Certain trails built in the past as political statements will be given back to the bushes and the refuge-seeking critters. Beaver Valley is not treated in these pages. The botanist-zoologist wanting to study that fascinating scene will have to do as the elder surveyor did on his 1970s journey of discovery—beat through thorns and the mud, over and under fallen trees. The place is too fragile for mass visitation. No trail will be permitted. Others are omitted from this guide and may be totally-partly deconstructed as DNR staff determines allowable levels of human impact.

Middle Tiger Railroad, round trip 10.2 miles

From Holder Gap ("Tiger Summit") on Highway 18, elevation 1350 feet, walk the gated West Side Road 3.6 miles to the trailhead in a brushy ravine. Elevation, 1200 feet.

Our mentor in logging history of the Issaquah Alps, the late Fred Rounds, informed us this rail grade emanated from the Hobart mill (the millpond, become a residential lakelet, can be spotted while driving by on the highway), crossed Fifteenmile Creek valley on the famous Horseshoe Trestle, and via switchback continued up the valley to Fifteenmile Pass. He and fellow loggers, based at the bunkhouse in Hobart, rode a speeder to work each morning. The logging ended with the Crash in 1929.

From the road ascend the slopes above a gully, in whose brushy depths can be seen the fallen timbers of a large trestle. At the top of a short, steep bit, where the Middle Tiger Trail proceeds ahead and up, the somewhat brushy lokie line diverges to the left on a railroad-typical easy grade. The path sidehills above Fifteenmile Creek 1½ miles to the creek, 1780

Forest scene on Middle Tiger Mountain

feet, a bully site for a wildland picnic beside the splashing stream, watching the dippers dip.

Near the creek are remains of the shack where the donkeyman slept; he had to rise early, while the loggers were still asleep in the bunkhouse at Hobart, to get up steam in the boiler. Other relicts are the 2-inch cable of the skyline that was rigged betweeen spar trees to carry the big sticks high in the air over the valley for loading on rail cars, and such uprights as remain of the ⅓-mile Horseshoe Trestle. At several spots the trail detours around fallen bridges. All were trestles because this rail line was engineered by "Trestle" Johnson. That other self-taught Swede engineer who with double-bitted ax and jawful of snoose laid out the West Tiger Railroad Grade favored stringer bridges. Whatever the comparative merits, it must be said that trying to bridge Fifteenmile Creek with a stringer would've demanded the ingenuity of more than one Swede, maybe even of a Norwegian.

Middle Tiger Mountain, round trip 10.2 miles

Walk the West Side Road (see preceding) 3.6 miles to the trailhead, elevation 1200 feet.

Located way out in the middle of the air between the deep valleys of Fifteenmile and Holder Creeks, equidistant from the hulking ridges of West Tiger and East Tiger, Middle Tiger is the best vantage for studying the architecture of the "Tiger Range." Of the several ways to the summit, the one described here is as popular as any and fits well into looping trips which will be left to the ingenuity of loopers.

The steep bit up the alder-choked ravine wall relents at 1300 feet, where the Middle Tiger Railroad goes off left from the site of the trestle. The way ascends fairly moderately in alder forest to ¾ mile, 1760 feet, where a sidetrail goes off right to hit the Tiger Mountain Trail; at 1 mile, 2120 feet, is the intersection with the Tiger Mountain Trail. Continue up into patches of bracken and stands of young firs, pass windows out on lowlands; pause to admire lichen-green granite erratics dropped by the glacier from Canada. The way switchbacks from a gully to a sky-open ridge and the summit, 2607 feet, 1½ miles.

Burned bare by fires, new growth discouraged by cold of winter and heat of summer and loud winds that blow the year around, the half-naked, mountain-meadow–like summit is bright in season with lupine and spring gold, paintbrush and daisy and goldenrod. Or used to be. Then, as it must to all clearcuts, young forest began leaping skyward, swallowing up the views. However, having determined that the site was subcommercial for tree-farming and absolutely splendid for scenery, the DNR decided the industry could spare a few twenty-second century trees and plans to open windows (as it will do when needed on similar spots, such as West Tiger 3).

For flowers and views do the climb on a sunny day of spring or summer. For mystery do it in a cat-footed autumn fog that mayhap settles into valleys to become a shining cloudsea. For arctic adventure come in winter when billions of flakes swirl around the summit or billions of sun-sparkling crystals are flung in your eyes by a northerly gale. Ascend (carefully!) when cloud castles are drifting, drifting nearer, nearer, slanting gray rain-lines to earth—and suddenly zapping each other and shaking the mountain and impelling your feet hastily downward.

Grand Canyon of Fifteenmile Creek, round trip 13 miles

Walk the West Side Road (see Middle Tiger Railroad) 5 miles and look sharp. If you find yourself crossing Fifteenmile Creek, you didn't look sharp enough. Before the drop to the creek, note an unused, gated, private road joining from the left—the Tiger Mountain Mine Road. In a short bit, where the West Side Road bends left, the Mine Road, here become a trail, goes off obscurely straight ahead, through a borrow pit into forest. Elevation, 800 feet.

Rising in the broad saddle of Fifteenmile Pass, which separates the bulks of West Tiger and East Tiger, Fifteenmile Creek is the central watercourse of the mountain, the longest and largest completely *within* the mountain. Beautiful and wild and exciting for all its deep-forested miles, the stream scenically climaxes in the Grand Canyon, where falls tumble down a slot steeply and gaudily walled by green trees and shrubs, gray and brown and yellow sandstone and shale, and black coal. Poking about (but *not in*) old mines and searching for yellow amber add interest. Though located in the "working forest" sector, the Grand Canyon never will see chainsaws or bulldozers. The law won't allow it. Too steep-walled and unstable of soil for even a trail.

At ½ mile is a large field; wander off left to peer down into a concrete pit formerly containing a device with large steel teeth that were meant to chew up the coal that wasn't mined by a stock operation of the early 1960s. The road-trail returns to forest and gently ascends along the sidehill of a splendid green valley, the creek roaring far below. At ¾ mile, 950 feet, the way bends in and out of the ravine of the South Fork, a delicious creek; look for a hole in the bank, either a coal prospect or an amber-miner's dig.

Around a corner at 1 mile is a Y, 980 feet. For the picnic trip take the left fork, contouring to concrete artifacts and rotten timbers and the end of the mining railroad; dating from around World War I and sporadically active in the 1930s, this operation produced little coal. A slippery path leads to the slot of the Grand Canyon where water sluices through trenches in the rock and swirls in potholes and splashes hikers' hot faces. In winter the slot is totally occupied by raging furies; in late summer a person can scramble and slither in, startling the dippers as they flit by.

The right fork passes the mine (rusty algae ooze out, maidenhair fern hangs over the black mouth), sternly climbs past the slot, then levels out at creek level and at 1½ miles, 1200 feet, deadends. Note timber footings of the vanished bridge; in low water hop across and investigate ironware and the collapsed tunnel, which was timbered only with alder poles and went in just far enough to extract cash from investors. In the early 1980s archaeologists of the Issaquah Historical Society excavated a mine cart, now on display at the museum in the building that used to be the Issaquah train depot.

Tiger Mountain Trail: South End

The Tiger Mountain Trail is a permanent feature of the "working" forest on Tiger Mountain, just as in the West Tiger Mountain Natural Resources Conservation Area. DNR timber harvesting either will leave undisturbed buffers along the trail route, or will be done from roads which avoid the trail and after the logging are put to bed, or, when a segment is deemed necessary to harvest, will be replaced by a relocation to a site harvested so long ago the second-growth (or third, or fourth) is older than trees ever get, nowadays, on a "private" forest.

To reach the south trailhead, drive Front Street–Hobart Road 7.2 miles south from Sunset Way in Issaquah and turn left on SE Tiger Mountain Road. At this writing the interim trailhead is over private land and cannot be signed or described (or used?). In 1995 the DNR will complete a parking area for twenty-five cars and a trailhead facility some ¼ mile from the Hobart Road. Watch for it on the right. The existing south end of the TMT and the South Tiger alternate TMT will then be rebuilt to higher standards.

Where "official" (on DNR land) trail begins is a sign, "Elevation 500 feet," and noting, "West Side Road 3.7, Middle Tiger 5.4, Fifteenmile Creek 7.4, West Tiger Railroad 11.6, High Point Trail 13.6, Tradition Plateau Trailhead 16.0."

Old logging-road-become-trail sidehills above a lush valley in virgin forest dating from a burn that got here before the loggers did. Giant sawn stumps begin, and the route becomes true trail and passes through Weedwhacker Gap, 1100 feet, and very shortly Hobart Gap, 1080. Here the way meets a 1920s railroad grade. The left, the alternate TMT (part of the South Tiger Loop) ascends a ridge of South Tiger Mountain (the summit, 2028 feet), crosses a 1700-foot pass, and drops past Otter Lake to the West Side Road. The right, the main TMT, contours on the rail grade along the opposite (east) side of South Tiger, crosses a powerline swath, and attains the West Side Road via a 1970s logging road closed to public vehicles.

Unless continuing on for the whole TMT, or intending the South Tiger Loop, a rewarding turnaround for an easy morning is a bit past Hobart Gap on the main TMT, a waterfall judged by the Chief Ranger to be Tiger Mountain's prettiest. Bring out the crackers and cheese, pickles and olives, jug of lemonade. Round trip from south trailhead a scant 4 miles, elevation gain 600 feet.

Northwest Timber Trail, round trip 5 miles

This brandnew trail, opened the summer of 1994, was built by the DNR for two reasons. First, few Tiger trails are on the Highway 18 side of the mountain, and that seems a recreational waste of some splendid country. Second, the new outdoor activity, riding off-pavement (fat-tire) bicycles, requires a new set of opportunities, since it cannot be permitted to run free on hiker/horse trails. This, and the also-new East Tiger Trail (see Longwell's guide), are DNR experiments. As the only trails on the mountain open to wheels, they provide a laboratory to determine through actual use, rather than courthouse trial, where and how off-road bike routes might be provided, and if they can be provided without unacceptable damage to forest communities. The two experimental trails are also open to hikers and horses, though it has been suggested the peacelover may wish to try them weekdays only, and best on rainy winter days in February—except the probability is high that when the tread is wet and fragile they will be closed to all travel in order to keep the experiment "clean."

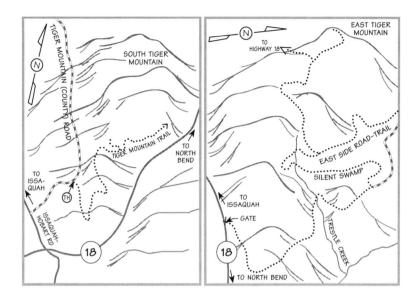

Drive to Holder Gap ("Tiger Summit") on Highway 18 and park in the large lot, elevation 1350 feet.

Walk the righthand of the two gated roads that start at the lot. In a short bit go off the road, right, on the signed trail, having to that point avoided the several unsigned paths bulled by motorcycles when they were tolerated here (as they are not anymore). The forest is instantly superb and unfolds one after another display of what Nature can do in three-quarters of a century of good tree-growing conditions. The scattering of monster Douglas fir stumps is all that tells this is not a virgin forest, and one getting along smartly toward becoming ancient. Should the laboratory experiment fail, this still will be a grand museum of "North-west timber."

Every step, going and coming, is a delight. If climactic moments must be cited, there is what has been called, aptly, "a Sargasso Sea jungle of moss-covered vine maples," an airy light-green interval between the darker solemnities of big firs and hemlocks and cedars. The bridges built by the DNR over the several creeks are enough to make an old Scout's heart leap (give the lads and lasses merit badges all around). The waterfall, issuing from a forest ravine to tumble over a wall of hard rock. Just beyond the falls and its companion, the High Bridge, the Pre-Columbian Tree, a Douglas fir some 40 feet in circumference, possibly the largest extant in the Issaquah Alps (certainly making the final cut in the Big Tree Pageant). And what amounts, now, to a historical note, at the end, 1800 feet, having gained an elevation of an easy 400 feet in 2½ miles, a surprise—the closed-to-public-wheels East Side Road (see East Tiger Moun-

Mount Rainier from Tiger Mountain

tain via Silent Swamp)—and through the up-sprouting alders of a 1980ish clearcut, window views over the Snoqualmie valley and the Cascades.

East Tiger Mountain via Silent Swamp, round trip to swamp 7½ miles, to summit 13½ miles

Drive Highway 18 to 3.1 miles west of I-90, 1.2 miles east of Holder Gap ("Tiger Summit"), and carefully make a treacherous turn off to a small parking space at a gated road, elevation 1100 feet.

The three forest-management roads from Highway 18 (Tiger Mountain Road, West Side Road, and East Side Road) became popular walking routes when they were built in the late 1960s to middle 1970s, but automobile recreation by view-seekers and family picnickers soon grew so busy that foot travel could only be recommended on weekdays. Then the

DNR, for reasons of vehicle safety and maintenance expense, was forced to permanently close all three roads to unauthorized motorized vehicles, which now are all-seasons, all-days joys to the non-motorized public. The wildlife also rejoices, secure as it is from weapons-carriers/meat-wagons.

Creek after creek tumbles though forest grown tall since the railroad logging of the 1920s. Harvesting will come again, but not of the bottom-line sort also seen on this road, dating from the last days of the cut-and-get-out Weyerhaeuser regime, "liquidating the inventory" by clearcutting from horizon to horizon. The DNR harvests will be restricted in size, will leave undisturbed strips along streams, and will save old snags—and even "make" new ones for birds to nest and perch.

At 2.4 miles from Highway 18 is the lower end of the Silent Swamp Trail, elevation 1420 feet. Ascend a short bit to a railroad grade. To the left it meets the East Side Road (for a reason to be explained below). Turn right on the grade, which makes a sweeping U-turn around the end of a low ridge, goes through a wide saddle at 1550 feet, and enters the valley of Silent Swamp. Hark! What is that new sensation that smites the ears? It is the sound of silence. The ridge has blocked out the din of I-90. Listen now to frogs and wrens. Gape at huge stumps of cedar and fir. Admire devils club and skunk cabbage of the lovely swamp, headwaters of North Fork Trout Hatchery Creek.

The grade sidehills from the swamp to a junction at 1 mile, 1700 feet, and a lesson in railroad history—and the reason this railroad grade, as well as those of West Tiger and Middle Tiger, is proposed for preservation as an Historic Site.

Whereas the Hobart mill engineered its rail approach to Middle Tiger forests with a long, gradual sidehill ascent, and the High Point mill built a tramway up West Tiger, the Preston mill that operated on East Tiger employed switchbacks in this manner: a stretch of grade angled up a slope to a deadend. At the distance of one locomotive and a train of cars back from the deadend, the next stretch of grade took off uphill at an acute angle in the opposite direction. A train climbing the mountain proceeded past the junction to the deadend, pulled by the locomotive. A switch was thrown and the train went into reverse and backed up the next stretch, pushed to another deadend by the locomotive, which on the next switchback again took the lead.

On the route thus far, the Silent Swamp Trail where first intersected had just completed a switchback from the stretch of grade now occupied by the East Side Road. The sweeping U-turn was used to obviate the need for one switchback. Here at 1700 feet is the next switch. The grade reverse-turning to the right leads ¼ mile in lovely woods to the East Side Road at 1850 feet—and another switchback, along the road. For the best walking, though, continue straight ahead to the deadend at the deep-woods ravine of South Fork Trout Hatchery Creek, 1¼ miles, 1720 feet. Why go on? No dandier spot for a picnic than by the splash of the creek. Watch dippers dart from boulder to boulder.

However, to rest is not to conquer, the summit lies above. Follow meager trail along and across the creek, then up the fall line to the deadend of a washed-out logging road. Turn right, back across the creek, returning to the East Side Road at 1950 feet, 1¾ miles from where it was left for trail. The road climbs steadily, swinging around the side of the 2786-foot satellite peak of East Tiger; views begin to open through young firs whose crowns are leaping up to block views. The road tops the saddle between the peaks and drops a bit to join the Crossover Road, an offshoot of the Tiger Mountain Road, at 2670 feet, 6 miles from Highway 18, 1½ road miles from the upper Silent Swamp trailhead.

The final ¾ mile is packed with entertainment. The Spring, source of the Spring Fork of Raging River; ponder where it gets its year-round flow, here so near the summit. The sky, which now grows enormously as trees shorten. Though there is never a single 360-degree panorama, views extend in every direction as the road winds south, west, north, west, and south again so confusingly that a hiker needs a compass to avoid mistaking Duvall for Seattle. At one time or other look over the Raging River to Rattlesnake Mountain and the Cascades, over I-90 to Lake Alice plateau, Snoqualmie Valley, Glacier Peak, and Baker, south to Rainier and the ruins of St. Helens, and over Middle Tiger to Seattle and Whulge.

At 3004 feet, 4½ miles from the upper trailhead for Silent Swamp, the road flattens on the bulldozer-leveled summit, trashed with metalwork. However, the tower people are cleaning up, revegetating and generally beautifying. A forest of huddled hemlocks blocks views north and east but horizons are open a hundred miles south and west.

Other Trips

See books and maps published by the Issaquah Alps Trails Club:

Cougar Mountain Regional Wildland Park, Coal Creek Park, and May Creek Park, a map

Guide to Trails of Tiger Mountain State Forest, a book and map by William G. Longwell, Jr., periodically revised

Guide to Trails of Squak Mountain Parks, a map by William G. Longwell, Jr.

For Rattlesnake Mountain, see *Hiking the Mountains-to-Sound Greenway,* by Harvey Manning (Seattle: The Mountaineers, 1994)

CEDAR RIVER

The Cedar is the most useful river in Puget Sound City. Rising on the Cascade Crest, it brings clean mountain water to Landsburg, where more or less of the flow, depending on the season, is diverted into the pipeline that empties into a reservoir, Lake Youngs, which fills the bathtubs and swimming pools, greens the lawns, and washes the dishes of the south sector of Seattle and satellite communities. The waters not so diverted enter Lake Washington, where they provide the flushing action without which the celebrated Metro sewage cleanup wouldn't have done the job of cleaning up Lake Washington. Exiting through the Ship Canal to Lake Union and Whulge, the river gives sockeye salmon a route from the ocean to spawning grounds.

Less known is the role of the 103,000-acre, closed-to-the-public Cedar River Watershed upstream from Landsburg, as a reservoir of wildlife that constantly replenishes the populations of birds and beasts in the Snoqualmie Valley, the Issaquah Alps, and the entire Lake Washington–Lake Sammamish–Cedar River–Green River area. The Washington State Department of Fish and Wildlife (formerly, Game) insists that recreation can coexist with potable water. However, that excellent agency has a traditional and powerful clientele for which "wildlife" means something to eat. If hunting were permitted in the watershed—now completely closed to all forms of recreation—the number of animals shot dead would be a small fraction of those well warned to be warier.

The watershed is the reason there are cougar on Cougar Mountain, and elk through May Valley nearly to Lake Washington, and lynx and coyote and bear, and bobcats dining on pussycats. No matter how thoughtfully a "harvest" hunt is controlled, it is bound to be

White-crowned sparrow

discouraging to the harvestees. Let it be noted that guns are not the only violent human intrusions. The fisherman storming paths to the riverbank, the hiker pounding the trail, throngs of bicyclers yipping and giggling at high speed through sanctuaries, the family circus spreading a blanket on the ground for a picnic lunch are, in sum, the equivalent in wild eyes of a Panzer division of motorcycles carrying attack rifles.

Seattle City Water is engaged in a study of boundary areas, looking to find an allowable route for the Cedar River Trail to detour to the north of Taylor and Rattlesnake Mountains to rejoin the rail-trail route east, as well as a pedestrian route along the slopes of Rattlesnake and the ridge east to the Cascade Crest. Such adjustments would not endanger the integrity of the wildlife sanctuary.

But wildlife-loving pedestrians want their boots banned from the heart of the refuge. To let in their boots would be to prepare the way for wheels, automobiles, guns. Mankind has virtually the entire planet open to his violence. The wild creatures are running out of escapes.

USGS maps: Mercer Island, Renton, Maple Valley, Black Diamond, Hobart

Echo Mountain (Lake Desire–Spring Lake Regional Wildland Park)

Drive 196 Avenue SE from Maple Valley Highway to SE 183rd. Turn right, then immediately right again on Spring Lake Drive 1 mile to the road-end gate, elevation 490 feet.

Narrowly rescued from a "planned community" of 900 homes and acquired by the King County open-space bond issue of 1989, these 371 acres

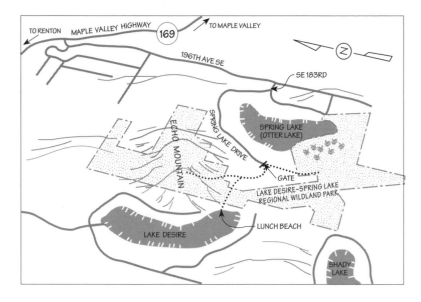

Echo Mountain

have been described as a "little Cougar Mountain." That is to say, a *wild-land*, not a gymnasium but a museum. In the midst of suburbia. All the better. How "little" *is* it? The novice explorer does well to have pockets crammed with cake crumbs to mark the return route through the maze of trails. Having a whole cake in the rucksack isn't a bad idea, in order to spend a full day following out every sidetrail to where the dogs announce the edge of private property. However, the basic trip is to the 899-foot summit (highest of the twin peaks), a nice 3-mile round trip from the gate, gaining 400 feet. The forest has had three-quarters of a century to grow tall and cool-shadowed since the loggers went away. And—oh!—the summit bald, the sedimentary rock rounded and scraped clean by that old Canadian glacier. Deep-forest flowers yield to rock-slab flowers. There even are some views—Rainier and Tiger.

The recommended choice is the "Main Trail." Though it's the service road to the water tank serving local homes, rarely is it traveled by service vehicles, and never by public wheels, and the width is trail-cozy. The light dressing of crushed rock underlying the needles and leaves readily distinguishes the route from old logging-roads-become-trails, excellent in their own rights. Explore them after the gipfelfest (summit lunch).

Main Trail sets out from the gate (just past a Wildlife Department boat-launch on Spring Lake, also called Otter), parallel to a woods path (onetime road) which soon intersects the Main Trail. Salmonberry, bleeding heart, candyflower, trillium, avens. The woods road-trail continues straight ahead, a lovely forest walk, eventually leading out of the park to houses. Main Trail horseshoe-bends right and climbs from the valley bottom of big cottonwood and cedar. At 590 feet, a trail (onetime road) goes left a scant ½ mile to a narrow sliver of park, "Lunch Beach," on Lake Desire, for those who need to look at civilization while eating. But you could be lucky and see otters at play or beavers at work. And/or the nesting pair of bald eagles. Great blue heron or osprey.

At 738 feet the Main Trail goes a short bit straight ahead to deadend at the water tank. Forget that. Turn right, steeply uphill, at a King County Parks trail sign, in blackberry and solomons seal, fairy bells and toothwort, out of the forest onto the rock bald. Walk softly! This summit area is very sensitive to human intrusion. Don't mash the flowers! In season for each, blossoms of Easter lily (mid-April), chocolate lily (May), seablush, kinnickinnick, strawberry, monkeyflower, nodding onion, and serviceberry bushes festooned with airy masses of light-green lichen.

Look out the open window through the trees. Expect to see Tiger. Instead, Rainier! But there also is Tiger, where Rainier ought to be. Thank golly for the cake crumbs. When sun is sparkling the water, see green-screened Lake Desire. From every side come noises of what we simians call civilization. But muted enough not to drown out the birds. (Some 79 species have been documented.) Here there is "wildness within."

Not to be described here is the largest, most pristine (never mined for peatmoss) sphagnum peat bog west of the Cascade front. Stay away, please! Eventually Parks should install an interpretive plank-walkway to keep visitors to a non-destructive route where they can have explained them the succession of post-glacial icewater lakes through marsh to bog to meadow to forest. The Labrador tea, swamp laurel (kalmia), cranberry, and sundew could then give a caring Public the best bog show within urbanizing King County.

Gene Coulon Memorial Beach Park

Bus: 210

Go off I-405 on Exit 5, turn right on Park Avenue, then right on Lake Washington Boulevard, then left into the park, elevation 25 feet.

What man has put asunder, man may sometimes have a chance to put back together. Renton Parks started with 57 acres of Lake Washington shore hemmed in by railroad tracks and mucked up industrially for a century. Guided by a Jones & Jones design, it fashioned a park that on fine weekends swarms with swimmers, sunbathers, fishermen, canoeists, stinkpotters, sailboaters, and little kids yelling—but on weekdays is as peaceful a lakeshore as one could wish, only the goslings and ducklings making a racket.

In an air distance of 1 mile are 1½ miles of in-and-out shore paths. For the full trip park at the south end in a lot serving South Beach. Walk to the water, passing the Shuffleton Steam Plant where Puget Power used to generate electricity by burning coal. The little Nature Island is often closed at the bridge to give the birds a rest. Views are impressive of the gaping maws from which issue just-built Boeing jets. The geographic panorama includes the mouth of the Cedar River, Beacon Hill, the south end of Mercer Island, and a glimpse of Seattle towers.

Shore paths lead northward past the kids' playground, the bathing beach (enclosed by a concrete walkaround excellent for out-in-the-lake viewpoints), coots, ducks, and geese to a bridge over the marsh estuary of John's Creek. A second parking lot serves the boat-launch and boat harbor. The Lagoon is enclosed by the 1000-foot floating boardwalk of the Picnic Gallery. The Gazebo, the Pavilion, the Ivar's Eatery all are in turn-of-the-century architecture recalling the waterfront amusement parks of

Gene Coulon Memorial Beach Park

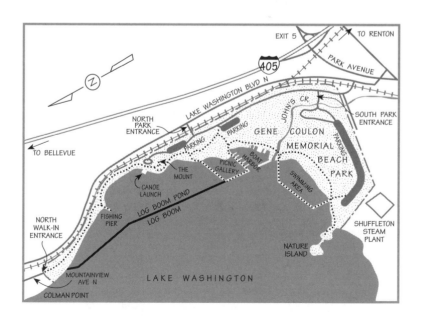

127

young Seattle. *Interface*, a bronze sculpture by Phillip Levine, demands a pause. The shore continues along the largest enclosure, Log Boom Pond, logs moored at the outer edge to fend off razzer-boats. Between water and railroad tracks are The Mount, a hummock that adds topographical interest, and a profusion of plantings of trees and shrubs, native and exotic, that ultimately will give the park innumerable sylvan nooks. In all, some 15,000 trees and 90,000 shrubs and water plants have been set out.

At an entry road from Lake Washington Boulevard is the third and final parking area, serving the Canoe Launch and the North Beach, ½ mile more of pathway. Granite boulders have been installed on the shore, as well as old timbers recognized as being rudely handsome and thus rescued from the dump. The concrete piers and rotting pilings of a booming ground remain; here the railroad used to dump logs for rafting to mills. A bridge crosses Trestle Marsh (cattails and blackbirds). A fishing pier lets a person walk on the water. The park ends at residences of Colman Point.

Cedar River Way

From points at or near the river-outlet end, three partly potential and partly existing non-motorized travelways would fulfill a wise logic: a route along the line of the historic Seattle & Walla Walla Railroad to Elliott Bay; a second up and along Beacon Hill, then down to the Skid Road and Elliott Bay; a third north beside Lake Washington to Bellevue, the Seattle & Walla Walla line branching off to May Creek and Coal Creek and to the Issaquah Alps.

From points along the river to the upstream end, non-motorized travelways to Lake Wilderness and Black Diamond; to Big Soos Park and Auburn; and to Snoqualmie Pass. On the Cedar River Way itself, choice spots to enjoy the windings of the stream through city, through countryside, and through wildland.

Eventually the river route will extend 22 miles from Lake Washington to the fenced boundary of the closed-to-the-public Cedar River Watershed. Most will be a bikeway/joggerway/runnerway. For walkers, most of the best—the "trail days"—lie in the past. However, there still are quiet and placid times, such as rainy Tuesday mornings in February.

Lake Washington to Cedar River Park 1¾ miles
Bus: 106, 107, 155, 240, 340, 912 to Renton Park & Ride

Drive Logan Avenue North from the city center north past Renton Stadium to the entry of Boeing Renton Plant. Turn left on North 6 Street, signed "Cedar River Trail," and proceed to a deadend at Lake Washington, elevation less than 25 feet.

In this age when Growth is coming to be seen as not worth it if it adds only flesh, no spirit, many a community is engaged in a quest for identity, a search for soul. Renton found part of its soul in the heart of town—the Cedar River—and built a splendid trail where citizens can walk close to home and where visitors can learn what Renton is all about.

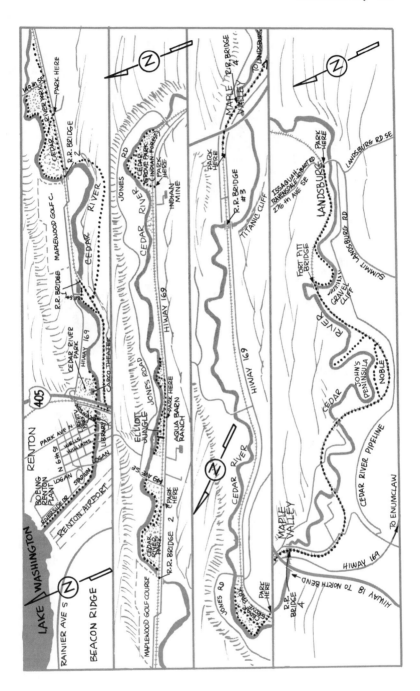

Cedar River Park

A Boeing fence unnecessarily blocks access to the absolute mouth, a few feet distant, but doesn't shut off views to Mercer Island, Beacon Ridge, Queen Anne Hill, and Cougar Mountain.

The wide path—blacktop, then cinders—parallels the channelized river in lawns amid new-planted trees and shrubs. The water floats ducks and gulls; thickets shelter flitter-birds. On every side are big tin pots sicklied o'er with the pale cast of watercolor—Boeing jets trundled across a bridge from the factory to Renton Airport to set off on maiden flights from which they never return because the field is too short for jets to land.

Listening to the thundering present, ponder the wild past. Primevally, the Black River drained from the lake hereabouts and flowed close beneath the steep slopes of Beacon Ridge to join the Green River; somewhere in the middle of the plain that until recently became part of the lake during the rainy season, the Black was joined by the Cedar River, which later was diverted into Lake Washington.

Note the future opportunity—the Seattle City Light powerlines descending Beacon Ridge, the potential link to Seattle and the Whulge Trail.

The park lane passes Renton Stadium, crosses under Logan Avenue, goes by a massive pier of the long-gone railroad bridge, and passes Renton Senior Center. The path enters a residential neighborhood and crosses under Williams Avenue, Wells Avenue, and Bronson Way to Renton Public Library—which bridges the river!

Past the baseball field, by the swimming pool, cross the street and go under the railroad and I-405 to Cedar River Park, mainly noted for Carco Theater. Here the river debouches from Maple Valley onto the Renton Plain, northern terminus of the Big Valley.

Cedar River Park to Maple Valley Junction 5 miles
Bus: 143 to Wilderness Village Park & Ride; 912 to Carco Theater

Drive Highway 169 from Renton under the railroad and I-405 to the mouth of Maple Valley and some 5 miles along the valley to Maple Valley Junction.

In 1994–95, Highway 169 is being widened and the Cedar River "Trail" relocated and tidied up as a bikeway more or less unpleasant for walkers except on those rainy Tuesday mornings in February. From Carco Theater to Maplewood Golf Course the route will be on the south side of the river. Bridges then will take it across to follow the north side of the highway.

The best walking in Maple Valley will be (as it is in 1994, before reconstruction) at the upstream end of the golf course, going off the bikeway into the old farm acquired by King County Parks and let go wild. An entry lane winds to the river through fields that grow only grass, broom, tansy, and hellberry constantly under the hungry eyes of touring hawks; something edible lives there, scurrying around in the weeds. The width of the fields so softens highway noise that the river readily drowns it out. From the far bank steeply rises a 325-foot wildwood wall. Peace.

The lane turns downstream on a short stretch of dike to a place where State Fish and Wildlife annually, October–November, installs a weir in the river to divert spawning sockeye salmon to a holding pond where eggs can be stripped—part of the Cedar River Enhancement Program which intermittently has been so successful that in spawning months of good years a person hardly can see the river bottom for the big red fish—and hardly can take a step along the banks without stirring up a gang of ducks, herons, gulls, and other fishers.

The downstream way enters a forest distinguished by monster cottonwoods; sidetrails lead out on gravel bars. Across the river are a magic grotto where a creek falls free into the green from a tall wall of sandstones and shales, a seam of coal at the foot. In low water one can wade.

The upstream way prowls through more cottonwoods to a river meadow and a look across the water to a sand wall pocked by swallow caves.

Wheelfree nature walks can total, upstream and down, some 2½ miles.

For another chunk of King County parkland along 1 mile of river, east from the entrance to Aqua Barn find a chance to bust through the snowberry and wild rose to the cottonwoods and proceed to the river.

Just east of a sprawl of buildings occupied (1994) by a roofing company, occupying the site of the old Indian Mine, find on the north side of the highway a gated woods road through columnar cottonwood to a dike that runs ½ mile upstream. Paths continue on, steadily more obscure. Between railroad grade and river lies nearly a square half-mile of floodway sloughs and floodplain forest, a wild tangle.

Maple Valley Junction to Landsburg, 5½ miles

The better start is upstream at Landsburg. Drive Issaquah-Hobart-Ravensdale road 3 miles south of Hobart to the Landsburg Bridge over the Cedar River. Park nearby, elevation 560 feet.

The start from Maple Valley will be the popular wheelway. However, the traveler on shanks' mare ever will prefer the lonesome wildwoods from Landsburg, the gravel bars to delight and the gravel cliffs to astound, and many an opportunity to distance the respectful feet from impatient wheels hasting along lest somebody preempt their grave.

For 1 mile a trackside path long has been beaten by fisherfeet, and branch paths lead to overlooks of dippers and ducks, mossy nooks among the maples, and picnic bars. On a survey in early October there were a gull or heron on every boulder, squadrons of ducks on patrol, raptors circling above, and pools so full of sockeye salmon they scarcely left room for the water.

Where the grade enters an odd little valley, turn off on a riverside path that follows the stream around a big loop for ⅔ mile (the railroad shortcuts to the end in ⅓ mile). Enchantment! Virgin-looking forests of big old conifers. Groves of giant cottonwoods. Understory of vine maple in flame (in October). Camps on the gravel. And across the river the Great Gravel Cliff rising an absolutely vertical 150 feet from the gulls. At first the way follows what appears to be an ancient railroad grade, then becomes a mixture of mucky woods roads and fishing paths. The segment concludes at a bridge signed "Fort Pitt Bridge Works Pittsburgh PA 1890."

Across the bridge are more deep-shadowed wildwoods, more sunny bars, but this vicinity is suggested as the turnaround for a neat 4-mile round trip from Landsburg—what with the sidetrips you easily could be the whole day at it, especially if the kids have anything to say.

Houses now enter the scene, across the river. And there are no more easy paths to the water. However, at a long ½ mile (as the rails used to run) from the first bridge is the Cedar River's most topographically exciting moment, a pair of peninsula ridges enclosed by giant meanders. John's Peninsula, on the far side, only can be explored when the river is wadable. The peninsula on the near side, a skinny ridge with cliffy walls, is strictly for the doughty.

Though wildwoods continue, interest diminishes. At ⅓ mile from the start of the peninsulas is a crossing of SE 248 Street, entry to the hideaway homes of Noble. Public feet are pretty well excluded from the river. At a second bridge, 1 mile from the Noble road, suburbia thickens. However, in the remaining long 2 miles to Maple Valley Junction are two more bridges worth photographing.

GREEN RIVER

The Big River of Pleistocene time issued from the front of the Canadian glacier, engorged mountain tributaries, and flowed on south, seeking a way open to the ocean. Among the myriad legacies prominent in the geomorphology of our Holocene time is the Big Valley extending south from the Seattle area to beyond Tacoma and Orting and, in a narrower version, to the Nisqually.

Streams very much smaller than the Big inherited its broad floodplain. When European settlers arrived, Mount Rainier's Puyallup entered the valley at Electron, turned north, at Orting picked up another Rainier river, the Carbon, and after a while turned west to Commencement Bay.

Green River and Mount Rainier

A third Rainier river, the White, debouched in the Big Valley at Auburn and during a dozen millennia sometimes turned south to join the Puyallup and sometimes north to Elliott Bay. The farmers wearied of the fickleness and after a switch from north to south during a winter flood of 1906 called in the engineers to build dikes to fix it in that southward course. At the point of diversion, where it exits from the Cascade front, the river changes name to the Stuck—golly remembers why.

Some maps of pioneer days had the White entering Elliott Bay. Others called the river in its final stretch to Whulge the Duwamish, the Anglicized name of the local Original Inhabitants. Once the White was out of the picture, geographers were torn between Duwamish and Green, the latter being the old White's chief tributary, also entering the Big Valley at Auburn. The ultimate consensus was to keep the de-Whited river Green to its Tukwila junction with the Black, the outlet of Lake Washington, then make it Duwamish the rest of the way to the saltchuck. (For a time after the ice went away, the saltchuck, Whulge, occupied what is now the valley of the Duwamish, wrapped around the south end of Beacon Hill, and filled the glacier-dug trough north of Renton. Sedimentation by the White, at that time containing the Green and Cedar, dammed off Lake Washington and pushed Whulge around the corner and north to today's Elliott Bay.)

The primeval Black River was the sum of the Sammamish River, Juanita Creek, Thornton Creek, Kelsey Creek, Coal Creek, May Creek, Issaquah Creek, and all other waters of the Lake Washington basin. Less than a mile from the lake it received the Cedar River and thus snowmelt from the Cascades. It was a substantial stream, indeed, when it met the White River to form the Duwamish. Of course, it couldn't compete with the White's spring floods from The Mountain and would then reverse flow and pour Rainier water into the lake. The Originals therefore called it Mox La Push, meaning "two mouths." In 1912 the farmers diverted the Cedar into Lake Washington, from which its waters quickly exited in the Black. In 1916 the new Lake Washington Ship Canal provided the lake a new outlet and the Black went out of the river business.

The riparian and human history of the Big Valley enriches the pedestrian experience. The recent and continuing chapters of the story are more saddening than not. The brown-black alluvium which fed Tacoma and Seattle, and the marshes which fed migrators on the Pacific Flyway, have largely vanished under blacktop and buildings. Flat ground, centrally located, is too expensive to grow food for man or beast or bird. The Big Valley has become the heavy-throbbing heart of Puget Sound City. Freeways rumble over the plain, unfruiting enough cropland to feed a Third World nation, and thunder up the valley walls. Jet airplanes rocket cloudward like so many Flash Gordons headed for Mongo and plummet forestward like so many gaudy baubles seeking Christmas trees, ceaselessly pummeling Puget Sound City with what the Port of Seattle and Chamber of Commerce hail as "the sound of progress" (money, that is).

Yet so far as the walker goes, none of this is fatal to whatever it is he/she seeks on a day's outing. The eye can follow a jet as well as a goose. (Milton wrote *Paradise Lost* and *Paradise Regained;* choose your paradise.) There is an esthetic of freeways, as there is of assault rifles and mushroom bombs. Human engineers are as entertaining as beavers, not the least because the busy-ness of both is in the using-up and ultimate destruction of their habitats. The editions of this book, which commenced in the surveys of 1976–78, were successively more bullish about prospects for foot travel in the Big Valley. But so much has happened in the past decade, events piling up year by year, that this edition must be tentative. The "worst of times"? Said the incurably ebullient Rabbi Ben Ezra, in the poem by Robert Browning, "Grow old along with me, the best is yet to be." Both of them later died. The fate of the River of Green awaits events now unfolding.

However, before it sorties out into the semi-anarchy, near-chaos of the Big Valley, the Green River courses riparian geography demanding no tentativity, naught but wonder and delight. One of the two greatest footlands of Seattle terra firma (the Issaquah Alps the other), an assured paradigm of "the wildness within." The Green River Gorge, that is.

USGS maps: Renton, Maple Valley, Black Diamond, Cumberland, Eagle Gorge, Auburn, Des Moines, Poverty Bay

Green River Way

The "River of Green," a non-motorized travel route from Whulge to the Cascade front, linking Seattle to cities of the Big Valley, to farms preserved as such, and to the Green River Gorge, has been a notion as exciting to walkers and horse-riders and bikers of today as the Oregon Trail was to nineteenth-century Americans. To hitch the saltwater to the wild highlands is necessary. Because they are there. The pedestrian whose religious needs are met by ceremoniously placing feet on the land, one at a time, one after the other, must at least once in his/her life perform the complete rite of passage. To be sure, the average walker will do a bit now, another bit later, and perhaps never the whole thing. Certainly the time of the walk will be chosen for those seasons, days, and hours when crowds of wheels are not socializing like so many flying ants. Admittedly, the multi-use route is mistakenly labeled "trail." But it surely is a way from here to there, and many good places along the way.

Black River

Bus: 108, 143, 145, 147, 148

From Martin Luther King Jr. Way–SW Sunset Boulevard (Highway 900) drive 68 Avenue S south to a crossing of the railroad tracks just beyond King County Public Works Pump Station No. 1 where Monster Road SW goes right. A beaten path through tall grass leads to pond and trail.

Railroads kept the memory alive by their signs, "Black River Junction," puzzling newcomers who looked in vain for a river. Yet the Black River does truly live! Just barely.

Two walks sample the Black. For the first, follow the service road down beside the riprapped ditch in which the river flows, when it has any water, to the Momentous Spot, the confluence with the Green River, the birthplace of the Duwamish. Let the eye slip into way-back focus. See the Duwamish people paddling or poling dugout canoes, taking the all-water route from Elliott Bay to Issaquah. See the barges carrying coals from Newcastle, the paddlewheel steamers bringing garden truck to market. See the ladies with parasols being paddled or rowed by their swains on Sunday voyages from Georgetown to Renton.

For the second walk, enjoy the parklet on the east side of the pump station, then follow the mowed lane down the slope to the enormous stormwater retention pond. The reason for this pond and the pumping station is that, though Howard Hanson Dam holds back mountain floods and dikes keep the Green in its channel, often the river flows so high that drainage from valley walls can't climb the dikes into the river. Without pumping stations the floodplain still would regularly flood. Once man starts messing around with Mother Nature's arrangements there's no end to it.

The mowed lane follows a terrace on the pond bank, secluded from the business "park" where used to be the Earlington Golf Course. Find a patch of shade under a new-planted tree and get out the binoculars. On a day in late June four separate, large families of Canada geese were observed.

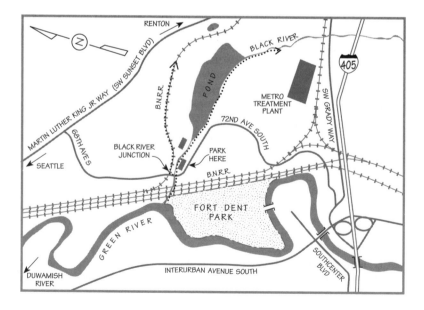

From the desk of

Joseph Becker

5 part Everett

rgt 194
left 99 194
rgt 92
to Granite Falls

Robe
Verlot
Silverton

Can take 194
from 5 to GF
or
left from 194
to 9
rgt on 9 to
GF
5
9
204
9
92

Ducks took off from the water, flopped in the water, quacked. Swallows swooped low over the surface, snapping up bugs. Killdeer ran about, squealing piteously. Mysterious splashings testified to creatures diving— or surfacing and pulling their heads back under before the binoculars could swing around. Who knows what secrets lurk in that opaque water? A chain of islets is brilliant yellow in summer in the bloom of deervetch. The far shore is a brooding jungle of tall cottonwood swaying in the breeze. Beware the "GARK! GARK!" of the dreaded GBH! In a scant ½ mile the pond bends to the south, to the mouth of a south branch of the Black that ditch-drains the plain beside and south of the now-Boeingized Longacres Race Track. At the far east edge of the pond, spot a bayou exiting from the cottonwood forest. This is the shrunken remnant of the Black as primevally it flowed from Lake Washington.

To these scant 1¾ miles of strolling and watching, a third walk adds 1 mile rich in history. Railroads! As shriveled as the Black but still alive, awaiting ultimate rejuvenation, and meanwhile, in that way-back focus, a bustling scene. Rails first reached the Black River in 1877, when the Seattle & Walla Walla Railroad arrived from Georgetown, headed for Renton and ultimately the Newcastle mines if never Walla Walla. In 1883 the Northern Pacific linked the Black River to Tacoma and Portland and the East. By 1909, when the Milwaukee came through, five lines passed the Junction. There still is a north–south mainline and, easterly toward Renton, the former Milwaukee, kept minimally alive by the mergerization known as the Burlington-Northern.

The view across the pond from the mowed lane compels the landscape detective to investigate the line east. The old Seattle & Walla Walla ran parallel a few yards to the south; from Renton to Newcastle the exact grade largely survives and has been walked on scheduled hikes of the Issaquah Alps Trails Club, which proposes that the rail route from the mines to Elliott Bay be declared a National/State/King County Historic Site.

Sorry to say, the cottonwood forest which from the mowed lane appears immense is seen from this backside to be a thin fringe, narrowed in 1987 for Blackriver Corporate "Park." Incredibly, a considerable stretch of the old Black channel had survived, to be logged and filled and blacktopped by the "Park," doubtless illegally, a partner in the crime being the City of Renton. That the cottonwood forest is 660 feet wide rather than the 250 feet intended by the developer and approved by the city is due to a troublemaking birder, Marty Murphy, who let the Audubon world know she had found a great blue heron nest in the doomed strip.

Above the tracks rises the mile-long green wall of the south end of Beacon Hill. Hemmed against the wall by the rail grade is a pond hiding behind thickets of willow and brambles. One ventures to guess that things live in and around that pond and on the wall above.

Near the start of this railway jaunt, accidentally (no doubt) spared from dredging for the storage pond, having the look of a cutoff meander, an oxbow marsh is a relict of the ancient river. The Black lives!

Tukwila, one way 2½ miles

Bus: 150; on Strander Boulevard, 240, 340

For the north end of the Green River Way, drive to just south of the I-405 bridge, elevation 20 feet.

From I-405 to the south city limits of Tukwila, the Green is channelized and diked and domesticated. The offices and warehouses and shops of Southcenter debouch swarms of lunchers every nice weekday and are busy morning and eve with joggers in sweatsuits and bikers in their sisters' underwear and doddering pedestrians brandishing quarterstaffs. Bicentennial Park boasts a log-cabin picnic shelter. In a long ½ mile the way passes under Strander Boulevard and becomes Christiansen Greenbelt Park. The storage pond behind Pump Station No. 17 floats a goodly number of ducks, though nothing like the tens of thousands that wintered or nested in the vast marshes paved to become Southcenter, or stopped off for a night's rest and a meal while migrating on the Pacific Flyway.

At 1¾ miles is "The End"; the dike continues but is gated. A pretty footbridge arches from true left bank to true right, and in ¾ mile more are the city limits.

Kent, one way from Tukwila to south end of Kent 7-odd miles

Bus: 34, 150, 154, 160 on West Valley Highway

Drive sidestreets off West Valley Road (Highway 181).

At a certain line beyond Tukwila, changing each year as the frontier advances, the rich black alluvium that fed Seattleites garden truck tastier than the bland agribusiness merchandise from Moses Lake and Califor-

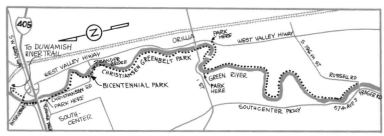

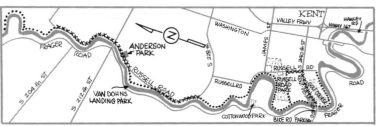

nia and Mexico, now grows naught but tansy and mullein and thistle and survey ribbons. Eventually farm fields begin beside the dikes on one or both sides of the river. In season, pick raspberries or buy fresh corn and cukes. Photograph cows, barns, and farmhouses. Inhale the heady fragrance of fresh manure. A little park at Van Dohns Landing commemorates the 1887 cable ferry. Russell Road Park, Kent's pride, has space enough for a cityful of picnickers and room, as well, for soccer riots of European magnitude. The river flows through it, floating waterfowl and rubber rafts. Always there are broad views across the Big Valley to the Issaquah Alps, Beacon Hill, and Rainier.

Mill Creek Canyon Park, round trip 4 miles

Bus: 150, 159, 161, 162

From Central Avenue on the east side of Kent turn east on Smith Street (Highway 516) to a stoplight. Turn south on E Titus Street to the parking area, elevation 50 feet.

A green gash in the Big Valley wall has been rescued from a garbage dump and restored and preserved in a 100-acre Kent city park, creek and forest 2 miles from upland down a canyon to the floodplain of the Green River. In 1982 the debouchment, four blocks from Kent City Hall, was transformed from a motorcycle-savaged field into an earthwork by the renowned Herbert Bayer; it serves as stormwater-retention pond and under-the-summer-stars concert hall, available for weddings and bar mitzvahs.

Mill Creek Canyon Park

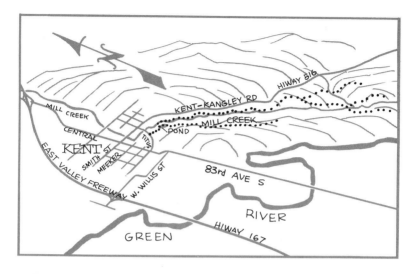

Two trails, one on either side of the creek, lead upstream. The north-side path is the suggested introduction. Now down beside the creek, deep in shadowed depths, now slicing the steep sidehill, now high on the rim, the path proceeds up the valley through a rich groundcover and understory beneath fine big cottonwoods and other deciduous trees, then a mix of cedars, hemlocks, and firs. Street noises fade. Glimpses diminish of houses on the rim. Feeder trails join from surrounding neighborhoods, sidetrails drop to creekside sitting spots, the main trail splits and unites, in a scant 2 miles ending at a paved road on the rim. However, by taking a sidetrail down to the creek and up to the opposite rim, the trip can be extended a bit to a field (and private property) where Mill Creek is no longer in a wide wild canyon but a narrow gulch fouled with farmers' garbage, elevation 350 feet.

North Green River Park, one way 4¼ miles

Bus: 150

From Kent drive Central Avenue, and turn east on S 259 Street, which becomes Green River Road S.

Having come so far upstream, it is meet to pause and reflect on the changes in river and valley since leaving the Black River. The Green is still rigidly channelized between dikes, frequently riprapped. But the water ... it's transparent! Not absolutely clear, yet boulders in the bed can be seen. There are rapids! And tidal mudbanks have yielded to fine sand. The elevation of downtown Kent is something like 35 feet.

Often called "Kent Valley," at this point the Big Valley is more than 2 miles wide from forested scarp to scarp, dominantly devoted to freeways. The city is a mixture of the industrial and commercial, old-residential detached houses with yards, newer-residential trailer courts with communal asphalt, and new-new semi-high-rise condos that face their little lawns and minute decks out upon the Green River where wild things swim and fly, creep and crawl. From some condo windows, farms can be glimpsed in the distance.

About 3 blocks on 259th from Central a sign on the right points into the "Bend of the River" apartments. From another sign, "Green River Corridor Park," paved trail goes a short way upstream.

Little shacks on (almost literally!) the river emit smoke from makeshift chimneys. Surely these are too picturesque to be legal. The mood of the route undergoes a dramatic and permanent transformation. Largely this is because though Kent gives way almost immediately to Auburn and the cities are virtual twins, the river has crossed the Big Valley to hug the east wall. Beyond the stream are Auburn and the 2

Green River near Isaac Evans Park

roaring miles to the west valley wall. Here there is King County Park, river, and river road that is almost walkable and genuinely is a "pleasure drive" and has many places to pull off on a shoulder and wander to the water. The subdivision of the Big Valley is at least half out of the mind because half the time the eye is on the wall of forest, as much as 400 feet tall. The houses lining the far bank aren't so bad because they are there and the public park is here.

Green River Road has many parking shoulders. Paths are frequent. Playfields and a King County P Patch lie between road and valley wall, and then the Auburn Golf Course. On the river side of the road are cottonwood colonnades, isolated meanders, quiet bars for sunning, wading, picnicking.

A final river path swings away from the road into a stupendous grove of cottonwoods, a parking area and picnic grounds and a sandy bar where children swim and splash. This is Isaac Evans Park, City of Auburn, connected to Henry Dykstra Park by a delightful swinging footbridge.

East Green River Park, round trip 4 miles

Drive east from Auburn on Highway 18 and just before it bridges over the Green River go off on the Black Diamond Road. Just before this road

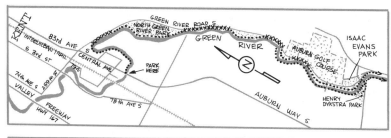

bridges the river, turn right on Green Valley Road and immediately pull off left on the fishermen's riverside parking area, elevation 75 feet.

A distinction must be made between the "Green River Valley" (Kent Valley, Kent-Auburn Valley, Big Valley) and the "Green Valley." The former is where the Big River used to flow. The Green River doesn't feel at home out there in the alien vastness of that 2-mile-wide expanse of floodplain made by far mightier floods than ever have been in its power. The Green River "belongs" to the homey little valley, the floodplain barely ½ mile wide at most, which extends some 7 air miles downstream from the exit of the Green River Gorge. A King County park upstream from the Big Valley lies within Green Valley coziness yet gives an outlook to the scariness.

Walk downstream beneath the Black Diamond Road bridge, the railroad bridge, and the Highway 18 bridge. Across the Green is the mouth of Big Soos Creek, babbling from the woods. Sit on the gravel bar and admire. Note that the river, at journey's start a pea soup, by Kent becomes a clouded limeade, now is clean and clear elixir—well, not for drinking, but inviting hot feet.

A broad dike guards the pasture to the left. In low water the hiker will prefer to walk gravel-sand bars, the river's width from the valley wall rising above streambank willow-cottonwood to Douglas fir of the Green River College Forest. Swallows flit, ducks quack, hawks circle, and pterodactyl-like herons implausibly lift from the gravel and ponderously flop to treetops. Remote, peaceful, idyllic.

The dike road swings left and fades out in woodland paths between a murky pond and the river. At 1 mile from the start a path reaches railroad tracks, the park boundary. Along the tracks to the right a short bit another road leads right to another dike. More pastures and birds and river. Now, as the Green River is entering the Big Valley, hugging the foot of the bluff for comfort, houses begin and the hike is best ended, 2 miles from the start.

For another experience of the Green Valley mouth, cross the railroad bridge at Big Soos Creek and explore the other side of the river.

Green Valley

Upstream from the Big Valley the valley of the Green River is as prettily pastoral as can be found so near Puget Sound City. When King County embarked on a Farmlands Preservation Program wherein owners would sell development rights to the county, thus getting the tax assessor and the developers off their backs so they could continue farming, the tragedy of the Big Valley was foremost in the preservers' minds. It had been a victim of the process which since World War II had gobbled up two-thirds of King County's farmlands, more than 100,000 acres, or 160 square miles, and was generally thought to be a lost cause. Happily, several in-the-nick coups in the Kent vicinity netted 989 acres on the banks of the Green, 1½ square miles which will remain green, growing good things to eat.

The protected acreage in the Green Valley is less—926 acres—but in those cozy confines is sufficient to keep in permanent green virtually the entire distance from the valley mouth to the gorge exit, on both sides of the river. Further, adjoining the 926 acres on the south are 4476 protected acres on the Enumclaw Plateau reaching south to and nearly encircling Enumclaw and guarding a great long stretch of the banks of the White River.

Grand news, indeed, that agriculture may prevail, that the agonies of Tukwilization do not lie in store here.

Sadly, a misunderstanding emerged. A final 8½-mile link in the trail from Elliott Bay to Green River Gorge was proposed through the Green Valley and included in King County's 1994 budget. Only then did it become publicly apparent that the transportation engineers who had been delegated to work out specifics of the trail corridor knew nothing about feet and horses. They had learned their trade building freeways and were now intent on building scaled-down versions for scaled-down wheels. Former enthusiasts for the King County Trails Plan were consternated to suddenly realize it actually was a Bikeways Plan. The Green Valley farmers who had happily accepted a narrow, quiet path through their fields saw that it was to be, instead, a wide swath to accommodate two-way 25-mile-an-hour traffic. In November 1993 the link was deleted from the county budget, done to death by the fear of hordes of bicycles. However, there is walking fitting the scene, savoring the close wildness of the valley-wall forests, the cows and corn on the valley floor, and the river. King County Parks has purchased segments for an Upper Green River Park through which there may or not ever be a trail. *However,* hostility has not subsided. Signs identifying easements acquired by the state Fish-

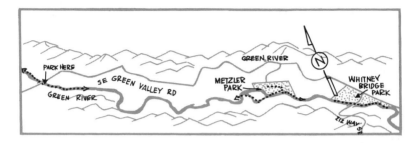

eries and Wildlife Department have been torn down, replaced by threatening proclamations certain to daunt walkers. Routes that were freely open to the public before the bicycle juggernaut of King County Parks threw off its mask and got up to speed have been removed from this book.

Metzler Park, round trips many miles

Drive Green Valley Road 4 miles from the bridge to the valley delight, Metzler Park.

Do not drive in haste. Go slow, to converse with the cows and horses. Keep the window open; in early summer the entire valley reeks of strawberries, in fall of corn. Real strawberries, real corn, not the watery synthetics fabricated in California.

A lane leads off to the parking area, elevation 150 feet. The path strikes off upvalley, at field's edge, bends right to cottonwood forest, and drops several feet to floodway terrace. The main route turns downvalley ½ mile to the riverbank; sidepaths go off upvalley to the bank. The cottonwood aroma overpowers the strawberries. The walker pauses to fill lungs.

Hark! What is this odd aural sensation? A person newly arrived from the rackety-bang of the Big Valley believes his/her ears have cut out. It is the sound of—no, not silence, but *quiet*. The green valley walls make no sound, nor do the green fields. Cars pass on the valley road only occasionally, muted by so much greenery. As many as a dozen minutes may pass without the brain being jellied by a jet. It is eerie to be able to hear faraway dogs barking.

The river is not silent. It is politely loud, but so clear and cool it tempts even the thirsty Sheltie usually too timorous to approach water that has a voice. The woods across the water are wild and green. The gravel bars and floodway forests invite the poking-about and wading foot.

Warning: Trail opponents have put up "bluff" signs claiming this public park is private property. Since King County has installed no boundary survey stakes, who knows? Don't argue with farmers who are so kind as to give us such good food.

Whitney Bridge Park, round trip 1 mile

Drive Green Valley Road a scant 2 miles from Metzler Park, to a scant 1 mile from Flaming Geyser Park. Turn south on 212 Way SE to Whitney Bridge and a parking lot, elevation 200 feet.

The park extends ½ mile along the river, fields ending at the shrub thicket on the riverbank. There are few gravel bars except in low water and a cursory survey revealed no paths. But there it is.

Green River Gorge

Immediately upon issuing from the Cascade front the Green River enters a canyon whose walls rise as much as 300 feet, always steep and often vertical, even overhanging. For 6 air miles, or 12 stream miles, its meanders are intrenched in solid rock, slicing through some 9000 feet of tilted strata of shale and sandstone, coal seams interbedded and fossil imprints imbedded of shells and vegetation.

There is absolutely nothing in the region that compares. (There used to be on the Nisqually and Cowlitz, but those canyons were drowned by Tacoma City Light.) From the time the coal miners arrived, a century and odd decades ago, the gorge has been a scenic attraction. Lacking permanent protection, however, it was sure to be exploited eventually for private profit. Then, in the mid-1960s, Wolf Bauer undertook a detailed survey of the gorge on foot and in kayak and drew up a proposal for "a unique natural showcase of free-flowing wild river and primeval canyon."

Green River from Flaming Geyser State Park

His lobbying brought the Legislature to establish a Green River Gorge Conservation Area.

The primary concern of the administrating agency, Washington State Parks, is acquiring and preserving the gorge from rim to rim. Appropriation by appropriation, State Parks is working toward that goal and expects to complete the initial program of purchase by 1996. The hiker, though gladly accepting the precedence of ecosystem protection, is served by a system of trails equalled only by the Issaquah Alps. Three sections of the gorge have major public accesses. In the middle is the Green River Gorge Resort, where private owners maintain trails in and around the gorge climax, the narrowest and most spectacular portion. State Parks has developed the gorge outlet and the gorge inlet and is holding for the future a number of other properties. As with the Alps, this book provides a sampling only, not an exhaustive inventory.

A trail has been talked about from one end of the gorge to the other. Someday such a trail may be built. Or maybe not. The route would have to stay on the rim in order not to molest the isolation of the river, and such a route has less interest than the bottom of the gorge. For much of its length this bottom is for floaters, not walkers, though a number of ways drop to the water. In late summer and early fall, when Tacoma is drinking so much of the Green there's only enough left to float the fish, much longer riverbank hikes can be taken than are described here. Conceivably a water-level route could then be walked (and/or waded, maybe partly swum) the full 12 miles.

Flaming Geyser State Park

East of Auburn, just before Highway 18 crosses the Green River, exit onto Auburn–Black Diamond Road and from that almost immediately exit right onto Green Valley Road. Drive 7 miles east to a Y and go right to the bridge over the river to the park. (Or, stay on the Auburn–Black Diamond Road to the Black Diamond–Enumclaw Road, follow it to 1 mile south of Black Diamond, turn west at the "Flaming Geyser" sign, and drive a scant 3 miles past the Lonely Red Schoolhouse of old Kummer to the bridge.) Parking is available at the park gates but most hikes are described here from a start at the far end of the park road, 1¼ miles from the gate, elevation 225 feet.

Romping the Riverside Fields, sample romp 1 mile

At the downstream end of the gorge, where the bluffs retreat from the river, which thereafter flows through the Green Valley over a floodplain ½ mile wide, is the site of an old resort now a state park. But before getting into its trails, park near the entry gate and strike off through the fields. Paths are mowed around the edges, by the river, and out in the middle. Strolling the "lawn" corridors through meadow grasses as high as an antelope's eye is an experience unique to this park, and people love it. Some love it so much they don't stay on the lawn strips but get down on hands and knees and creep to hideaways.

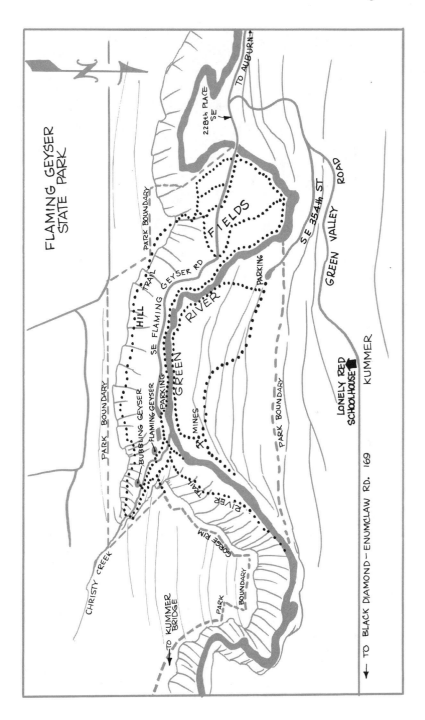

Kayaking in Green River Gorge

Perimeter Loop 3 miles

Having driven to the picnic area parking lot, walk upriver past a series of concrete fish ponds. At the fence corner, turn right up Christy
Creek. Pass a pool bubbling gas, the flow from a pipe ignited (sometimes)
to form a flame 6–12 inches high. In 1911 a test hole probing coal seams
was drilled 1403 feet down. At 900–1000 feet were showings of methane
gas. In early days of the former private resort the "Geyser" was flaming
many feet in the air; now it's pretty well pooped out.

Continue over a bridge and up the creek in mossy-ferny maple woods,
the trail dividing and uniting, passing a bridge and stub trail to the gray
mud of Bubbling Geyser. Up a short set of stairs and then again upstream,
the main trail recrosses the creek and ascends the bluff, topping out at
425 feet, and begins a long upsy-downsy contour along the sidehill in a
green tangle of maple and cedar and alder and lichen and moss. Views
(screened) down to the river. Sidepaths to nooks for lunch or rest or small
adventures suitable for small folk. The way at length drops to the floodplain and road, the trail now a mowed strip (or strips) in pasture grass.
Cross the road and walk out in the field to the park-entry bridge. Turn
right and follow the riverbank upstream to the picnic area, by sandy
beaches, through patches of woods, meeting ducks and dippers, gulls and
herons, and kayakers landing after voyages down the gorge.

Gorge Mouth, round trip 1½ miles

Beginning as before, past the fence corner cross Christy Creek to a Y. Go straight on the right fork (the left quickly ends at the river) and then left (the right ascends to the rim) up the old road-now-trail, climbing 100 feet above the river, contouring the sidehill, then dropping to a sandy flat in fine woods. The width of the floodplain dwindles to zero, the walls crowd the river, and upon entering the gorge the trail ends. Admire the 100-foot cliff of stratified rock, the river cutting the base. In low water a hiker can round the corner and snoop into the gorge.

Across the River and into the Trees, complete tour 4 miles

Drive back across the river on the entry road, turn right toward Kummer, and in 0.4 mile up the hill turn right off the Green Valley Road onto SE 35 Street. Descend to parking on the valley floor, elevation 200 feet.

Half the park is across the river, in a wildness that holds memories of a long human past. Pass the barn and keep left, crossing the green floodplain at the foot of the bluff. At ½ mile are an old orchard and Y. Take the road-path straight ahead and downhill into the woods. In a short bit is another Y. The right fork goes ¼ mile through forest to the river and a sandy beach for kiddies to safely wade, and a luscious pool of limeade for anybody to deliriously swim; a trail is planned downstream along the bank 1 mile, looping back to the parking area. The left fork goes a similar short way past interesting coal mine artifacts to the river; a trail is planned upstream to the outlet of the gorge.

Gorge Rim, one way 3 miles

The State Park Conservation Area is intended to protect the gorge rim the full distance from Flaming Geyser to the Kummer (Black Diamond) Bridge. Will it? Will the final acquisitions planned by 1996 fulfill the 1960s vision of Wolf Bauer? We hope. The elder surveyor once walked the 3 miles, not often on public land and largely in a bewilderment of logging roads. Rangers say the only hikers ever lost in the park have been attempting this route. However, the wily brush-buster can find vantage points for impressive views from the rim, which tops out at 525 feet or so, straight down to the river. Paths beaten by insane fishermen slippety-slide into the wild gorge otherwise known only to kayakers.

Kummer (Black Diamond) Bridge

Drive Highway 169 south 2½ miles from Black Diamond.

The view of the gorge the best-known to the most people is from the walkway of this bridge. Giddy gazing into the vasty deeps.

From the parking area on the north side of the bridge, elevation 450 feet, several paths dive to the river. Fishermen! A person managing to arrive intact at the river finds paths downstream about ½ mile and upstream a short way to a handsome sandstone cliff. In low water the walk can be extended indefinitely in both directions. On the south side of the bridge a plummet leads to upstream-downstream boulder-hopping. While a Boy Scout rock nut, the elder surveyor carried up this plummet a 50-pound chunk of lignified tree. (Well, his father carried it most of the way. A fisherman.)

South from the bridge ½ mile on the highway a gated road takes off south. An explorer from Flaming Geyser would come out here. Or from here the search parties would set out. If and when State Parks acquires this 650-acre property from Plum Creek (the current heir of the local loot from the Northern Pacific Land Grant) it will make the mine-treacherous terrain visitor-safe and perhaps build an interpretive center. Presently, fishermen walk the road, bend right past the mine workings, and descend the gorge wall to a riverbank path downstream to tumbled timbers of a mine structure and upstream ½ mile nearly to the bridge; at low water the gravel bars extend the route.

Hanging Gardens (Cedar Grove Point), round trip 1½ miles

Drive Highway 169 south from Kummer (Black Diamond) Bridge 1.5 miles and turn east on SE 358th (Enumclaw-Franklin Road). At 1.7 miles see two gated roads on the left. One leads to a fish hatchery, the other to the river. At 2.3 miles note, on the left, dumped stumps and heaps of trash. Park here, elevation 680 feet.

The State Parks Conservation Area has nearly 3 miles of river and gorge rim here, across the river on the northwest side (for a sampling, see Franklin, below). It has half that much length on this southeast side. Short walks give tastes.

Walk the road into the woods, shortly reaching the chain-link fence of the Black Diamond Watershed. Follow the fence to where it turns right; at a Y there, take the right fork down into lush mixed forest. The road soon yields to a trail down the bluff, following the crest of a finger ridge around which the river makes a sharp intrenched-meander bend. The point is distinguished by a grove of big cedar trees. It also features a sandy beach at the tip directly across from the Hanging Gardens, a vertical wall from which jut ledges sprouting shrubby trees and (in season) gaudy splashes of flowers—a phenomenon not unusual in the gorge but rather especially nice here.

Green River Gorge Resort

From Highway 169 in Black Diamond turn east on Green River Gorge Road 4 miles to the Franklin Bridge. (Alternatively, from Highway 169 at 1.5 miles south of the Kummer Bridge take the Enumclaw-Franklin Road 4 miles to the Franklin Bridge.) Park near the inn, elevation 580 feet.

In the 1920s the Diamond Stage Company began running Studebaker buses to the Green River Gorge, described in promotional brochures as possessing "a beauty that far surpasses any other scenic attraction in this Charmed Land." Resorts proliferated in the vicinity. Lake Retreat, Lake Sawyer Paradise, Lake 12 ("A delightful family resort—a rest room beneath the stars—a trysting place for man and health"), and Ye Olde

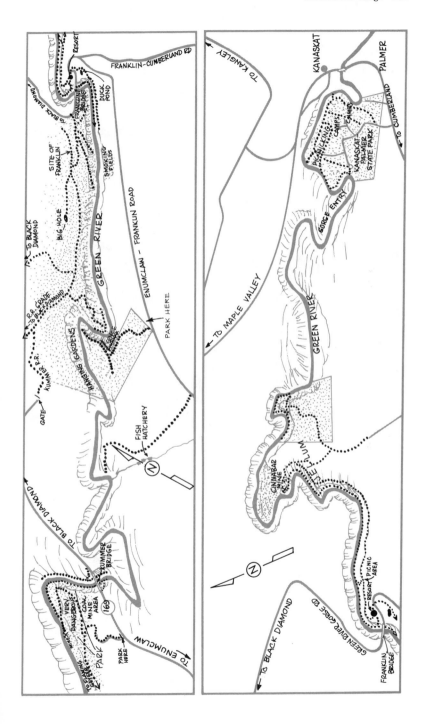

Green River Gorge Resort

Green River Gorge Resort, which was "so crowded on weekends that you barely had room to move," recalls old settler Tom Zumek. "On Sundays we had motorcycle races up the slag pile." There were a Knights of Pythias hall, a baseball field, a saloon (until Prohibition, when bootleggers met the demand, and so pugnaciously that revenooers abstained from visiting the coal country), and a dance pavilion "where bands strained to be heard above the din of the falls."

When the range of automobiles reached beyond the coal country to the mountains, the resort declined to a dark and seedy time. In the 1970s it was taken over by new owners who have turned down offers to buy by State Parks because they have too much fun busting brush to improve old trails and build new ones. The trail fee charged for the path down into the Quintessential Gorge is a small contribution to their efforts.

Yes. The Quintessential. As of this writing, off limits.

Two deaths, rowdy parties, boozing and drugging, and the liability

152

insurance forced the private owners to close the resort and forbid public entry. One way or another it will be reopened, perhaps in 1995, perhaps not. Before planning an outing there, call Jimmy Carter, (206) 886-2302.

From the snackery gate (solidly closed and non-detourable) the way drops to a Y. The downstream route turns left down a staircase-path over the brink of a waterfall to the river. There's too much to see to go fast and that's good; speed kills. Dark clefts between huge mossy-green boulders, slippery slabs by churning green pools of The Chute, under fern-and-moss cliffs and Rainbow Falls.

The way upstream from the Y turns right and in ¼ mile descends a staircase to a forest flat by the river. This is a loop trail—but only at low water because at high water a stretch of several hundred feet requires knee-deep wading. For seasons when the trail is submerged, a straight-up path climbs to the gorge rim. The other end of the loop trail descends spectacularly on staircases to the river and a T. The left fork goes downstream (the loop way) to a high-water end at a wonderful great cave. The right fork, a delight every step, proceeds to exposed coal seams and—it is rumored—all the way to the Cinnabar Mine.

Franklin Bridge

In the late 1880s an impressive engineering feat emplaced a wooden span over the Quintessential Gorge to link Black Diamond to Cumberland, Bayne, and Palmer. In 1915 it was replaced by a Baltimore Petit truss, the sole example of that design in King County. Closed for repairs in 1987, it reopened in 1991. The walk-across views into the gorge depths shiver the imaginations of gazers recalling the bridge's past as the region's favorite Lover's Leap.

Franklin

The Johnson girl was born in 1896, died in 1897. Edey Standridge came to the world in 1892, left it in 1893, "Asleep in Jesus, blessed sleep, from which none ever wakes to weep." Mary Llewellyn's dates were 1890–92. Francis Marie Myers lived from March 13 to May 24 of 1901. Alice Johnson knew 6 days in January of 1902. Something like half the headstones in the Franklin Cemetery are of infants; the recumbent lamb was the stonecutter's top seller.

The other half are for men in their twenties and thirties. On August 24, 1894, there died Luici Farro, 32; Rocco Tittara, 37; and Filippo Dimarino, 27; the three are memorialized by a single stone. Another stone states that on the same day James Gibson, 27, died. An historian poking through the hellberries and nettles, ivy and periwinkle, might find others of the thirty-seven who met their ends that day.

The site of Franklin Cemetery will not be described here, though the secret is pretty well out since the newspapers publicized the 1993 cleanup by the eighth-grade class at Cedar Heights Junior High School in Covington. One must hope their Franklin Project does more to get the site on the National Register of Historic Places than it does to guide ghouls on midnight plunders.

Though the Green River Resort is entirely surrounded by State Parks land, it beat the public to the punch in purchasing the field (elevation 608 feet) beside the Green River Gorge Road across the bridge from the resort. There thus are "No Trespassing" and "No Parking" signs at the State Parks gate barring the road into the field. Beyond the field, is State Parks.

Just inside the gate from the Green River Gorge Road, three sideroads-trails in quick succession turn off left into the flats of "Lower Franklin" and down into the gorge.

In a scant ½ mile from the gate the road Ts with the Franklin–Black Diamond rail line. Turn right over a flat bench where ivy climbs high in the poplars, hellberries daunt the most fanatic pothunters, and white roses blooming in wild greenery give the heart a pang. (Were they brought here by Paddy the Welshman? Or by the 600 black miners recruited from the Midwest, not knowing until they got off the train, no money for a return trip, that they had been hired to break a strike?) A gash in the hillside can be recognized as a collapsed mine mouth. A hillock reveals to the investigating boot that it is composed of waste rock and clinkers (from coal that was burned by spontaneous combustions in the dump). Three masonry masterpieces testify to the craftsmen who cut slabs of sandstone and concreted them together, brick-like, in Mayan-like temples. This is about all that remains of a town founded in 1885 by the Oregon Improvement Company, at the turn of the century home to some 1200 residents, and closed and vacated in 1924.

Franklin-to-Black Diamond Railroad, round trip 6 miles

At the T in Franklin turn left on the rail grade, now a woods road closed to motorized public vehicles. In a few steps is a Y. The right ascends a long ¼ mile to an elevation of 800 feet, ending abruptly at the Big Hole, a mine shaft grated in 1987 by the federal Office of Surface Mining. Gaze into a blackness said to go straight down 1500 feet.

Left (straight ahead) from the Y is the way (the rail grade now a service road) to Black Diamond. Diverging to the left is a stretch of railroad which never has been recycled into a wheel road. The level grade of the vanished rails has become a foot-only trail. Treasure the thought that the Franklin railroad was engineered in 1884 and hasn't seen choo-choos since 1924, and this particular stretch hasn't seen wheels since then. The grade is sliced through a cut, then in sandstone walls. A window opens in the superb mixed forest to views across the gorge to the Smoking Fields. The river can be heard if not seen. The cliffs drip maidenhair fern. The boots stir the scent of crushed mint. A path into and out of a gully whose trestle has been missing half a century crosses a cool ooze of water down mossy slabs.

At a scant 1 mile from the highway, the rail grade is joined on the right by the powerline service road of the Black Diamond Water District. The road, firmly gated on the Black Diamond side, climbs to the city's reservoir and a 1025-foot ridgetop in views over Puget Sound lowlands to towers of downtown Seattle.

The trail-grade rejoins the powerline service road, which at a long 1 mile from the highway takes off left from the rail grade, elevation 700 feet, and in ¾ mile of fine, cool forest displaying nicely big cedars drops past a pumphouse at the powerline end to one of the gorge's very few sizable river terraces, elevation 375 feet.

The hiker's imagination is certain to have been inflamed by the "footbridge" shown on the USGS map. He is sure he'll find nothing more than naked cables. He is virtually consternated to find the bridge is intact—a genuine swinging bridge. Especially if accompanied by a pair of cowardly dogs, he will not cross the bridge and that's just as well. It is a bridge to nowhere—to no trail. It is the pipeline (plus walkway for maintenance purposes) that brings water across from the Springs on the other side of the gorge (see Hanging Gardens), thence up to the pumphouse and onward to the reservoir.

A short bit upstream from the bridge are mossy masses of old concrete and a new grate over a pit of black water. In 1987 the Office of Surface Mining installed the grate after a horse fell in this pit, a mine airway, and drowned.

Black Diamond Museum

Downstream the road-trail ends in a grove of great cottonwoods and a path drops to the gravel bar. On the other side of the river a creek tumbles whitely out of the greenery. Sandstone walls leap up. See the fishermen. Watch the kayaks slide by.

At 1½ miles from the highway, where the grade continues ahead to Black Diamond, another grade, improved to a drivable (State Parks) service road, turns off left. This is the railway grade to Kummer.

At the turnoff, fields open out in the forest to the left, the Black Diamond Gun Club. In ½ mile the road is absolutely barred to public wheels by a sturdy gate of the State Parks variety. This gate can be reached from the other side. From Highway 169, where Green Valley Road turns off west, turn off east on a road signed "Black Diamond Gun Club Inc." In 0.3 mile the gun club road swings off right and the old rail grade proceeds straight ahead, reaching the gate at 0.6 mile from the highway. Park here, elevation 666 feet.

The old rail grade used to extend west of Highway 169 close to and partly on the modern Green Valley Road. In ½ mile is a little building with a school bell atop, prominently signed, "This is Kummer. Formerly School Dist. 123. Home of the Lonely Red Schoolhouse."

What about the ultimate destination, Black Diamond? That's less easy. At a long ½ mile from the Kummer Y the path enters private property. In another ½ mile, where the grade used to be until obliterated by houses and driveways, and where now a trespasser is liable to be torn to pieces by packs of savage dogs, is Highway 169. Just on the other side is Railroad Avenue, which in ¼ mile leads to the world-famous Black Diamond Bakery.

Black Diamond Museum

Bus: 147, 912 (weekdays only)

Drive Highway 169 to Black Diamond.

Before software and latte, before aircraft, before timber, fish, and Alaska, King Coal ruled King County. Axis of the industry was the railroad from the coal dock on Elliott Bay, up the Duwamish to Black River Junction, a branch to Newcastle, the main line through Maple Valley to Black Diamond, Kummer, Franklin, Cumberland, Durham, Hyde, Bayne, Palmer, and the rest. In 1880 the Black Diamond Mining Company of Nortonville, California, discovered the McKay Seam, the highest-quality coal ever found on the Pacific Coast, and in 1884 the rails reached the new town of Black Diamond, which in a year grew from a tent village to a population of 3000 and by the turn of the century 3500, the biggest producer of coal in the county. In the 1920s petroleum elbowed coal off the throne. The old Pacific Coast Coal Company shriveled. In 1933 the new Palmer Coking Coal Company bought up much of its property and in the 1980s, through a subsidiary nostalgically reviving the name of Pacific Coast Coal, opened the John Henry, an enormous open pit and one of two active coal mines in Western Washington. The other, at Chehalis, feeds a monster of a steam plant. The John Henry, partly owned by Mitsubishi, fills trucks for hauling to Ravensdale to be loaded on trains to British Columbia for shipment to Japan.

Historical societies thrive in Issaquah, Newcastle, Renton, and Maple Valley as well as Black Diamond. In 1976 the last-named society, its founding occasioned by the nation's bicentennial, undertook restoration of the railroad depot, abandoned for that purpose since the 1930s. In 1982 the museum opened. Days and hours are Thursday, 9:00 A.M. to 4:00 P.M., and weekends, noon to 3:00 P.M. For special tours call (206) 886-1168. Thursdays are work days when society members continue the refurbishing. The visitor may then find them with free time to explain the adjoining jail, wash house, "model mine" with mine cars and electric locomotive, and other displays, inside and outside the depot and in the caboose permanently parked on the rails. They may tell tales of the "bumps" that killed miners in the mile-deep No. 11 Seam, of the strike in 1921 when locked-out miners moved a short way west to found Morganville, named for the hospitable farmer who let them squat on his land, and of the product which gave Black Diamond a new fame in Prohibition, not necessarily because it was so much better than could be obtained in Seattle, but because it was sold so openly, lawmen knowing better than to mess with these miners.

To tour the museum at leisure—and to buy bread from the bakery next door—come any time except the weekend of the second Sunday in June. However, by all means come then for Black Diamond Day.

Jellum Cinnabar Mine, round trip 5 miles

From the junction just uphill and east from Green River Gorge Resort, drive east on Green River Gorge Road 0.5 mile. At the top of a rise, in an enormous clearcut of the mid-1980s, spot a road left barred by a gate. Park here, 789 feet.

The road, on private land but with easement for public feet, not wheels, crosses the clearcut plateau 1 scant mile to a Y. The right fork goes to the bluff rim, sidehills down to a broad bench, and in ½ mile ends in a fir-grove camp, once the site of some complicated activity (mine-related?). A trail goes over the brink, instantly splitting in two pieces, left and right, the two ends of a loop demanding to be hiked in its entirety. It is, however, the left fork that leads directly to The Place, featuring one enormous boulder that has atop it 18-inch hemlocks whose roots reach 25 feet down the rock to find nutritious earth. Not so much a trail as a clambering route, the way proceeds downstream, dodging through clefts, passing under a great overhang sheltering a ramshackle cabin, crossing sandy beaches, to a high-water end ½ mile from Camp Flat.

The left fork from the plateau Y passes ruins of an old shack on a jutting point and switchbacks on road-trail down to mine timbers and garbage. A path drops to the mine mouth (collapsed) and the waste rock sloping to the river. Mine artifacts and cinnabar ore mixed with coal are interesting, and the bouldery river, and the forest, displaying one 8-foot cedar. But the scene for soft summer days is the sprawl of sand dipping into the slow flow of river, a place that demands taking off shoes and rolling up pants and wading—if not taking it all off and thrashing around, crying "Evoe!"

Kanaskat-Palmer State Park, two loops 3½ miles

Drive via Enumclaw or Black Diamond to old Cumberland and thence to old Palmer. Alternatively, drive from Issaquah-Landsburg or Kent to old Georgetown (that is, the Ravensdale Market). Turn east 1 mile on Kent-Kangley Road to a Y. Keep right on Retreat-Kangley Road 3 miles and turn right on Cumberland-Kanaskat Road. Proceed 1.7 miles, passing through old Kanaskat and crossing the Green River to old Palmer and the entry to Kanaskat-Palmer State Park.

If the two state parks located at the exit and the entry of the gorge have the least gorge to show, they have the most easy river walks. The paths in this one are thronged on fine summer weekends, as are the deep pools of cold limeade.

Trails take off from a number of points on the park's road system and all are excellent woods walks, totalling some 3 miles and lending themselves to any number of loops. To go straight for the best, at a Y in 0.6 mile, where the road right leads to campsites, keep left. In 0.2 mile more pass a sideroad left to the downstream kayak put-in and take-out. In a final 0.2 mile is the turnaround at the picnic area and midway put-in and take-out. Elevation, 740 feet.

To the right, by the bulletin board giving boating information, a path enters the woods and leads upstream, keeping mostly at some distance from the river. Sidepaths go off inland to the camping area. A path goes off left to the upstream put-in and take-out. At 1 long mile the route intersects the entry road not far from the entry. A deadend path starts from the garbage cans at the turnaround circle, passes picnic tables, and drops to a gravel bar—the put-in and take-out spot. Just upstream the river falls over sandstone slabs into a spacious swimming pool.

The major trail downstream diverges from this deadend path a few steps from the parking lot and passes a privy, a picnic shelter in a broad lawn, and dozens of picnic sites tucked into a forest new-growing after a semi-clearcut in 1976. Sidepaths from the table go a few steps to the brink of a bank dropping steeply to the river. At the end of the picnic area the blacktop trail veers left to the entry road; the river trail, now plain earth, enters mixed forest, the alders and vine maple particularly fine. Rude sidepaths demand sidetrips to choice spots to sit beside the river. In ¾ mile the trail ends at the downstream put-in and take-out. Walk from the path out onto sandstone slabs beveled flat at the base of sandstone cliffs—not high, but announcing what lies just ahead. Stand at the edge of the beveled slab and look down into the water. E-gad! Retreat! The bottom can barely be made out, perhaps 12 feet down. The water is quiet, twigs fallen onto the surface scarcely moving. It is impossible not to wish one were a good enough swimmer to dive in. But one can be quite content gazing upstream to a jut of rock and a picturesque fir whose roots clutch the rock, barely keeping the leaning tree from falling into the water, and downstream, where the beginnings of the gorge can be guessed just around the horseshoe bend.

On the elder surveyor's first exploration here, before the park was developed, he found paths to the top of the cliffs of the incipient gorge and followed them along a bench in virgin forest of giant cedars, firs, and hemlocks. In ½ mile the terrace and trail ended at a lovely camp. The surveyor proceeded without trail toward Jellum and got so splendidly lost that his compass read 180 degrees wrong, no matter how hard he banged it. The vicinity has been so completely scalped in the last decade that the virgin forest probably has been relocated in Japan.

Nolte State Park (Deep Lake), loop and sidetrips 1½ miles

From Cumberland drive south 1 mile to the park, elevation 770 feet. The park is officially closed September to April but the trail always is open to feet.

Not in the gorge but near it is 39-acre Deep Lake, owned by the Nolte family since 1883, operated as a private resort since 1913, and in the late 1960s willed to the public by Minnie Nolte. During olden-day logging only the cream (the huge cedars) was skimmed and the forest of Douglas firs up to 6 feet in diameter appears virginal, fit companion for the quiet (no motorboats) water.

The trail loops 1 mile around the lake, through the big firs and 5-foot cedars and 3-foot cottonwoods, crosses the inlet, Deep Creek, and passes a number of birding paths to the shore.

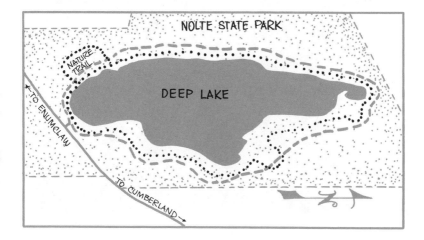

Mount McDonald

The trailhead can be driven to by any number of routes, all easy to find and confusing to describe. Use a road map. At 0.7 mile past a Bonneville Space Station on the Kanaskat-Kangley Road, spot a narrow lane on the east, SE Courtney Road, elevation 874 feet. Park on the highway shoulder, not up the lane.

An 8-mile round trip, elevation gain 2400 feet, is a succession of chapters in the geography of Whulge country. From the Cascade front between the valleys of the Cedar and Green Rivers, look across the upland sliced by the Green River Gorge to the Osceola Mudflow and The Mountain from which it gushed. Look to the peninsula thrust of the Issaquah Alps touching shores of Lake Washington. See Seattle and the Olympics and the steam plume rising from the Tacoma pall.

Walk up Courtney Road a short bit through the barking dogs. Cross the rail grade, which had tracks until the late 1970s. Turn left on a woods

Mount Rainier from Mount McDonald

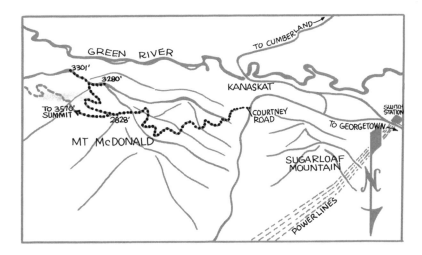

road to a gate. Climb steadily in mixed forest, spurs going off left and right. In ½ mile a window opens to pastures below and out to the Olympics and Rainier. At 1 mile is a waterfall-creek. As the road twists and turns around the mountain, the forest changes to young conifers, mostly hemlocks, and views commence over treetops and through them. At 3 miles, 2828 feet, is a Y where both forks are major. Go right, climbing. The views on this trip are cafeteria-like—something of this here, a bit of that there, never everything at once. In this stretch are the best views north, down to the Cedar River and out to Taylor and Tiger and Squak and Cougar, as well as to Rattlesnake and Si, Baker and Index and Three Fingers.

In a final 1 mile, with a couple more switchbacks, the road passes a deadend right to a gravel pit, stays left to a gate, and in a final ⅓ mile tops out on a clearcut plateau atop McDonald Point, elevation 3280 feet. Here, formerly the site of a fire lookout, is a TV repeater. Enjoy the grand view off the edge of the scarp. Then, for a variation, follow a sketchy road ¼ mile through small silver firs and western hemlocks to a 3301-foot point. See huge Rainier and nearby Grass. See the Enumclaw plain and silvery meanders of the Green River and hear the trains blow, boys, hear the trains blow.

Soos Creek (Gary Grant) Park

Bus: 158

To begin from the south, drive Highway 516 to Lake Meridian Park. Turn north on 148 Avenue SE 0.4 mile to 266th. Though the park continues south to Lake Meridian, the 266th trailhead is recommended to visitors from afar. Elevation, 400 feet.

Big Soos Creek is an example of the "undersized" stream not big enough

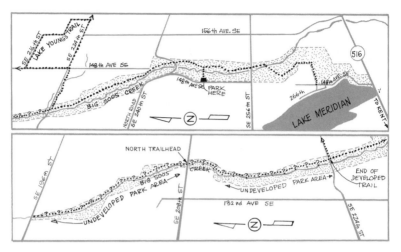

for its inherited britches. The valley it follows was dug by a far mightier flow of water, gone these dozen millennia. Gravels of braided channels that once swung from valley wall to valley wall have been buried by peaty bogs, cattail marshes, willow swamps. The usual fate of undersized creeks is to be filled, water ditched or sewered, houses and shopping center built. The Forward Thrust of the 1960s saved a long strip of Big Soos from such a fate—5 air miles, up to ¼ mile wide. In the late 1980s King County Parks began building an end-to-end trail, a blacktop lane for bicycles and wheelchairs, a dirt lane for horses, walkers welcome to both.

The good news: a sidehill forest of tall firs, a bottom woodland of willows, a striking bridge over the creek by a children-friendly wading pool, pastoral vistas, ponds dredged to retain stormwater already filled with cattails, blackbirds harassing walkers, and salmon fry leaping for mosquitoes. When complete, a 10-mile round trip of good news.

The bad news: King County Parks waited too long, houses got built, a public trail is not welcome in front yards and not ecologically tolerable or legal in the wetlands alternative. And bicycles ... the skinny-tires and fat-tires speed along the 4.4 miles of blacktop from Lake Meridian to the north trailhead at SE 208 Street and King County Parks stands by, eyes closed and hands folded, chanting its mantra, "Multi-use, multi-use."

But the county has nothing else like the Big Soos. Not anymore. It's much too precious to be a bikeway only. The walk in the wet must not be abandoned. For now, though, it cannot be recommended to pedestrians who live at a distance unless their masochistic itch needs a scratching.

Other Trips

Duwamish River. A sewage pipeline from a secondary treatment plant in Renton to the outfall at Duwamish Head will be utilized as a 12-mile non-motorized travelway.

Duwamish Viewpoints. The Port of Seattle has yielded to the City of Seattle's insistence that public accesses be provided to the working waterfront of the Duwamish Waterways. The choicest of the half-dozen or so is at Terminal 107, in close view of Kellogg Island. The Port of Seattle, having obliterated most of the island, was forced to spare the shrunken remnant as a wildlife refuge. The Duwamish people had a village here from approximately A.D. 670 to the Holocaust of the nineteenth century.

The Meandering Duwamish. Beginning in 1913, the river was straightened, channelized, and converted to a pair of industrial waterways bracketing Harbor Island. Starting 6 air miles from Elliott Bay, it was allowed to retain river status. Allentown Bridge lets the walker peer into olive-green water. The Allentown Pea Patch is an anomalous relict of the farming frontier. The railroad tracks let feet explore nearly 2 miles of the Old Duwamish from the Seattle Rendering Works past the Foster Golf Course to Black River Junction.

Big Soos Railroad Trail. From the rail bridge over the Green River, the living rails and ties give 4 miles of wild woodland walking up the Big Soos valley, in a secluded ravine to the start of farms at the confluence with Jenkins Creek. Far more attractive to a pedestrian than Big Soos Park as it now is.

Duwamish River viewpoint

Green River College Forest. The teaching forest, extending from the high promontory of the campus steeply down to the Green River and Big Soos Creek, has some 4 miles of trails maintained by students as part of their curriculum. A sidetrip on river gravels and dikes connects to parks of Auburn.

Lake Youngs Perimeter Trail. The fourth-largest lake in lowland King County has no swimming beaches, no hydroplane races, and as the holding reservoir between the Cedar River and Seattle City Water mains is rarely seen by the public, though sipped and swallowed by it daily. Forests cover three-quarters of the 4 square miles of the reservation. A 9-mile King County Parks trail on a Seattle Water Department 25-foot-wide dedication follows the fence, permitting the wildland to be visually enjoyed by clever householders and by walkers and horsefolk. Unfortunately, though the plague of motorcycles has subsided, it has been succeeded by the pandemic of fat-tire bicycles. The intent of planners was to exploit this centerpiece as a connection between Big Soos Park and the pipeline east to Landsburg, a "multi-use" trail. The refusal of government to control the fat-tire conquistadores has trashed this and many other splendid concepts.

Interurban Trail. Another dream that went sour. The Seattle-Tacoma Interurban Railway, killed in the late 1920s by the building of the Pacific Highway, was envisioned in the 1970s as a multi-use non-motorized travel route the 15 miles from Tukwila to the Pierce County line and ultimately on into Tacoma and north to Seattle. Segments were opened in the 1970s, signed "Bicycles Horses Hiking." Omitted from mention were the service truck parade of Puget Power and friends. The paved route has nevertheless gained favor of cyclists, skinny-tire mainly, and commuters mainly. Horses have not been seen for years. Pedestrians are kept under police surveillance as candidates for the loony bin.

Maple Valley to Black Diamond. Grade of the old coal railroad, once hoped to connect the Cedar River Trail to the Green River Gorge. From Lake Wilderness Park it's 2½ miles in one direction to where the rails used to cross the Cedar River, and 5 miles in the other to the outskirts of Black Diamond. The best walking isn't on the grade, it's by the lake—a 40-acre arboretum of native plants displayed on 1¼ miles of paths.

WHITE RIVER

Something scary here. Arriving on the lower White utterly ignorant of the region, a perceptive visitor quickly—and nervously—would note the difference between this river and those to the north. The black sands, the black and red boulders. That's lava rock. There's a volcano upstream. And the murky water, the wide gravel bed of interwoven channels old and new. That's rock milk and channel-braiding. There's a glacier upstream. A dangerous combination, a glacier and a volcano.

Tell it to the Original Inhabitants who were going about their business 5800 years ago when the steam bomb exploded 30 miles away, melting thousands of tons of snow and ice, sending down the valley to Whulge a roaring slurry of muck, perhaps 2.5 billion cubic yards of it, three-quarters of a cubic mile of rock debris. The Osceola Mudflow. Leaving in the lowlands a deposit up to 70 feet thick. A once-in-a-dozen-millennia rarity? No. The Mountain has spewed 60 such "lahars" in the last 10,000

White River from Game Farm Wilderness Park

165

years. Just 600 years ago the Electron Mudflow rumbled down the Puyallup to saltwater. Come the next big show and real estate in Enumclaw, Buckley, Kent, Auburn, Sumner, and Puyallup—all of whose sites were buried by the Osceola—won't be worth a nickel. A 113-page scientific study published in 1994 warned that "A major volcanic eruption or debris flow could kill thousands of residents and cripple the economy of the Pacific Northwest."

If man has performed no single so dramatic a stunt of river manipulation, he's puttered for decades, tinkering this way and that with the White. The diking by King County farmers to transfer flooding problems to Pierce County farmers has been discussed earlier. In 1914, arguments between the counties over whose fault it was emerged from the courts to an agreement for joint management and cost-sharing.

A disastrous flood of the 1930s, demonstrating the limits on Commencement Bay's industrial potential, couldn't be blamed on anybody but Nature, whose ever-doughty foe, the Army Engineers, answered the bugle call by heaping up the Mud Mountain Dam; the river is no longer permitted to flood and in flood season often is reservoirized by the dam, whose fate in the next Osceola unfailingly amuses congregations of Luddites.

Last, in 1911 Puget Power put the White to work, at Buckley diverting water through a flume to a reservoir, Lake Tapps, thence into turbines at Deiringer and a return to the White (Stuck) in the Big Valley. As a consequence, when everybody is cooking supper and taking a shower and watching TV and making aluminum all at once, the White-Stuck between Buckley and Deiringer dwindles to the minimum legally required for the comfort and convenience of fish.

The White thus is a tame and useful river. But it doesn't feel tame. None of these tinkerings diminish its excitement for the hiker, who keeps an ear cocked, alert for dull distant booms up thataway.

As the northernmost of Rainier's great rivers, the White is the shortest route for the most people to the national park. But outside the park, along the White, are many pleasurable walks closer to home, lonesomer, and open all year.

On the north side of the valley is a continuous ridge which as it moves east is successively called Boise Ridge, Grass Mountain, Huckleberry Mountain, and Dalles Ridge. On the south side are outer buttresses of Rainier cleaved by the tributary valleys of the Clearwater, West Fork White, and Huckleberry Creek. In this intensively exploited country, where plantations range in date from the 1930s to a few minutes ago and the clearcutting is proceeding now to elevations above 4000 feet, are hundreds of miles of scenic footroads. Down low, hikable except in dead winter, are green tunnels in second-growth forests. On high are freshly scalped ridges with views from here to forever, always dominated by the immense white heap.

The limiting factor (a straitjacket) is that most of the Cascade front hereabouts is in Weyerhaeuser's White River Tree Farm (Timber Mine), whose management knows how to whack down Nature-grown forests and spend a fortune in newspaper and TV ads trying to convince the Public of its ability to assure a national timber supply over the centuries, meanwhile proving to the satisfaction of qualified observers it cannot. Meanwhile, penuriously refusing to hire rangers to control recreation, the company gates the access roads shut and locks them tight. The serendipity of closed gates is that they exclude motorized vehicles. But except for destinations near the gates they effectively exclude pedestrians as well. (In October 1994, Weyerhaueser announced it would open up the White River and Snoqualmie Tree "Farms" to recreationists at controlled gates. Fee, $55 a year. Cheap for meat. Costly for feet. For information, call 1-800-433-3911.)

Among the most popular trails of the White River, lauded by earlier versions of this book, were those at and around Camp Sheppard of the Boy Scouts—Skookum Flats, Snoquera Falls, Snoquera Palisades. But returning in 1994 the younger surveyor found U.S. Forest Service signs not merely permitting but specifically welcoming fat-tire bikes. We cannot advise walkers to drive this far to get hassled.

There used to be opportunities hereabouts for establishing exciting new trails. In 1978 the elder surveyor proposed to the U.S. Forest Service that it exchange some lands and acquire some easements for a trail corridor from a Metro bus stop in Buckley up the canyons of South Prairie Creek to what has become the Clearwater Wilderness. These slot canyons of cliffs, jungle, rapids, and cataracts were literally wilder than the interior of the North Cascades and Olympics. Forest Service officials were enthusiastic. To what end? Scenes that were praised by us have been clearcut. The key Forest Service officials, terminally disillusioned, have taken early retirement.

USGS maps: Lake Tapps, Auburn, Sumner, Buckley, Enumclaw, Cumberland, Greenwater, Lester

Game Farm Wilderness Park

Bus: 150

From Auburn drive south on Auburn Way toward Buckley. Exit on R Street and continue about 1 mile to the bridge over the Stuck-White River. Turn left at the park sign to the entrance, elevation 100 feet.

Downstream, the Stuck River flows south through the Big Valley in a tidily diked channel between rows of houses and fields of cows. Upstream the White River issues from a wildland where braided channels migrate back and forth across a floodplain/floodway between tanglewood walls. Here, several minutes' walk from a Metro bus stop, a person might be in Mount Rainier National Park.

Though the park (State Parks/City of Auburn) is not quite 0.5 mile long, before there was a park the elder surveyor walked the dike 3 miles

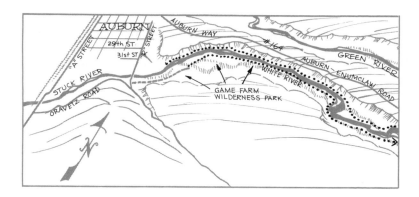

and only turned back because the school bell rang, warning that the motor-cycle hoodlums were being let out of their daytime detention center. They now are excluded, the river on one side, a chain-link fence on the other, rangers in between. The river is, of course, the best walking route, below the dikes of columnar basalt on bars of black sand and boulders of black andesite and red andesite. Exactly as in the national park, the walker feels close to volcano and glaciers, the Osceola Mudflow.

The river flow at any given hour is determined by how much water Puget Power is diverting into Lake (Reservoir) Tapps to serve the Deiringer powerhouse. Often the river has barely enough water to float the fish, as the State Fisheries folks are wont to complain. But one sunny day in 1976 the river was turned on full flow without notice and two children were drowned in their frontyard. Keep in mind the possibilities of unannounced "walls of water."

The route upstream soon leaves the wide-open spaces of the Big Valley for the cloistered White Valley. Ducks swim, fish jump, kingfishers dive. In low water (when the glaciers aren't melting and all the TV sets are turned on), the river is a safe and easy wade from side to side, back and forth. Follow a bar until it pinches out, wade a channel to another bar. Above the Puget Power diversion intake you'll have to cut that out, of course, but by then you're almost to Mud Mountain Dam.

The "Game Farm" of the name derives from the pens where the State Game Department raised shotgun targets until the site was taken over for Auburn playfields. Dikes on that side of the river are a popular Sunday stroll and a good jump-off for river-walkers. Calling the park "Wilderness" seems cheeky until a person has gone adventuring upstream.

One would never guess, driving through farms on the plain of the Osceola Mudflow, that a stone's throw distant, down the 125–250-foot bluffs, is a river bottom where the human presence is virtually unfelt. Old and very old woods roads wander this way and that, and fishermen's paths seek riverbanks, and gypos cut alder and river-rafted cedar logs, and here and there are small pastures and glimpses of houses on the brink of the bluff. But most of the time, down there in the broad bottom up to 1 mile wide, amid braided, shifting channels, marshy sloughs, tanglewoods, and beaver ponds, one could imagine the year to be 1850—or 1650.

In 1977 the elder surveyor found a woods road descending to the river and walked and waded 5 miles downstream, wondering if he'd somehow missed Auburn and might soon meet Dr. Livingston. Not so cheeky after all.

Mount Pete Park-to-Be

Drive Highway 410 to the eastern outskirts of Enumclaw, and at the Enumclaw Park swimming pool (formerly Pete's Pool) turn south on 284 Avenue SE. Follow it 1.5 miles and turn west (right) on SE 472. In 0.5 miles, at a sharp bend right, park on the shoulder by the obvious trailhead, elevation 770 feet.

What accounts for the "Enumclaw Blobs," the miniature mountains pimpling the pastured plain? The Canadian glacier and its Big River explain their existence. Hearts of hard basalt explain their steepness. The Osceola Mudflow provided the surrounding flatness. What accounts for the survival on the biggest of the blobs, Mount Pete, of a grand stand of virgin forest, a veritable wildland arboretum? Well, in 1979 the state DNR proposed to log it, and one would have thought from the instant uproar the proposal was to install Golden Arches in the Garden of Eden. Somebody loves ol' Pete. Lots of bodies. And they know how to yell. By 1988 they were heard in the King County Courthouse, the County Council traded lands with the DNR, Weyerhaeuser, and a smaller owner and created (or will) Mt. Pete Park.

Aha! Will it be "Pete"? The tin ears of local folks have introduced a variation, "Peak." "Mount Peak" indeed! Further, some stolid geographer has persuaded the official maps to call it "Pinnacle Peak." What have all these people got against the fellow the blob was named for—Pete? Of the

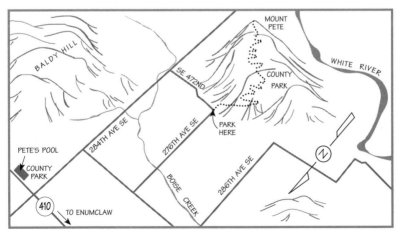

Columnar basalt on Mount Pete

formerly famous "Pete's Pool"? In 1986 another name was put forth by the Washington State Senate—"Mt. Frances"—to honor former Representative Frances C. North. Golly knows her labors to create the Mt. Si Conservation Area and protect other natural habitats richly deserve commemoration. But again, what about Pete?

The 1-mile trail is very steep and can be slippery but is wide and well beaten. At Christmas of 1983, the Great Enumclaw Hurricane destroyed a portion of trail with a mudslide 75 feet wide and 450 feet long. However, the Outdoor Bound class of Enumclaw High School built a detour. Beginning in lush undergrowth of a moist, mixed, second-growth forest displaying at least four species of ferns and lots of frogs, the way quickly ascends to startling big Douglas firs, up to 4 feet thick, plus a full assortment of other good green things suitable for a virgin forest. In ¾ mile the path joins the old road built to serve the lookout tower, removed in the mid-1960s. Narrowed to a trail, in ¼ mile the road, after passing the finest of many displays of columnar basalt, curves around to an end close under the summit, 1801 feet.

With the tower gone and the trees a-growing, the panorama ain't the 360-degree circle of yore. King County Parks may be expected to open windows to beautiful downtown Enumclaw and other points west, to vistas from the Issaquah Alps to McDonald, Boise Ridge, Grass—and Rainier, the Clearwater River valley and Three Sisters prominent. In mind's eye one can see the Osceola Mudflow surging down the White River valley, dividing to sweep around both sides of Baldy and Pete and overwhelm villages of The People. (Is the racial memory responsible for the name, "Enumclaw," which means "place of the evil spirits"?)

Grass Mountain

Drive Highway 410 east 5.9 miles from the turnoff to Mud Mountain Dam. Turn left on Clay Creek Road to a gate always closed to public vehicles. Elevation, 1500 feet.

Grass Mountain is some 15 miles long, rising from the Green River at the Cascade front and extending far into the range, for most of its length forming the north side of the White River valley. The only reason it's not longer is that at a certain point, for no apparent reason, the map gets tired of Grass and starts calling the ridge Huckleberry Mountain. This much mountain obviously provides material for any number of hikes, mostly in the stark landscapes of recent clearcutting, the views beginning early and growing and growing as elevation is gained.

Because the way is open to feet at any time of week or year, it can be done when you please. A snowline-prober unmarred by snowplaying 4x4s is a splendid notion, climbing until the kids have thrown all the snowballs they want and the dogs have filled up on white candy and the snow becomes more nuisance than pleasure. Choose a delicious meltwater torrent or an especially big viewpoint and call it a lunch.

The narrow, rough, steep road ascends Clay Creek valley, at ¾ mile, 1900 feet, swinging under a basalt cliff to splendid views down to the highway, Stink Lake, Philip, and Rainier. Now on a flat railroad grade in second-growth from the 1930s, the road contours east 1 mile to the edge of Cyclone Creek valley. Bending left, in ½ mile it comes to a Y, the right fork dropping to the creek; go left, climbing to a railroad grade that contours west at 2300 feet a scant 1 mile, then switchbacks east onto another flat grade for ½ mile to a series of view windows. Here, at 2500 feet, 3¼ miles from the highway, is a satisfying turnaround.

For a time the views get no better—rather, worse, as the slope lays back. But the top of the world awaits the long legs. Proceed from the windows across a cutbank of rotten lava rubble on a steep sidehill. The road switchbacks west and ascends to a T at 2650 feet. The

Grass Mountain engulfed in clouds

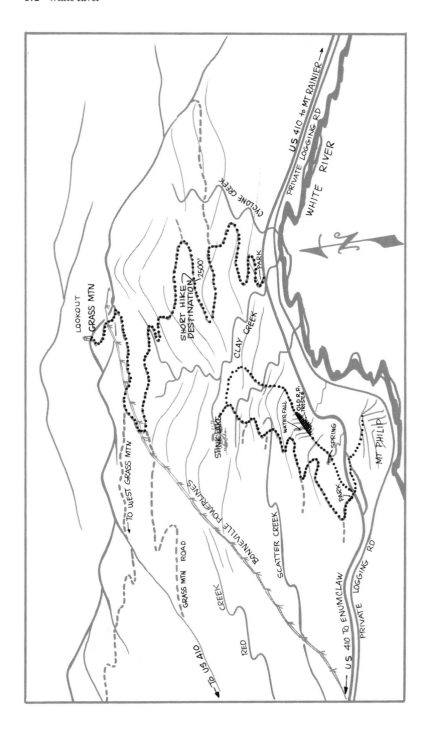

right fork drops to Cyclone Creek; turn left on another railroad grade that goes on and on—and on—swinging into a number of creeklets feeding Clay Creek, each with its ghosts of old trestles. Windows open on Rainier. And now from nice young forest begin views to the scalped ridges of Grass.

Approaching a Bonneville powerline which crosses Grass from the Green to the White, pass a sideroad right to the powerline. Now climbing, pass a gravel pit and at 6½ miles, 3100 feet, meet the Grass Mountain Road, which is gated against public vehicles.

Turn right on this wider road and settle down to grind out altitude. During the first ½ mile, keep right at two YS; from then on simply forge ahead, passing many obviously deadending spurs. The road starts up across the steep final slopes of the mountain, clearcut in the 1960s, the new plantation a sprinkling of shrubs. Views become continuous and overwhelming. At 4000 feet is a saddle; now there are views down to the Lynn Lake basin and north to the Green River. The road ascends the ridgecrest on top of the stripped-naked world, to the summit at 4382 feet, 8½ miles.

What a world! Out the White River to Enumclaw, Whulge, Seattle, the Olympics. Across the Green River to McDonald, Issaquah Alps, Si, Baker, Glacier, and beyond the Cascade Crest to Stuart. Let's see, there must be something else. Oh yes, The Mountain.

Three Sisters

Drive Highway 410 to the southwest corner of Buckley. Turn south on Highway 162 for 1.5 miles, then left another 2.5 miles on Highway 165 to Wilkeson. Turn left at Railroad Avenue, passing historic Wilkeson School to the end of paved road. At 1.6 miles from the school, pass Sunset Lake Camp (Seventh Day Adventist). Continue on the obvious main road, passing many sideroads, some gated, to a fork 5.4 miles from the school. Turn left. In 1.4 miles, take the lower of two roads, the left, and in 0.2 mile cross South Prairie Creek. Beyond the crossing is the first (and last) sign, road No. 7710, so full of bullet holes it may not last to see this book published. At 0.9 mile from the creek, take the sharp left switchbacking up through ongoing (1994) logging. In another 2.8 miles, continue straight (right) where Weyerhaeuser road No. 3011 goes left. In 0.8 mile, 11.4 miles from Wilkeson School, cross East Fork South Prairie Creek. In the next 2.3 miles five waterfalls cascade down rock faces. The road becomes a steep slice in the sidehill. Great views of Puget Sound and the Olympics. At 14 miles from Wilkeson School, the survey wheels were halted by snow, elevation 3600 feet. The logging road continued.

Hikers driving toward the virgin forests and flower meadows and dazzling glaciers of Mount Rainier may not notice, just as they leave the lowlands, a huge bulk of landscape lofting steeply above the White River. If they do, they may wish it weren't there, so they could see The Mountain. What they don't realize is that this *is* The Mountain, the outermost

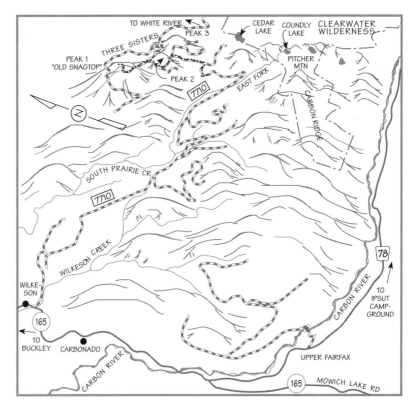

bulwark. Another distinction is that its summit provides the most stupendous panorama anywhere of the northern hinterland.

Eventually the Northern Pacific Land Grant and related nineteenth-century embezzlements of public land will be taken back from the heirs of the criminals. Until that time, the hiker wishing to ascend Three Sisters must choose among several ways, none exactly a Sunday-afternoon stroll.

From Weyerhaeuser's White River Tree "Farm" Bridge Camp Gate, on a spur road 5.4 miles east of the turnoff to Mud Mountain Dam, it is 18.3 miles to the summit of Three Sisters 1, "Old Snagtop." More of a round trip than the average pedestrian can leg in a day. By consulting the 1990 Mt. Baker–Snoqualmie National Forest map of the Clearwater Wilderness and Norse Peak Wilderness, showing the private logging roads which infest the tree "farm" as densely as worms do a corpse, a person who doesn't flinch at the sound of gunshots and ricocheting bullets can find the drivable way. (See earlier note on fee-access. For details, call 1-800-433-3911. For $55 a year, a person perhaps can drive across the Clearwater River and Canyon Creek, up onto Three Sisters Ridge, and conclude with a 1½-mile walk, gaining 900 feet, to the 4980-foot summit.)

When the U.S. Army Corps of Engineers, in a spate of benevolence triggered by a Congressional order to perform "mitigation," built the White River Rim Trail (later obliterated by Weyerhaeuser logging), its public relations twinkies floated the notion (a soap bubble, but very pretty before it popped) of a trail over Mud Mountain Dam and up the canyon rim. Logging roads exist over there on Champion and Weyerhaeuser booty lands and could be hooked up (if a way were provided over the dam) to climb via South Prairie Creek and New Pond Creek and a ridgetop spur to the 3969-foot summit of Three Sisters 3, perhaps 12–15 miles from the dam, elevation 1300 feet. A bit of trail-building could shortcut this to about 5 miles.

In 1978 the elder surveyor, guided mainly by his nose, supplemented by flashes of supernatural revelation, puzzled out the "Interesting Way." Starting from Wilkeson, a maze of unsigned logging roads was solved to an end up South Fork, then East Fork South Prairie Creek. The latter was waded to a 1930s logging railroad grade from which genuine Forest Service trail ascended into an astonishing scrap of virgin forest, emerged at 3800 feet into the awesome devastation of a 1970s clearcut. Nothing thereafter to obscure the routefinding except stumps, elk paths were followed through the slash to the top of Old Snagtop, sprouting a hairpiece of snags of trees the loggers didn't want so they burnt them. Railroad logging ended here on the Three Sisters ridge in the 1950s, the scalping completed by truck logging. No need in this out-of-the-way corner of The Mountain's ecosystem to fret about public relations; the surveyor looked down from the summit, aghast to see chainsaws slaughtering a patch of short but thick-butted and very ancient trees at the edge of a subalpine meadow-marsh. The surveyor numbered Weyerhaeuser foresters among his friends and knew them to have the consciences of decent humans. But this view from Old Snagtop illustrated the fact of life that corporations are not human, that where people have a conscience they have a profit-and-loss sheet.

In 1993 the Photographer and Mrs. Photographer, while searching for the old Forest Service trail to the Clearwater Wilderness loop (see *100 Hikes in the South Cascades*) got lost and accidentally retraced, sort of, the elder surveyor's 1978 route. That scrap of virgin forest was gone, and the trail through it. But the camera found itself atop Three Sisters ridge. The younger surveyor was intimidated by logging trucks on her first sortie but on a second (a Sunday) found herself. However, beware of the Bottom Line. Remember, timber companies have no shame.

Ascend a straight-up boot-beaten path through the stumps, gaining 300 or so feet to intersect a Weyerhaeuser road. Follow it left some ½ mile to another road. Turn right if you seek traces of the old ridgecrest trail to the Clearwater Wilderness boundary above Cedar Lake. For Three Sisters, turn left, then right-left–this way–that way, wherever elk-stomped lanes provide easy walking through stumps and brush, to Old Snagtop, reached at about 2 or 3 miles from the road at 3600 feet.

Beyond the millions of stumps on private lands are more of the same on Forest Service multiple-use lands, and then the Clearwater Wilderness and Mount Rainier National Park. The tree "farm" (never to produce, up here, a second commercial "crop") contrasts shockingly with the virgin green of Carbon Ridge, the dazzling white of The Mountain's Winthrop Glacier, Little Tahoma, Curtis and Liberty Ridges and Willis Wall, Ptarmigan Ridge and Echo and Observation, Mowich Face and Sunset Ridge. South over Carbon and Puyallup and Nisqually valleys, Spar Pole Hill and The Divide and Bald Hills and Black Hills. North over the White valley, Boise Ridge–Grass Mountain–Huckleberry Mountain–Dalles Ridge and high Cascades beyond, from Stuart to Chimney to Glacier to Baker. West, Tacoma and Seattle, Whulge and Olympics. The circuits overload. The brain explodes.

Had enough? If not, logging roads, then a gated service road, lead several miles, depending on the route chosen, to a radio tower atop Three Sisters 3. It's one long step down to Enumclaw, Buckley too. And bug-infested Highway 410. The Weyerhaeuser mill. The reservoirized White River. All around is the immense second-growth wilderness of South Prairie and Canyon Creeks. And out there beyond the mountain front are the Osceola Mudflow, Lake Tapps, Big Valley, cities and towns and farms, Issaquah Alps, and Whulge.

Federation Forest State Park

Drive Highway 410 east from Enumclaw 17 miles to the Interpretive Center parking area, elevation 1650 feet.

The twentieth century was only just getting up a full head of steam when the Washington State Federation of Women's Clubs realized there eventually would be no low-elevation ancient forests except in parks. To let the masses see what they would be missing, a stand of big old trees was acquired beside the Snoqualmie Pass Highway east of North Bend. But Weyerhaeuser badly wanted those trees, so handy to its Snoqualmie mill, and warned the women that since the company was clearcutting up to the preserve on all sides, the wind soon would blow down the ancients. The beneficent Bottom Line offered to exchange for a forest in the White River boondocks.

Boondocks no more. A highway has since been built over Cayuse Pass and Chinook Pass. Side-highways lead to the Crystal Mountain Ski Area and Yakima Park in Mount Rainier National Park. Having skinned the White River valley, Weyerhaeuser has turned the stumps over to its Real Estate Division, serving the demi-urge of the "Tree-Eating and Subdivision-Growing Company." The traveler's brain reels as his car carries him out of this "daylight in the swamp" to the 612-acre preserve, the "Land of Giants."

From the Interpretive Center (open to group tours by appointment only; call (206) 663-2207) the two Fred Cleator Interpretive Trails, both

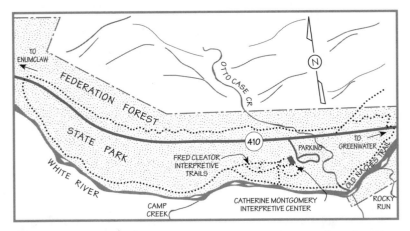

loops, the West Trail a scant 1 mile, the East ½ mile, introduce five distinct forest communities on a broad river terrace perched 30 feet above the present level of the White River. Also preserved is a stretch of the Naches Wagon Road, or Naches Trail, route from the east of the Longmire party in 1853. The nature trails and the plantings around the Interpretive Center are a fine classroom for learning the native shrubs and trees, including ancient Douglas fir, western red cedar, western hemlock, grand fir, and (uncommon this far inland) Sitka spruce.

A 1-mile River Trail takes the feet to gravel bars of the White, which might be followed upstream to the glaciers, downstream to Auburn. The 5-mile loop of the Hobbit Trail tours the park from one end to the other on both sides of the highway. Trees, springs, marshes. The walker surfeited of ogling and gasping at forest giants and ghostly saprophytes can burst free from green twilight and be struck blind by the bright day of the glacier-fed river.

Other Trips

Baldy Hill. The 1580-foot east summit of Mt. Pete's twin (except it has lost all its hair) is attained via a gated logging road in a long 1 mile from the White River Mill.

Boise Creek Trail. A 1-mile, self-guided nature trail from the White River Mill to swamps and views.

Boise Ridge. The 3000-foot ridge hangs in the sky at the Cascade edge, no trees left to block views over the Osceola Mudflow to everywhere. But when the gates are open the logging road is a motorized playground, and when they are not the walker has a one-way trip of 11 or more miles, which is almost too much peace and quiet for the average set of legs.

Grass Mountain, West Peak. Little lower than the Main Peak, the West Peak is far enough removed to be a whole different thing. From the ever-closed gate, elevation 1180 feet, just off the Green River Mainline

Federation Forest State Park

(reached from Cumberland), it's 8 miles to the 4000-foot summit. However, any number of big-view clearcuts can be declared The Destination, starting at a saddle, 2550 feet, 3 miles from the gate.

Mud Mountain Dam. The Vista Trail descends ⅓ mile to dam views. The White River Rim Trail, briefly the most popular low-elevation walk in the area, was obliterated by a Weyerhaeuser clearcut and not replaced by the Corps of Engineers. But service roads descend to the river, where the reservoir is filled only in flood time, and gravel bars can be walked 5 miles to the terminus of the destroyed Rim Trail at Scatter Creek.

Stink Lake and Goodwater Railroad. At 3.4 miles east of the turn-off to Mud Mountain Dam is a gated woods road, elevation 1450 feet. In a moody 3 miles through claustrophobic young forest is a group of marshy potholes and beaver ponds, elevation 2300 feet. An obscure loop link descends Clay Creek ¾ mile to the grade of a logging railroad abandoned in 1950, one of the last to operate in the state. In 2½ more miles it passes a trestle on which the rails bypassed an imposingly vertical lava cliff, a waterfall off the overhang, and famed Goodwater Spring, gushing from the forest floor and asserted by locals to have the best flavor in the country.

Mount Philip. Across Highway 410 from the start of the Stink Lake road, a ½-mile trail winds in dense forest around a little knoll to a flower-bright rock garden that looks down to the White River and across to the mouth of the Clearwater.

PUYALLUP RIVER

As the Puyallup is Tacoma's river, Tacoma is the Puyallup's city. The prominence given the river here may seem to imply that Tacoma has little good walking elsewhere. That is not so. Any community fortunate enough to be on Whulge cannot fail to be dominated by it, and a companion book treats Commencement Bay, Point Defiance Park, and Chambers Creek, enough in themselves to keep the feet busy many a day.

Whulge, of course, gave Tacoma its reason for existence. And historically, of course, the city has claimed special rights to The Mountain from which it took its name. But there is, as well, The River, the sum of many rivers.

The White River issuing from Emmons and Winthrop Glaciers, the Carbon River from Carbon Glacier, the Mowich River from Mowich Glacier, and the Puyallup from Tahoma and Puyallup Glaciers, all flow as one to Commencement Bay, the sum of the rock-milky melt, snowfield trickles, and rainfed springs from the entire northeast and north and most of the west slopes of The Mountain. One wants to be respectfully humble when discussing this mighty river. Down it from the White 5800 years ago rumbled or squished the Osceola Mudflow. And down the Puyallup proper a mere 600 years ago the Electron Mudflow buried Orting under 15 feet of boulders and muck; floods devastated the rest of the valley, dumping 5 feet of mud at Sumner. Another bad day for the Indians.

The proposition in these pages is that there should be a Tacoma-to-Tahoma Trail, open the whole year, mostly within minutes of major neighborhoods of Puget Sound City. Extending from The Whulge to The Mountain. Of more than local or regional significance—a national trail.

USGS maps: Lake Tapps, Enumclaw, Wilkeson, Buckley, Orting, Sumner

West Hylebos State Park

Bus: South Federal Way Park & Ride on 348 Street and 9th Avenue—174, 194, 195, 196, 197

Drive I-5 to Exit 142B, signed "Federal Way," and go off on 348 Street. Pass three stoplights, the last at 9 Avenue S. In a long block from there turn left on 4 Avenue S, signed "West Hylebos Wetlands State Park," past a couple houses to a "Parking" sign just beyond the Marlake houses on the right. Elevation, 220 feet. This is the temporary entrance, until the interpretive center is built. In the interim, please check in with the Marlakes or the people in the little house below them.

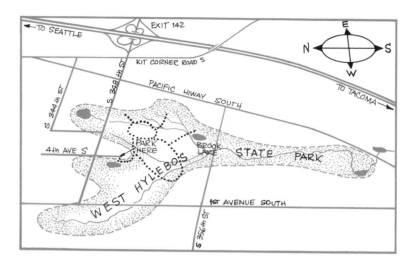

Northernmost of the eight fingers of Commencement Bay pushing into the Puyallup River delta is the Hylebos Waterway, the dredged-out lower extremity of Hylebos Creek, a stream whose three forks and five tributaries drain the glaciated highlands between Federal Way and Milton and west Auburn. The wetlands at the headwaters of the West Fork stretch credibility just about to the limit. Not that they should have been left behind by the Pleistocene glacier, but that they should still be *here,* not industrialized, urbanized, highwayized, and generally drained and paved. Various fortuitous accidents preserved them into our time. Then came Francis and Ilene Marckx to make life so uncomfortable for public officials that in the end they established—starting in 1981 with a gift of land by the Marckxes—a state park.

Walk down the road by the little house and orchard to the start of the 1½ mile loop trail. Do not omit the sidepath, the Trail of the Giants, featuring huge old Sitka spruce (one of the smaller trees was cored and found to date to 1662) and a sand boil, active from November to June, the dance of the grains of

Wood duck on Snake Lake

sand so mesmerizing that susceptible people might well go into a trance.

Look for quaking bogs with Labrador tea and kalmia and swamp birch; big western red cedar and hemlock (only one corner of the park was logged, in the nineteenth century) and a fallen Pacific yew (an estimated 500–1000 years old), Oregon ash, and cottonwood; the deep sinks, a pole provided here to let you measure the depth (17 feet!) for yourself, and giving an air to the scene by bubbling up fumes of sulphur gas. The tally of birds is 114 species, of mammals in the dozens, flowers (uncounted), shrubs (18), mosses (25), liverworts (6), lichens (18), plus fungi, and "unidentified aquatic forms" (the Loch Ness Monster?).

Returned from the loop, visit the display, "Beginning Growth of Fossil-Related Trees," including the Gingko and dawn redwood formerly native to Washington; Man Lake, to see Canada geese, ringnecks, golden eyes, buffleheads, wood ducks, and nearly every local waterfowl; and the arboretum, containing three of every conifer found in the state (twenty-three in all) and a variety of rhododendrons.

Swan Creek Canyon Park

Bus: 41 to Portland Avenue to Harrison Street and walk ¾ mile to Pioneer Way and the park

Drive I-5 to Exit 135 and go off to Highway 167, following "Puyallup" signs. Well out of the interchange, 162 bends left; diverge right, past Puyallup Tribal Smoke Shop, on Pioneer Way. In 0.7 mile, just before Waller Road, note an old farm on the right and a chain-closed lane signed "Swan Creek Trail," entry to a Tacoma–Pierce County park of 200-plus acres. Park on the wide shoulder near the gate, elevation 20 feet.

A wildland's value varies inversely with the square of the distance from home. What would be merely nice in the heart of a national park is beyond price in your backyard. Thus is magnified the preciousness of Swan Creek Canyon, a refuge of green wild peace on the exact city limits of Tacoma.

Follow the lane through pastures and orchard into woods. As the canyon is entered the roars and growls and belches and sneezes of civiliza-

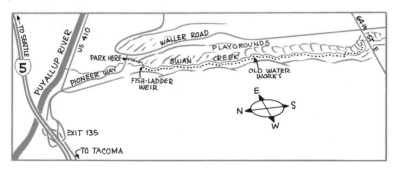

tion are muted, letting through to the walker's ear the creek chatter and bird babble. In a scant ¼ mile the way touches the creek, here flowing over a fish-ladder weir. Though the road-trail continues, cross the weir to trail nicely graded but defensively constructed to exclude wheels.

Now beside the gravel-rattling creek, now contouring high on the sidehill, the upsy-downsy path ascends the valley in the snug isolation of a spacious wild living room, a green grotto under arching maples and alders. The way burrows through vine maple, passes giant cedar stumps, trickling tributaries. The forest floor and understory are an arboretum—skunk cabbage and maidenhair fern, youth-on-age and ginger, devils club and elderberry—and escaped exotics to knit the brows of wildflower watchers. Of historical interest are relics of an ancient waterworks—wire-wrapped wooden pipes, mossy concrete cisterns, and a springhouse. (Additional historic interest: Under an older name, "Bummer Gulch," the canyon was Tacoma's largest hobo jungle.)

The creek dwindles, the canyon narrows. The forest changes from fern-hung maples to Douglas fir and hemlock and salal. At a long 2 miles the trail ends, where an old road (for pioneers' wagons?) once dipped into the

Swan Creek Canyon

canyon to cross. Hippety-hop over the creek and proceed on lesser trail a final scant ½ mile to trail's practical end where the creek flows in a culvert under 64 Street. In all this distance not a house is to be seen and the rantings and ravings of civilization are far away.

In 1994 the process is beginning of developing a master plan for the future of a park enlarged to encompass the former gravel mine on the flats above the canyon. Playfields yes but also strolling paths over lawns in new-planted groves of trees. Little change is expected in the canyon.

Snake Lake Nature Center

Bus: 27

Go off I-5 on Exit 132 to Highway 16. In 2.7 miles turn right on 19 Avenue. At Tyler Street turn right and then immediately left into Snake Lake Nature Center, elevation 300 feet.

Snake Lake is interesting on several counts. For one, it is not notable for snakes—the name is for the shape. Second, it is fed by a 1200-acre watershed to the north—the streets of Tacoma! Water that once filtered through swamps and marshes over weeks and months now flushes through the pipes in hours. As a consequence, the lake is changing in character from open to closed—to marshes and swamps. The city uses it as a detention basin to regulate flow down Flett Creek to Chambers Creek. Third (and hurrah!) the 54-acre reserve of the Metropolitan Park District of Tacoma has been set aside as an ecological study area. "The park is not a playground. The visitor is reminded that the park belongs to the plants and animals. People are visitors in their space." Some twenty species of mammals, from red fox to flying squirrel to voles and shrews. Birds—more than 100 species. The surveyor's favorites are the ten pairs of wood ducks nesting at the lake.

The three self-guiding nature trails total 2 miles.

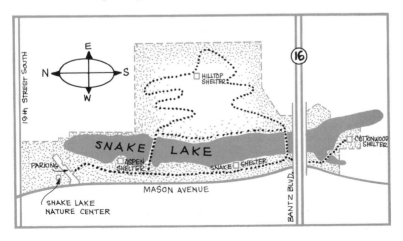

The short loop is from the parking lot to the Heron (1st) Bridge, loop trip ½ mile.

The medium loop goes down the west side of the lake to Blackbird (2nd) Bridge, crosses, and returns on the east side of the lake-swamp along the old grade of the Tacoma–Lake City Railway, built in 1890 from Old Tacoma to a resort on American Lake, way way out in the country. The route returns to Heron Bridge, where the wood ducks were hanging out, and to the parking lot. Loop trip, 1 mile.

The longest loop is the bestest. It sets out down the west side of the swamp-lake, passing shelters for birders, and goes under the freeway bridge to Mallard (3rd) Bridge and Cottonwood Shelter. Next, back to Blackbird Bridge, across and up switchbacks from wetlands habitat to forest habitats, through Douglas fir, madrona, and a few Pacific dogwood (check to see how they are coping with the current Dogwood Plague). The trail tops out at 423 feet, soon after passing a kettle left behind by the glacier some 12,000 years ago. The descent passes a few Oregon white oak on the way back to Heron Bridge and the parking. Loop trip, 1¾ miles.

The self-guiding pamphlet explains the bee tree, black cottonwood, cascara buckthorn, bitter cherry, poison hemlock, Goose Prairie (mowed for the Canada geese), filberts, green heron, open water in scoops dug out by peat-mining, an ancient ant hill, and the greater yellowlegs. Fun and instruction for the whole family. (But be *quiet,* children.)

Tacoma-to-Tahoma Trail

Tolmie went this way on his botanizing trip in 1833, the first European to walk the slopes of Rainier—or Tahoma as some think it is better called. It's a way that walkers of today can take as well, following banks of the Puyallup River from Commencement Bay by industrial plants to pastoral floodplain to forests of the mountain front, and thence via several alternatives to wilderness of the national park. Close to where people live, open the whole year, the Tacoma-to-Tahoma Trail is an idea whose time should come. But a pedestrian needn't wait—the trips described here sample the river's moods.

Commencement Bay to Fife 2½ miles

Bus: 400

Drive Highway 167 to about halfway between I-5 and Puyallup. Between Mileposts 3 and 4 at 66 Avenue E, turn north over the river on narrow old Melroy Bridge. Turn west on North Levee Road 3 miles to its end at a railroad bridge. Park here, elevation 20 feet.

The best grimy-industrial trip in the book, this walk over the Puyallup delta—the Port of Tacoma—is most exciting on a work day when all the satanic contraptions are bumping and grinding and honking and bellowing, infernally fascinating. Yet serenely sliding through is the river, green-

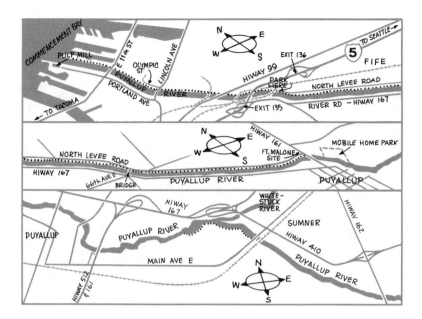

brown from pollution by glaciers and farms, afloat with ducks and gulls and fishermen, but not with ships because the river—or Puyallup Waterway as the final stretch is called—is rarely used for docking; a half-dozen busier waterways are dredged in delta silt.

Cross the railroad tracks, drop to the dike, and away you go downstream. The levee is unobstructed, the gravel road little used. This is the premier walk for bridges, some old, some new, some supported by piers of wood or concrete, others on concrete pillars. In sequence there are a railroad bridge, I-5 monster bridge, another railroad bridge, old Highway 99 bridge, a third rail bridge (there's a lot of good train-watching), Lincoln Avenue Bridge, a fourth rail bridge, this a swing-opener to let ships through, and finally the classic 11 Street Bridge with a tower-lift center section.

Along the way are views to downtown Tacoma on the bluffs above the delta. At the end are views over the bay to ships coming and going and sitting at anchor, and to Point Defiance, Vashon and Maury Islands, and the Olympics. Also at the end is the star entertainment—the Katzenjammer Kastle pulpmill, hissing, squealing, humming, and roaring, pouring clouds of steam from a dozen stacks and a hundred cracks in the walls.

Fife to Puyallup 5½ miles

Waterway narrows to River, sedately but powerfully flowing between dikes. Industry ends and not-quite-yet-platted farms begin. Birds flit in riverbank brush, fowl fly and dive, fish swim. The view of Tahoma is famous.

Puyallup River and moon rising over Mount Rainier

To do the complete route, drive as before to the west end of North Levee Road. Walk back east on it, passing the first farm, and in a short bit drop to the waterside footroad, where just about any day of the year fishermen are parked.

There's time for pondering, looking across the foreground of murky stream to the far glaciers. This is one of only three outlets of The Mountain's water, the others being the Nisqually and Cowlitz Rivers.

At 5½ miles is the Highway 161 bridge, the proper turnaround. But first visit the historical marker noting the constuction here by U.S. soldiers in February 1856 of Fort Maloney to protect the John Carson ferry, thought necessary after Indian attacks of the previous October. Here the Military Road from Steilacoom to Bellingham crossed the river. For more history, enter Puyallup and in ½ mile from the bridge turn left to Pioneer Park and the restored seventeen-room mansion of Ezra Meeker, who arrived in Puget Sound by wagon train in 1852 and platted the town in 1877.

Puyallup to The Turn 1¾ miles

From Highway 410 drive Highway 162 to the bridge over the Puyallup and park on the south side of a fishermen's lot.

Though a walker with as much gall as the surveyors can do every step of the route from Puyallup to Orting, it is a tour unlikely to become wildly popular until cleaned up for a National Historic Trail. There are, however, limited objectives worthy enough for the present, starting with two

Momentous Events. First, at the downstream end of the Sumner peninsula, is the confluence of the Puyallup and the White-Stuck. Stop the car to listen for loud noises, a distant explosion followed in an hour or so by a huge squishing, or whatever sound is made by a wall of mud doing 50 miles per hour. Cock an ear up the Puyallup, the source of the Electron Mudflow, and up the White-Stuck, whence came the mighty Osceola.

Then drive on to enjoy the second Momentous Event, The Turn. From Sumner to Commencement Bay the Puyallup flows in a west–east valley. But here it issues from the north–south Big Valley of Pleistocene time. A footpath drops from the fishermen's lot to the riverbank slope and follows the river bend (first of three in less than 1 mile) north to a sand point jutting splendidly into the angle. The path is forced from the water by brush and enters a magical place, huge old maples arching over the greensward, a fit picnic spot for Robin Hood and his merry men. Next to the maple grove, and part of the large farm to which all this belongs, operated by Washington State University as the Puyallup Research and Extension Center, is an experimental plantation of cottonwoods in neat rows. Just short of a barb-wire fence a path turns left to the river, the stock fence easily crossed. Soon comes The Turn—an abrupt 90 degrees—and another dandy jutting sandbar. Bar-walking can be continued a bit farther, the river flowing through wildwoods on both banks, before a farmhouse interrupts.

The Turn completes the transition backward in time to the past-lingering-in-present—a farming valley, fields of crops and cows, picturesquely framing old homes and barns, little old country stores. But of course, the 7-11s are coming, Tacoma is coming.

The Turn to the Carbon River

Don't bother trying a through-walk, not yet. But in driving through on Highway 612, see, still existing, what the portion of the Big Valley south of Seattle looked like just a flash of years ago. The traveler's spirit leaps in joy to revisit the Living Past, plunges to despair at the prospect of déjà vu all over again. What will Pierce County do? What *will* Pierce County do?

Make two stops for short walks. At the Alderton grocery, turn east on 96 Street 0.5 mile to a large (but no longer signed, probably) Department of Fish and Wildlife "Public Fishing" parking lot just before the bridge. The dike north has a public walking easement donated by Sumner Sportsmen Association. The green way passes a large marsh-lake (not visible enough for the Photographer to spot it) abounding in birds, river and wildwoods, glimpses of farms.

At McMillin turn east on Colburn-McCutcheon Road, 128 Street E, 0.5 mile to the bridge. Cross and park on a shoulder. Note the pipeline carrying the Green River to slake Tacoma's thirst.

A gated road lets quiet walkers amble downstream on the lonesome dike, past a slough-marshy forest which has forbidden agriculture, pre-

Cottonwood plantation at Washington State University's Puyallup Research and Extension Center

served solitude. A sandy trail beyond the road-end proceeds into poetry. Out from under arching alders stealthily sneaks Canyonfalls Creek. Birds flit in secret shadows. The sand peninsula at the creek mouth, ¾ mile from the gate, is a grand spot to eat peanut butter-and-pickle sandwiches and watch the river run.

Upstream, the dike road, boulder-blocked to halt wheels, begins with a pasture left, a magnificent bar right. Both sides of the river are now wildwoods. At a scant 1 mile is another Momentous Event, the confluence of the Puyallup and Carbon Rivers. The walk can continue up the Carbon 1 mile to dike's end at the rearing up of a gravel-and-forest cliff across the river from Orting.

Carbon River to Canyon Bridge 7 miles

Bus: 403

Drive Highway 162 southeast of Orting 1 mile and at the Crocker Grange y turn south on Orville Road. In 3.3 miles as road and river are partway through a horseshoe bend where Orville Road bridges the river, park on a large shoulder, elevation 350 feet.

Due to private roads and fences, the only practical access to this segment is the upstream end. But that's good—difficulties pretty well exclude any foreign travelers except very quite, polite, and inconspicuous ones on foot.

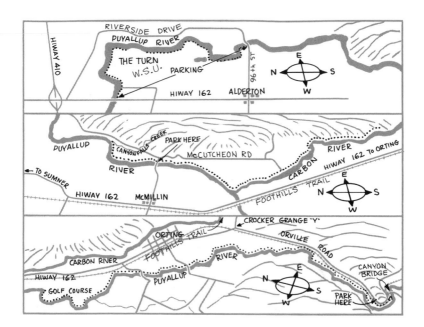

Drop to the gravel lane below the road. Follow it down to a lane entering from the highway. Turn downstream on the abandoned rail grade. You're on your way. The dike goes on and on, crossed by frequent stock fences easily circumvented, the lack of signs demonstrating a high level of toleration of pedestrian trespassers. Except for the occasional farm vehicle, wheels rarely roll the road.

At the start the Puyallup valley is canyon—narrow, soon widening to a modest floodplain, then abruptly to a mile from green wall to green wall, the veritable Big Valley. Cows moo, dogs bark, guns of Fort Lewis boom. From cottonwood forest the river emerges to farms and sorties out to the middle of the broad plain. Off east can be seen the Carbon valley, Microwave Hill and Spar Pole Hill, and—gasp—Tahoma.

Gravel bars and beaches of black volcanic sand are alternatives to the dike. Marshes and sloughs are passed, barns and more cows, and, at a scant 4 miles, the bridge of the Orting-Kapowsin Road, which due to fences is not an access.

Now, the best part. The river turns westward to the foot of the high, steep wild-forested valley wall and at a scant 2 miles from the bridge reaches Hi Cedars Golf Club. For 1 long mile the neat greensward is on one side of the dike, the river and green-tangled wall on the other. Where Orting High students of the Class of 1941 put their numbers on a boulder (as have other classes on other boulders the entire route) is the proper turnaround. It is 1 more mile to the Carbon confluence, all except the last bit walkable, but made unpleasant by mean-it fences and hellberries. The main attraction is the boulder of the Class of 1937.

Canyon Bridge to Electron 3½ miles

Suburbia, innocently trusting to the dikes and ignorant of the Electron Mudflow, is invading exurbia's stumpranches. The crops here are those of the Kapowsin Tree Farm. Sad to report, the peaceful railroad now is a furious truck road. But the dike portion of the route is as good as ever. Start from the only reasonable access, the same spot as for the previous segment.

Walk the railroad grade upstream through the short stretch of rock-walled canyon, a brief little spectacularity. Just past the bridge drop off the tracks to river sand, leap or wade Fiske Creek, and scramble onto the start of the dike. For a scant 2 miles the elevated causeway proceeds by marshy woods and stumpranch pastures, the last habitations. (On the far bank home construction is madly in progress.) Sands and gravels offer alternative walking. Across the river the torrent of Kapowsin Creek gushes in.

When dike ends, clamber boulders to the abandoned rail grade, which here returns to the river after an absence and provides the rest of the route. The way joins a log-haul road and enters clearcuts. However, a fringe of fine trees has been left on the riverbank. In a long 1 mile is the crossing of Fox Creek, which cuts the base of a rock wall; beavers have dammed the small stream. The road leaves the river, whose forest invites exploration of a riverside route. In a final long ½ mile, the road returns to the river and crosses it—precisely where it exits from the mountain front, here consisting of the Kapowsin Scarp.

At the bridge are houses. Electron. But you can't get there from here—the bridge is gated and guarded.

Electron to the Glaciers

From the bridge it's 1 mile upstream on river gravels to Puget Power's Electron Powerhouse at the foot of Kapowsin Scarp. A cog railway once carried tourists to a vista point beside the reservoir. This was a pretty impressive hydroelectric operation in 1904.

The fascinating Electron Flume enters the reservoir, often carrying most of the Puyallup River from the Headworks weir 10 miles upstream. An expedition up the flume was aborted by umbrella weather that made the narrow plank walkway treacherous; Puget Power probably wouldn't have been too crazy about the scheme anyway.

Yet here, along the 10 miles of the Puyallup valley wall, paralleling if not actually somehow using the flume, the Tacoma-to-Tahoma Trail must ultimately run. This is the wild side of the river, steep and jungled and frequently cliffy.

For the interim, the Kapowsin Tree Farm is the way to go. From the King Creek Gate, the Access Road follows the valley upstream to the confluence with the Mowich River. Sideroads lead to or near the river at a number of points. At the confluence of the Puyallup and the Mowich begins the home stretch to Mount Rainier National Park, in the Rushingwater Foot-Only Zone.

Foothills Trail

Cued by the nation-wide Rails to Trails movement, the Pierce County Parks Department proposed to put feet, hooves, and bicycle wheels on the abandoned 21 miles of Burlington-Northern (née Northern Pacific, of land-grant infamy) railroad grade from McMillin to Orting to South Prairie to Buckley. Stepping forth in support were walking, cycling, horse-riding, birding, and poeticizing groups. Standing in opposition were abutting property owners who sought to claim the grade. In November 1991 Pierce County voters said "Yes!" to the trail. Privatizers have stood on constitutional right to which the courts have said "No!" Volunteer work parties began clearing the grade in 1992. Parks Department crews likely will finish up before the turn of the century.

In the 1970s, in the course of plotting a Carbon River Parkway Trail, the elder surveyor walked the route as far as Cascade Junction. In 1987 the younger surveyor retraced his steps, except where frightened off by barricades and threats. At this writing, the trail is coming-into-being, but not everywhere at once. If hollered or barked at, don't holler or bark back. Go away and bide your time.

McMillin to Orting 3½ miles

Bus: 403

For the north end of the trail, drive Highway 162 to McMillin, elevation 110 feet. For the south end of this segment, drive to Orting, and turn north on paved Calistoga Avenue to the trail, elevation 180 feet.

The official start of the Foothills Trail is McMillin. The grade runs close by the highway, then veers toward the Carbon River, and remains there to Crocker.

The surveyors prefer an off-trail route starting at Orting. Beyond Calistoga the road becomes River Street, which ends at a blockade to keep wheels off the dike. Pent between the dike and the gravel-forest precipice noted earlier, the Carbon wends its final 2¾ miles to the confluence with the Puyallup in green lonesomeness, the walker scarcely aware Orting is near.

Walk downstream on the dike or, when available, on bars of gravel and black volcanic sand tracked by deer and ducks and raccoons. The dike is hedged by forest broken now and then by pastures. On the far side the river cuts the foot of a cliff of gravels and jungle rising as tall as 400 feet. A waterfall plumes down. On a log in the middle of the river sits a heron.

A gravel bar thrusts out to a tip between the Puyallup and Carbon Rivers, the former often yellow-green murky with rock milk while the latter is crystal clear—or sometimes brown with glacier-milled rock flour. The presence of The Mountain is closely felt. A dandy spot for lunch.

Orting to Crocker 3 miles

The trail leaves the Big Valley of the Puyallup River for the Carbon's cozier valley—and so does the foot-only (unofficial) alternate on gravel bars and dikes. Park as before and walk upstream, admiring river and birds, wildwood wall, columnar basalt of the dike, and bullet-pocked con-

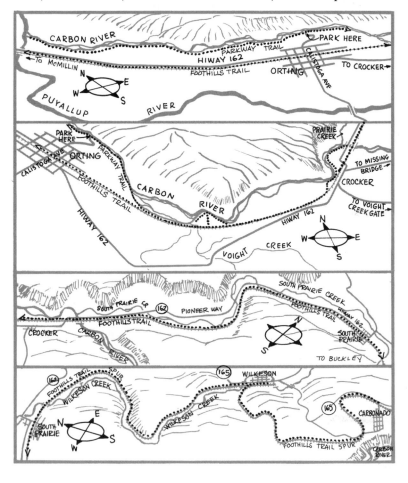

crete piers of some ancient mystery. Ahead rise Microwave and Spar Pole Hills and, farther along, the Park Boundary Peaks and Rainier itself. In ¾ mile a stock fence halts wheels; footpath continues ¼ mile to the rail-road-trail grade. The river is joined by the alder-arched birdlane of Voight Creek.

The best part of the trip is a sidetrip. Dive off the trail on a fishermen's path through the woods to river gravels. Walk the wild island downstream ¼ mile to the junction of Voight Creek and the river, then upstream to a point where the trail can be regained at a point 1½ miles from Orting.

Riverside houses keep the walker on the Foothills Trail the next 1 mile, which cuts inland. Gravel bars and dikes resume for ½ mile to South Prairie Creek. The walk can start here, parking by Highway 162.

Crocker to Cascade Junction 3 miles

From Crocker the Foothills Trail crosses the Carbon River and leaves it to ascend South Prairie Creek. For a bit the grade is beside the high-way, but when that crosses the river, the trail is near and often beside the creek for a while, until the highway recrosses to parallel the grade into the hamlet of South Prairie. In 1 mile more is Cascade Junction, 480 feet.

The surveyors beg off describing this vicinity, as well as the 12 miles to the end of the Foothills Trail at Buckley, waiting for the smoke to clear. Up-to-date information can be obtained by calling Pierce County Parks or attending a hike scheduled by the Tacoma branch of The Mountain-eers or any other of the supporting organizations.

Cascade Junction to Wilkeson 5 miles

The main line of the railroad extended from Cascade Junction to Buckley, and so will the main line of the Foothills Trail. A branch line went off up Wilkeson Creek to Wilkeson, Carbonado, and Fairfax, and so will a branch of the Foothills Trail (maybe and someday).

Due to the ticklish diplomatic situation, in 1987 the younger surveyor let this stretch alone, and that seems the best policy for other non-residents in 1995. In the more relaxed 1970s the elder surveyor plunged through a daunting thicket to a bridge over South Prairie Creek a bit above its confluence with Wilkeson Creek. A large, slow, cool pool in the river obviously was the local Ol' Swimmin' Hole.

At ½ mile from the junction, the line touched the bank (riprapped with—what else?—Wilkeson sandstone) of Wilkeson Creek. Here at a bend in the stream, in a splendid forest starring enormous cottonwoods, was a fitting spot to sit and watch spawning salmon, dippers, or whatever other traffic was on the water avenue.

The survey assault thrust some distance farther but ultimately was hurled back by nettles-salmonberries-burdock. However, the grade was intact—in fact, ties and rails were in place—and it was plain that an armed band rather easily could slash a path the 3 miles from the Fitting Spot to Johns Road on the outskirts of Wilkeson, 780 feet.

Wilkeson, walkabout 4 miles

Drive Highway 410 to a complicated, confusing junction at the southwest edge of Buckley. Turn south on Highway 162-165 for 1.5 miles, and then follow Highway 165 as it swings left, proceeding to Wilkeson. For the full tour park near the timber arch welcoming you to town, elevation 780 feet.

In 1869, inventorying the booty heisted 5 years earlier in the Northern Pacific Land Grant, railroad surveyors found sandstone and coal on a tributary of the Carbon River. From the company treasurer the resulting town took its name, Wilkeson. The place reeks of history, a century and more of artifacts lurking in the bushes. And it's pretty, too. To better enjoy the town and its surroundings, read *Carbon River Coal Country,* by Nancy Irene Hall.

Muse through the cemetery; there's another off the highway on Johns Road. Poke into sidestreets for nineteenth-century architecture, including the handsome building signed "Holy Trinity Orthodox Church in America 1900." At the far edge of town turn left onto Railroad Avenue, past the striking Wilkeson-sandstone school.

Where Railroad Avenue turns left over rusty tracks, a sideroad goes right; park here for an alternative start. The sideroad forks; do both. The low road, left, goes by the coke ovens, beehive-like mounds of brick, their

Abandoned coke ovens near Wilkeson

age shown by the size of the trees atop them. The high road, right, climbs a blacksoiled hill one abruptly realizes was not erected by nature but rather is a 100-foot heap of waste rock; look down to Wilkeson Creek, which long ago was pushed to the side of its valley floor to make room for mine, railroad, and town.

The main attraction of the town nowadays is the region's largest quarry, off-limits to visitors unless prior arrangements are made. However, there is no objection to walkers politely following the road of Wilkeson Cut Stone Company ¼ mile from Railroad Avenue to the fringe of the stone-cutting works. The quarry can be glimpsed, far up the hill. Overhead cables (used to) bring monster slabs down to the shed where gangsaws patiently cut into the stone at the rate of 4 inches an hour. The first use of the stone was by the railroad, for fill and riprap, widely utilized around the region. In 1883–84 the first stone was taken out for construction—of St. Luke's Episcopal Church in Tacoma. A man named Walker quarried blocks from 1911 on, taking them to Tacoma by rail for splitting. In 1915 the present plant was built, the machinery pretty much devised on the spot by self-taught engineers, a time-warp trip to early days of the Industrial Revolution. Until the 1920s, most Seattle streets were paved with Wilkeson cobblestones. In 1982 the company went bankrupt and the quarry was closed, whether permanently or not remains to be seen.

Across Railroad Avenue from the quarry entrance a sideroad switchbacks off the main road, up the hillside, into the canyon of Wilkeson Creek; the black slope on the far side was the location of one of the several coal mines in town.

From Wilkeson the old railroad and the to-be spur of Foothills Trail crossed and will cross a minor height of land to Carbonado-atop-the-Bluff, 1200 feet. The route onward to Fairfax is next on our agenda.

Carbon River Parkway Trail

In 1881 Bailey Willis opened a tourists' horse trail to the Carbon River from the new coal-mining town of Wilkeson, and next year cut a way over the ridge to the Mowich, where (or perhaps on the North Fork Puyallup) he erected the cluster of log cabins grandly called Palace Camp. Prospectors later built a spur to Mowich Lake and Spray Park; a grindstone they left at the spur junction gave it the name of Grindstone Trail. When the railroad was extended to new mines farther up the Carbon, the Bailey Willis Trail became known as the Fairfax Trail, ultimately extended through Puyallup country to the Nisqually River.

Except for bits in the national park, the old trail system—here and throughout the Carbon province—has been obliterated by logging. Hikers long ago gave it up as a lost cause and herded into the park. However, the short hiking season there, the driving distance from cities, and the boots-boots-boots marching up and down are reviving interest in the hinterland. Its time is coming—again.

The notion propounded by the 1979 predecessor of the present book was this:

Here is a green-jungle, white-water lane of lonesome wildness reaching out from Mount Rainier National Park nearly to the lowlands. The gorgeous gorge and splendid forest, the colorful rocks, both sedimentary and volcanic, the foaming cataracts, the old coal mines and coke ovens and vanished villages are at an elevation open to walking the year around. What to do with them? How about a Parkway Trail? Connected to the Tacoma-to-Tahoma Trail? A continuous route from saltwater to volcano icefields. The Whulge to The Mountain!

Look from Seattle/Tacoma to Mount Rainier. The footings of The Mountain itself are hidden by Carbon Ridge, whose peaks are, west to east, Burnt Mountain, Old Baldy, "Old Nameless," and—highest and most prominent—the half-horn of 5933-foot Pitcher Mountain, which everybody sees and nobody has ever heard of. Much of Carbon Ridge has been put in the Clearwater Wilderness. Draining its north slopes is a stream nobody has ever heard of—South Prairie Creek.

This trail would lead to that country, would get the feet to where the city eyes look.

Crocker to Missing Bridge 3 miles

From Orting drive Highway 162 south 1 mile to Crocker Grange Y and then east (left) 2 miles. Turn east (right) on Alward Road (177 Street E), past a row of coke ovens. In 0.5 mile, where the road touches the river, park on the shoulder, elevation 330 feet.

Wild river, solemn gorge. A green Eden surviving in the universal clearcuts. Elves, gnomes, sasquatches, lions, and tigers, and bears.

In the forest live people who accept (or don't know) they are certain to be occasionally wiped out; their floodplain habitations are hidden from a

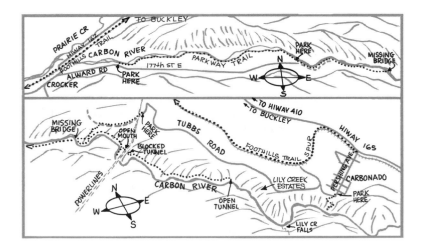

person walking gravels of the braided channels. The splendid stream brawls through boulders of black and red Rainier andesite, iron-yellow Wilkeson sandstone, white granite, black coal, gray lignite chunks of petrified trees, gaudy clinkers from coke ovens, plus rusty artifacts from old towns. A scant 2 miles of ecstasy for a pretty-rocks fan leads to another contact with the road, where it ends. For a shorter walk park here, elevation 440 feet.

No houses now, because 300-foot walls of lush forest and outcropping sandstone press close to the river. And no wheels because boulders at road's end, 520 feet, block them off. Only feet continue into the utter wildness, following the ancient railroad grade cut in the jungle slopes. (Note: This is not the rail line to and beyond Carbonado-Atop-the-Bluff but a deadending spur at a whole other settlement, Carbonado-in-the-Canyon.) Fern-hung rock ribs

Carbon River Parkway Trail

jut into green pools. Black-sand beaches invite children to build castles and everybody to take off shoes and wade.

All too soon it's over. In a scant 1 mile the rail grade runs out in the air; on the far side is the causeway-abutment of the missing bridge. So, turn back. But first descend to the abutment of quarried Wilkeson sandstone resting on an outcrop of the same rock to the large black-sand beach overhung by maple. Except for the river, quiet. Having walked the grade upstream for the sake of trees and ferns and flowers, walk the gravels downstream for the sake of boulders and dippers.

Missing Bridge to Blocked Tunnel 1¼ miles

Drive Highway 165 to Carbonado and turn right, into and through town, on Pershing Avenue. Just past Carbonado Tavern the road (now Tubbs Road, though unsigned) bends sharp right along the canyon rim, joins another road from the right, and passes the sewage-treatment plant, swinging left and becoming narrow and gravel. At 2 miles from the tavern, where Tubbs Road crosses a wide powerline swath, turn left on the service-and-logging road to the gate. Park here, elevation 837 feet.

Or, if the gate is open, perhaps drive on. Follow the logging road as it veers rightward from the powerline and in a scant ½ mile reaches the canyon rim. The rail grade is 300 steep feet below. You can't miss it.

The surveyors freely concede that until the bridge no longer is missing, the tunnel unblocked or detoured around, this will not be a place to take your Sunday school class for a picnic. Presently the scene is strictly for brushapes and history fanatics.

No way down to the old grade is dangerous if care is taken. Most, though, are mean and nasty medleys of thorns and logs and muck. The single neat way is the crest of an indistinct ridge, easily found from below (making the return a cinch) but requiring luck to find from above. The recommended procedure is to continue a couple hundred feet from where the logging road hits the rim, plunge over the brink, and look for the best. If fortune smiles, in several minutes you'll reach the grade precisely where it leaves the valley wall and strikes out across the floor on a causeway.

First walk downstream, out on the causeway to its end in rotting trestlework. Game traces lead easily to a wonderful wide gravel bar. Ah, solitude! Ah, pretty rocks and pools! Ah, dippers dipping, sandpipers peeping! Ah, salmon spawning! Ah, picnicking, wading, napping! Ah, wilderness!

Now, upstream, resolutely cheerful as a gap in the grade puts you on game paths through a creek's brambles and slop; if only the deer were taller their routes would be more satisfactory but soon the pain is re-

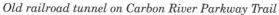

Old railroad tunnel on Carbon River Parkway Trail

warded by the open end of the blocked tunnel, the interior heaped with old rail ties. By clambering over the dry-rotting jackstraw, a person might explore the Stygian depths. A happier tour is along the foot of the sandstone cliff to the river and upstream on a bar. The cliff overhangs 20-odd feet at the bottom, sheltering an alcove garden of maidenhair fern and dangling shrubs. Ah, charmingness!

When the river is very low, or the walker totally insane, the cliff corner can be rounded. To what purpose? Around the corner the rail grade resumes and in 1 mile (don't expect a rose garden, but plenty of thorns) is a walk-through tunnel 90 feet long with a 30-foot-high ceiling. On the way are lovely gravel bars that invite picnics, and cliffs of Wilkeson sandstone stupendously overhanging the grade. Then, bah, humbug. See below.

Blocked Tunnel to Carbonado 1½ miles

In 1978 the elder surveyor hailed this as the narrowest chasm, the steepest walls, the canyon climax. And here was the busiest walking, trees and flowers and rocks, loud waters of the river and white ribbon of Lily Creek Falls, coke ovens, an old mine mouth, and railroad tunnels.

In 1980 a sign was erected, "Lily Creek Estates," and a fellow sat in a lawn chair on Sunday smoking a big cigar, cooler close to hand, offering lots to prospective buyers and hollering at hikers.

The road slid out and the cigar and cooler went away and hikers returned. Then, in late 1987, the younger surveyor found the gorge forest logged, the coke ovens and other artifacts of Carbonado-in-the-Canyon demolished, and earthmoving monsters poised to do golly knows what awfuls.

Carbonado to Fairfax 5½ miles

Drive Highway 165 past Carbonado 0.7 mile. Look sharp just at the far end of a wide shoulder, just before a sign, "Speed Zone ahead, 35 mph," and spot a gated road leading to a log-haul road that utilizes the old rail grade. Park on the shoulder, elevation 1209 feet.

Walk clearcut, then forest, on the railroad grade sliced in canyon cliffs; far below in lush forest is the river. At 2 miles the grade passes under the Fairfax Bridge (Highway 165). The walk thus far is a pleasant, peaceful stroll on a weekday.

For the shorter version, drive over the Fairfax Bridge to parking on the west side, elevation 1324 feet. Walk back across the bridge and skid down to the railroad.

The highway is across the valley, unseen and rarely heard; this is the wild side. In a few yards look to the left for a dark hole that goes down, down, down to the coal. At ¼ mile is a ghost—sandstone foundation of some unguessable structure; old maps show a mine downhill here. At 1 mile the ghosts throng—above the tracks, and also below, are fields of an abandoned homestead. Ascend the hill to concrete foundations of the house. Descend to pastures on a wide alluvial terrace. Beyond lichen-hung fruit trees find a rude path dropping to the river in an enchanted spot, canyon walls plunging to pools of glacier limeade. What went wrong in Shangri La? Aside from the train quitting and the house burning down?

What went sour beyond Shangri La? A new clearcut starting ½ mile past the farm. End of the story? At least until pioneers whack and ribbon a passage, permitting reasonably easy travel the final 1½ miles to Fairfax. Before the clearcutting happened the grade touched the river and the route left the grade, here blocked by slides and washouts. Game traces on riverside flats led the short bit to trip's end.

The elder surveyor, on his 1970s expedition, had no notion where he was. He pondered the non-natural shape of the terrain. Then, from the black black earth of a mountain-beaver excavation, from tree roots wrapped around clinkers, he figured it out. Mind's eye stripped away half-century-old forest to reveal rail spurs and bunkers and buildings and machinery and waste-rock dumps of the Fairfax Mine. He followed the rail grade to pilings and sandstone blocks pushing out into the river—another missing bridge crossing to remains of the hamlet of Fairfax, where in olden days tourists got off the Northern Pacific train and were conducted by packtrain to The Mountain.

Fairfax to National Park

Drive Highway 165 a long 0.5 mile past the Fairfax Bridge to the y and go left, toward the Carbon River entrance to Mount Rainier National Park. In 3 miles, shortly after passing a couple of roadside homes and the clearing where the school stood until a decade or so ago, and just after crossing Evans Creek, is a y with no signs; go left, switchbacking downhill 0.7 mile to a valley-bottom t. The cluster of houses here is the center of Upper Fairfax. Unfortunately, the inhabitants don't take kindly to prowling strangers, even if they are harmless history nuts, so drive on, right, past a two-storey brown house that was the railroad station, and shortly cross the Carbon River. Park out of the way on a shoulder, elevation 1400 feet.

The final segment is noted only for completeness, since it'll not be a popular walk until the Parkway Trail is built. The ultimate route should stay on the wild side of the river, not crossing to Fairfax; at present, however, the brush is too much.

Proceed upstream from the bridge, partly on woodland paths, partly on river gravels; just here the riverbed widens out to a "valley train" of braided channels that continues to the Carbon Glacier. In 4 miles the river can be crossed on the road No. 1811 bridge to the park boundary. In some 8 more miles on park roads and trails is the terminus of the Carbon River Parkway Trail, which is to say, the snout of the Carbon Glacier.

History is thick hereabouts. The railroad continued 2 miles past Upper Fairfax to the hamlet of Carbon, which then had a school and a ranger station. From there the "incline" of a logging railroad went 1500 vertical feet up the south valley wall to a logging camp. On the north valley wall, 150 feet above the river, was the enigmatic Cliff House. At various times there were several logging railroads, on both sides of the valley, and three lumber mills. Before that were the coal mines and coke ovens, still to be seen, as are the old cemetery and remains of logging camps moldering in second-growth forests. And in just about the beginning there were Bailey Willis and his trail.

Kapowsin Tree and Meat Farm

Logging began hereabouts early in the century; the spar pole atop Spar Pole Hill at the mountain front dates from around 1910. Year by year the railroads of St. Paul and Tacoma Lumber Company pushed up the Puyallup River valley, the ridge between it and the Carbon River to the north, and the ridge between it and the Mashel and Nisqually Rivers to the south. At a certain point St. Regis assumed the corporate responsibility and trucks took over from lokies and climbed higher and higher—incredibly, to the very boundary of Mount Rainier National Park, and into valleys and onto peaks that belonged in the park—and still do, though scalped.

The company banned public vehicles beyond the firmly closed gates. Hikers, though, were welcome. To be sure, it was a tree farm, not a wilderness, and the ancient trails had been obliterated. But except for the very occasional company vehicle the roads were *footroads*. The elder surveyor walked hundreds of miles on them, sometimes 25 or more in a day which ended in a jog through the twilight, howled at by coyotes and stared at by bands of amused elk, and pursued by goblins. He walked from Voight Creek Gate to Montezuma Gate, on the return staggering under a rucksack load of chanterelles, from King Creek Gate to Sparpole Hill, from Ohop (Camp 1) to St. Paul Lookout and Ohop Lookout, and from Mowich Gate (Camp 2) to the confluence of the Puyallup and Mowich Rivers.

In 1984 Champion International bought the 135,000-acre property and on September 1, 1987, announced a bold experiment. The roads were

opened to public vehicles through two controlled gates. Seven parcels totalling 30,000 acres were, at the insistence of the State Wildlife Department, to prevent an immediate wholesale slaughter of a semi-protected
animal population by roadside guns, set aside as "road-management areas," which translates to "foot-only zones." Walkers exulted. They weren't
even soured by the dropping of the other shoe, an entry fee.

After 7 years, preliminary judgment can be rendered. Champion is

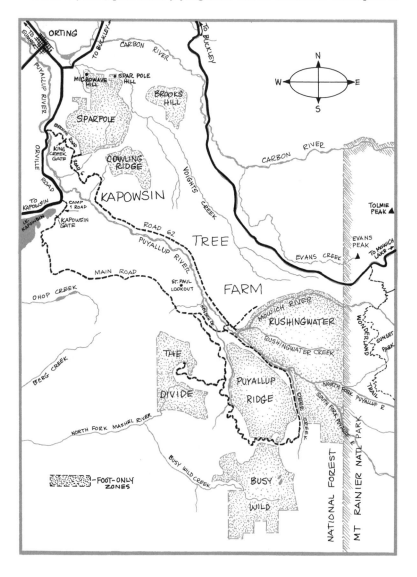

not operating a recreation Safeway, trails for the hiker, campgrounds for the family. It is running a meat market. The information brochure (for a copy, write Champion International, 31716 Camp 1 Road, Orting, WA 98350) is headed, "At Champion, we are concerned about managing our forests for trees and a lot more." Yes, more, namely, 400 carcasses of deer and elk a year, odds and ends of bear, coyote, cougar, bobcat, beaver, and whatever targets might entertain a plinker.

Is Sparpole Hill worth $10 per hiker per day? Some trips require an overnight—is The Divide worth $25 per hiker? (In 1994, Weyerhaueser was sufficiently enchanted by the Champion Bottom Line to open up some of its meat/farm roads, for $55 a year. See the White River chapter in these pages.)

The gate hours and days are fitted to a hunter's schedule, not a hiker's. The fire season closure doesn't intrude on the shooting season but cuts the heart out of the pedestrian season. How does the wildlife feel about it? The plants are not what they were primevally and won't ever be again on a "farm." In summary, Champion's big new idea is no substitute for placing all this country, from the slopes of The Mountain out the valleys of the Puyallup and Carbon and Mashel—the Greater Mount Rainier Ecosystem—in a national park reserve for eventual addition, when restored to sufficiently primeval condition, to the park.

In the interim, other accesses exist to the meat farm. The Sparpole, Cowling Ridge, and Brooks Hill Foot-Only Zones protect wildlife from motorized weapons-carriers, but at $10 a walk are pricey for a hiker. The Divide Zone features a unique geographical spectacularity, but it is most interestingly approached by Weyerhaeuser roads (however, *that* tree-farmer has decided to get into the meat business). The biggest brag of the Puyallup Ridge Zone is the Bell System relay to Jupiter, atop the 4930-foot former site of the Puyallup Ridge Lookout. Everything in the Busy Wild Zone is readily reached from Forest Service roads above the Nisqually River.

Probably worth $25 a customer, at least once, is the Rushingwater Foot-Only Zone. First off, it's the most infuriatingly scandalous, and should be studied by the camera of a muckraking environmentalist engaged in documenting the necessity of the Greater Ecosystem concept. On an October day, in the low country, walking the Main Road from Ohop, the elder surveyor watched truck after truck roar by at 50 miles per hour carrying Douglas fir logs that by their size had to be ancient and by their thick coatings of fresh snow had to have come from on high; new snow like that doesn't happen in October except at elevation, and Douglas firs don't grow at that elevation at all unless they took root in the warmer climate prior to the Little Ice Age. Those firs were *relicts*. The Bottom Line was shipping our botanical pre-history overseas.

Second, three great rivers brawl from the glaciers on this face of The Mountain—the Mowich and the North and South Forks of the Puyallup. The two ridges on either side of Rushingwater Creek rise to the border of Mount Rainier National Park; no walker who climbs through that butcher

Small stream near Fairfax

zone to the border of ancience can remain neutral in a righteous crusade for revestment.

Third, way back before the logging began, way back before there was a park, Bailey Willis built his Carbon River-to-Nisqually River trail through here, from Grindstone Camp (modern Camp 2) through the Mowich-Rushingwater-Puyallup valleys and ridges. Ruins of his Forest Castle might be found on the North Fork Puyallup, or possibly the Mowich.

Other Trips

Pitcher Mountain. The footings of Rainier are concealed from Seattle by Carbon Ridge, whose highest and most distinctive summit is the half-horn of 5933-foot Pitcher Mountain. Views extend from glaciers of The Mountain to waters of Whulge. Walk logging roads above South Prairie Creek to the edge of the Clearwater Wilderness.

South Prairie Ridge. Logging roads out of Wilkeson climb to a boggling desolation of clearcuts far up onto the mass of Mount Rainier. Stumps of relict Douglas firs which grew to ancience in the warmer climate predating the Little Ice Age and were logged in the 1970s are passed; pause to count rings. On the crest of Carbon Ridge is intersected a remnant of a trail (to where?) which started in Wilkeson.

Gleason Hill. The old CCC Fairfax Truck Road from Wilkeson to Upper Fairfax has in recent years served as the region's premier 4-wheelers' "mud run." When the runners are absent a solitary walker can get very moody ascending from Upper Fairfax through ruins of moonshine factories to the top of Gleason Hill. The trail from Wilkeson presumably passed through here to Carbon Ridge, which connects to Independence Ridge, which connects to Sluiskin Peaks to Old Desolate to Curtis Ridge to the summit icecap.

Spar Pole Hill. Marked by the surviving spar pole of the 1910 railroad logging, its views reopened by the second-growth clearcutting of 1977, this final blip of Ptarmigan Ridge long was the classic mountain-edge walk of the Kapowsin Tree Farm. When that boodle of the Big Steal was sold to Champion, the popularity of Spar Pole dropped to zero. That is, via the $10 gate. The old entry via the now-closed-to-the-public Voight Creek Gate is being remembered and the popularity restored, as is that of adjoining Microwave Hill. Powerlines are a handy way to dodge around the gate onto Fox Creek Road, which leads to Beane Creek Road, and thence through old stumps and new to the spar pole and the 360-degree panorama.

Confluence of the Mowich and Puyallup Rivers. An upside-down hike starting in a descent from old Camp 2 (still older, Grindstone Camp) to the Momentous Union. The view of 12,000 vertical feet of The Mountain is considered by the few hikers who have seen it to be the most stupendous Rainier picture there is.

Evans Peak. The 5000-foot westernmost summit of the "Park Boundary Peaks" straddles the park boundary. Clearcuts and an official ATV Hell on national forest land to the west demonstrate why there has to be a national park system and why the entirety of the Greater Ecosystem must be added to Mount Rainier National Park. This farthest-out high point of Ptarmigan Ridge, which extends from the summit icecap to Spar Pole Hill, has nothing in the way to block views to the Big Valley and Seattle.

St. Paul Lookout. By driving the Camp 1 Road to or near Camp 1 (Ohop), then walking either the little old semi-abandoned North Ohop Road the long way, or the big wide truck-thundering Main Road the short way, and then finding the little old abandoned sideroad to the lookout site at 2970 feet, a person can experience a religious transport gazing over the broad, flat valley where Mowich and Puyallup Rivers and Niesson Creek join (and where the Electron Mudflow did flow) to 13,000 feet of icefalls and lava ramparts (and a foreground of seventeen googols of stumps, of which some eight googols of trees should have been preserved from the robber barons for inclusion in the national park). For $10 per hiker the transport can be achieved with much less physical exercise.

NISQUALLY RIVER

Southernmost of Rainier's great ice-melts to enter Whulge, the Nisqually for generations has been the world's way to The Mountain. Now it is in process of becoming a Parkway from The Mountain to the delta's National Wildlife Refuge and as such will in its own right (assuming the Private Greed Doctrine of the Bottom Line is whipped back into its cage by the Public Trust Doctrine) catch the world's eye.

Of the several subprovinces, the South Puget Plain is largely Fort Lewis, where the U.S. Army used to prepare for battles on the North German Plain and now, the Evil Empire having self-dismantled, is flailing about for a credible foe.

Ohop Creek evidences derangements of the landscape by glaciers from both Rainier and Canada, as well as Electron and other mudflows. Just an itty-bitty thing, the creek holds title to two oversized valleys, in its

Nisqually River near Wilcox Farm

upper length occupying an apparent former valley of the Puyallup River (and Glacier), and in its lower the mountain-edge valley of the Really Big River.

The largest subprovince is that of the Mashel River, a stream known to hardly anybody but loggers; with its major tributaries, the Little Mashel and Busy Wild Creek (poetry does lurk in the hearts of loggers), it drains a broad stretch between the Puyallup-Ohop valley and the Nisqually. Few areas of the Northwest are so totally privately owned and so absolutely skinned. But oh the views in the big-sky, moorlike land of 50 billion stumps! Among them are supreme vantages for planning the ultimate westward expansion of Mount Rainier National Park—out on Ptarmigan Ridge to take in the Park Boundary Peaks, out along Sunset Ridge and Rushingwater Creek to the confluence of Mowich and Puyallup Rivers, out across the South Fork Puyallup to take in Puyallup Ridge and Beljica— though it wouldn't be inappropriate to go one more ridge west, over Deer and Neisson Creeks, to take in Busy Wild and Thing Peak and The Divide. Mashel ownership is split between Weyerhaeuser and Champion International. Each in its own manner exhibits the trait of corporations that distinguishes them from the people who run them and who act in their TV idylls: they have the legal rights of humans but are not human, have no human morals, no human soul, are as intelligent as (and no more so) than a computer. Their Bottom Line cannot be allowed to inherit the Earth. Gazing over Mashel country, we hold these truths to be self-evident.

USGS maps: Nisqually, Weir Prairie, McKenna, Harts Lake, Bald Hill, Tanwax Creek, Eatonville, Ohop Valley, Mineral, Morton, Kapowsin, Mt. Wow

Nisqually River Not-Quite-Yet Parkway

When a governor of Washington proposed a parkway from the Nisqually National Wildlife Refuge to Mount Rainier National Park, environmentalists clapped politely, feeling he'd done nothing more creative and courageous than praising Mom's apple pie. But from the uproar of the big bucks and little pols you'd have thought he'd taken the pie and slammed Mom in the face. The governor withdrew. But the notion was in the air. Other leaders more adroit in working the system convinced the big bucks that a few small displays (immensely magnified by skillful PR) of inexpensive virtue would reward them with more bucks, and the little pols that the reflected glory would make them look tall.

In 1987 the legislature adopted a Nisqually River Management Plan recognizing the unique cultural, historical, environmental, economic, esthetic, spiritual, and blah-blah-blah importance. The twenty-one-member Nisqually River Council was appointed, composed of the bureaucrat pack, the Nisqually Indian Tribe, and the U.S. Army (the irony of *these* two at the same table!), and assorted do-gooders (many of them genuine). The council's twenty-one-member Advisory Council was formed to represent citizen interests along the river, "citizen" being defined as property owner, that being the American Way, the Public Trust Doctrine developed in the English common law and so pungently expressed by the likes of Benjamin Franklin suspected of being an invention by Marx or Lenin.

The Nisqually Delta Association is, on the delta scene, the environmental coalition's thrust point, and a sharp point it is. A companion book to this tells how at river's end publicity and the law are being stuck to the 700-pound gorillas who upstream are playing nice-nice for fun and profit. The Nisqually River Basin Land Trust, which employs donated funds (tax-deductible) to acquire title or easement to maintain green uses, since 1989 has gained protection for a half-dozen properties totalling 100 acres, 2 miles of river front.

The 1987 Management Plan was developed by the Department of Ecology, instructed to do so by a 1985 act of the legislature. A Nisqually River Task Force was appointed, six technical advisory subcommittees and two citizen advisory committees, a roomful indeed. The elder surveyor was twice invited to Olympia (and even paid gas money), presumably because he had plucked the governor's soap bubble out of the air and by foot and beetle traced the 78 miles from Whulge to ice, as well as many of the 331 tributaries adding up to 715 miles of streamway. The 1979 edition of *Footsore 4* presented the results of his survey, describing a dozen-odd walking tours of regional attraction in areas of ecological significance. Of these, three were selected as superstars of the Nisqually project and are described here. (Two of them, that is; Tacoma City Light belatedly decided not to play; see below.) Interestingly, *Footsore 4* is not to be found on official bibliographies. But a rude surveyor gets used to that.

Wilcox Farm, round trips 4 miles

From Highway 7 south of Spanaway turn off on Highway 507, signed "Roy, Centralia." In about 1 mile turn left on Harts Lake Road, signed "8 Avenue," and proceed due south for miles and miles, through Fort Lewis, over the vast South Puget Plain. The road bends west around the rim of the amazingly cirque-like (but that's ridiculous) basin of Harts Lake. At a Y where Harts Lake Loop Road (an alternative approach, from McKenna) proceeds west, turn south, downhill, on Harts Valley Road, signed "Wilcox Farms." From the Y drive 1.5 miles, passing the Wilcox Farm Store (eggs, milk) and farm headquarters (see Rainier!) to the plain. Just after passing the foot of the last hillock and crossing the ditch of Harts Lake Creek, park at the gate, elevation 354 feet.

What's the explanation of this horseshoe bowl cupped in 150-foot drift bluffs, this inlet-lacking lake, this wide, river-lacking plain extending from the lake to merge with the Nisqually floodplain? The plunge basin and outwash plain of a great falls of a great river issuing from the ice front? Well, whatever. The result has been a large expanse of un-Nisqually-like rich black soil. In 1909, to quote the milk carton, "Grandfather Judson Wilcox established the Wilcox Farm on the fertile land around Harts Lake."

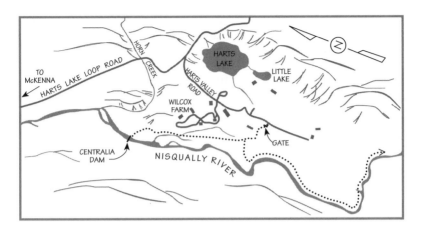

The third generation now operates a family factory-farm of 1000 acres, 1,000,000 chickens in dozens of enormous metal coops, cows of the largest dairy ranch on the Nisqually, and crops all over the emerald plain. It's a scene from another world. Someplace in Europe, maybe. Farm policy bans public vehicles on lanes but hospitably welcomes well-behaved public feet.

From the gate walk the lane right, through fields by the creek, ¼ mile to a Y. Take the left and at the next right go straight ahead another long ¼ mile to field's edge, woods, and the trail through the brush to the river.

A downstream dike ½ mile, wild forest on the across-river wall, and then 1 scant mile on a farm lane lead to the Centralia Dam, the 1930 weir that diverts water into the Centralia Canal for the "Yelm Hydro Project." A gravel bar below gives a view of the structure and a nice picnic.

On his first journey of discovery, the elder surveyor explored lanes up the river to Tanwax Creek. On the way he passed enormous structures from which continuously emanated a strange, loud, rather scary sound. Not until he walked by a ventilator fan and was nearly felled by a chicken wind did he recognize the sound. A chicken farmer himself as a youth, but never more than a dozen hens at a time, he had failed to identify the birth celebrations of 600,000 eggs a day.

School or other groups wishing a guided tour, write (two weeks in advance) Wilcox Family Farm, 40400 Harts Lake Road, Roy, WA 98580.

Nisqually State Park, round trips 3 miles

For now, forget it.

When the trip becomes possible, drive Highway 7 to a few yards south of the Highway 161 turnoff to Eatonville. Turn right on road No. 200 and proceed 1.2 miles, winding down into the canyon of the Nisqually River. But road No. 200 is gated and the bridge is out and the area is a hangout for drunks, druggies, and gun-toting punks. Two murders, countless assaults, and menacings and rioting make it a place the police take pains to avoid. Presumably the law will arrive on the scene someday, but not until State Parks and Pack Forest and third and fourth and fifth parties work out a deal on purchase or trade of lands.

The description below was written after lofty pronunciamentos by the grand poo-bahs. File it away. By the time the River Council and the Advisory Council and the State Parks Commission get through their quadrille, the turn of the century likely will be a fading memory.

The confluence of the Nisqually and Mashel Rivers is truly a Momentous Spot. No less so, if less picturesquely dramatic, is the confluence of the Nisqually and Ohop Creek, at the south end of the Big Valley (here, much shrunken) beginning on the north at Lake Washington. For 20 years Weyerhaeuser permitted campground use of a 330-acre forest across the Nisqually from the mouth of the Mashel. Keggers, muggings, shootings forced closure in 1988. In September 1991 the site was acquired by State Parks. To this key parcel, 3 miles of riverfront and ancient forest, additions have been and will be made for an ultimate 1400 acres. Not enough. Should be 2000 acres at least, to the edge of Ohop Valley.

The confluence will be a day-use area. Some time after 2001 a major campground will be developed on uplands of the Mashel Prairie. River accesses will be provided at the confluence, Ohop Creek, and the Piessner Road bridge.

For walking, the top of the list is the ¾ mile upstream, through trees so big one marvels that Weyerhaeuser spared them. Above the river leaps a 200-foot cliff of iron-stained gravel pocked with bird caves—swallows' apartment houses. The forest floor is carpeted in season with blossoms of starflower and candyflower, lily of the valley and trillium, solomons seal and Oregon shamrock. Myriad paths branch off, and gravel bars also can be walked, as well as a cutoff river channel. In ¾ mile the last path peters out on a "beach" of rock shelving into the water. Above are green shadows of La Grande Canyon and only ½ mile away is the powerhouse, but you can't get there from here. Not unless you're a fisherman, and insane.

Downstream are ½ mile of old roads through second-growth, passing old camps, long since barred to wheels by backhoeing. Trail burrows another ¼ mile, ending on mossy slabs dipping into rapids. Lovely! Lonesome! Scrambles in steep brush take the explorer to a gravel bar. Doughty fishermen doubtless proceed into wildness beneath the 200-foot canyon walls whose jungles guard the solitude.

The prize is across the Nisqually at the mouth of the Mashel, fortunately acquired by the University of Washington for its Pack Forest before Weyerhaeuser's Bottom Line went ape at the prices the Asians would pay for new logs from ancient forests. Whether or not there ever will be a trail along the Mashel depends. The canyon has broad river terraces but also precipitous walls. The vegetation is formidably healthy. A 5-mile loop from the Pack entrance to the canyon floor, and through the incised meanders to the Nisqually, might be an ecological disaster.

Speaking of disasters, the Original Inhabitants, the Nisquallies, remember how one fine day in March of 1856 a doughty company of real estate speculators, calling themselves the Washington Mounted Rifles, mostly colonels, rode into a village on the Mashel, discovered the men were away, and vented their frustrated patriotism by murdering seventeen women and children. If the site can be identified, a sidetrail would be appropriate, and an interpretive center for the Mashel Massacre. The names of the Mounted Rifles should be listed and a tally given of how much of Washington they stole from their victims.

Northwest Trek Wildlife Park

Drive Highway 161 south from Puyallup toward Eatonville. (Or, drive Highway 7 south from Tacoma and at a Trek sign opposite Highway 702 jog to 161.) Just south of Clear Lake turn in on the park entrance and drive 0.7 mile to parking areas from which paths lead to Trek Center, elevation 760 feet.

No zoo, this, but rather a unique 645-acre wildlife park of Tacoma Metropolitan Park District, maintained in cooperation with Tacoma Zoological Society. Northwest Trek was begun by the loving care of Dr. David and Constance Hellyer, who acquired the property in 1937 and in 1972 gave it to the public. Hundreds of thousands of visitors a year take the 5½ mile, 1-hour Trek Tour, riding quiet trams through areas where animals roam free— only people are fenced in. The park is open daily February through October, Wednesday and weekends November to January.

Take the Trek Tour to see deer, elk, moose, woodland caribou, bison, wolverine, bighorn sheep, mountain goat, and Pennsylvania wild turkey, roaming gone-to-nature farm fields and second-growth wildland woods.

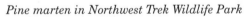

Pine marten in Northwest Trek Wildlife Park

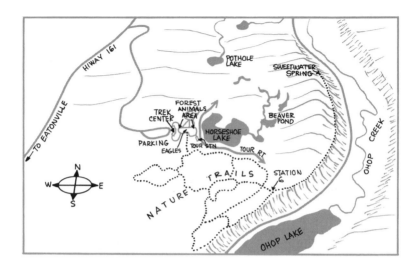

Do some walking, too, on the 5 miles of nature trails; these are in a different area from that of the Tour, which cannot be visited on foot. For openers, near the main entrance is Cat Country, pairs of bobcat, cougar, and lynx. Left from the Center is a loop of blacktop paths totalling ½ mile, passing animals in natural habitats (beaver, porcupine, otter, fisher, mink, skunk, weasel, marten, raccoon, a children's Baby Animal Exhibit, and—supreme thrill—an overlook of nonchalant bear—and wolves loping through woodlands.

For the long walk, go right from the Center toward the Tour Station above Horseshoe Lake, beyond which loom summit snows of Rainier. On the way, opposite uncaged, unchained bald eagles and golden eagles perching there watching the parade, is the trailhead. From it are a number of loops of various lengths, sampling the various forest systems—marsh, young fir, alder-maple. For an introductory tour, do the perimeter loop, taking all right turns, and thus in about 1 mile reaching the brink of the plateau, the Ohop Valley scarp, and screened glimpses of Ohop Lake. In about ⅓ mile more, at Station 6, starts a sidetrip, the best part. Turn right and proceed along the bluff in cool green lush forest, past the end of Ohop Lake, out along the slope of Goat Ridge, to Sweetwater Spring, 1 mile from the loop. Sit a while, imagine how sweet it was (before the Great Giardiasis Pandemic) to dip a delicious sip or so from the boxed-in pool. Return to Station 6. Again on the perimeter, return to the eagles in a final ⅔ mile.

Dress and behave appropriately and you may be taken for one of the exhibits, as was the elder surveyor, who was eagerly asked by a party of foreigners, "Sir, are you a logger?" The honor modestly accepted, there is now some corner of England where his photo is displayed as representative of the species.

Pack Forest

Drive Highway 161 through Eatonville to Highway 7 (or drive 7 direct from Tacoma). At 0.2 mile south on 7 from the junction is the Pack Forest entry. At the gate (open weekdays to 4:30 P.M., closed weekends) is the parking area, elevation 800 feet.

At the interface of lowlands and foothills, on a "mountain island" enclosed by Mashel and Nisqually Rivers, is Pack Forest, a 4250-acre laboratory of the University of Washington's College of Forest Resources. Miles and miles of lonesome footroads wind around hills and valleys in woodland and meadow and views from Rainier to Puget Sound, a walker's paradise. Snowline-probing and animal tracks in winter, flowers in spring and summer, colors and mushrooms in fall. And—peace be with you—on weekends the gates are closed to public wheels, but not feet.

Aside from pedestrian pleasures, Pack is a unique opportunity to observe a wide range of forest-management techniques and experiments. Tree-farming was pioneered here, including some of the earliest plantations in the Northwest. Thinning began in 1930, and in the 1940s the first forest-fertilization studies anywhere in the world. Through the years there have been programs in forest nutrition and in harvesting methods, clearcut and shelterwood. The largest research project ever undertaken at Pack Forest is a 20-year study of the effects of recycling biosolids as a

Pack Forest

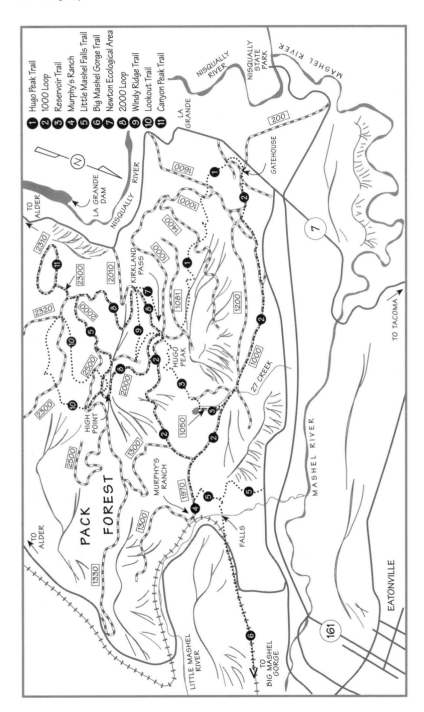

Key to trails:

1. Hugo Peak Trail
2. 1000 Loop
3. Reservoir Trail
4. Murphy's Ranch
5. Little Mashel Falls Trail
6. Big Mashel Gorge Trail
7. Newton Ecological Area
8. 2000 Loop
9. Windy Ridge Trail
10. Lookout Trail
11. Canyon Peak Trail

forest fertilizer. ("Biosolids" are treated wastewater solids, as distinguished from untreated "sludge.") It was for such purposes that Charles Lathrop Pack made the initial gift of land in 1926, establishing a teaching and research laboratory for teachers and students, a demonstration area for the forest industry, and, for the general public, a living textbook.

The andesite ridges of Pack, glacial drift-covered down low, rock-outcropping up high, were thoroughly burned about 1800, only a few relict trees escaping. Some of this 1800 forest survived the big Eatonville Fire of 1926 and other blazes of the period. A management plan has been adopted to increase age diversification of Pack's forest groups and thus enhance the educational value: 10 percent of the land, including the 42-acre relict-tree Ecological Area, will be reserved in a natural state; 14 percent, including the 940-acre Hugo Peak Transect of 1800 forest, will be specially managed, only limited salvage logging of fire-damaged trees; and 76 percent, including the almost two-thirds of Pack burned since 1920, will be intensively managed on a conifer rotation of 80 years, approximately 30 acres to be harvested annually. A single walk passes trees from seedling age to centuries old and a variety of planting and tending and harvesting methods.

Change is a constant on Pack Forest. Roads are improved or built; each year clearcuts open new views—as the growth in plantations is closing old ones. Pack, however, is much more than a cellulose factory. Though 95 percent self-supporting from harvesting, the income is incidental to the teaching, the research, and the "demonstration," which is so integral to the purposes that visitors are not merely tolerated but warmly welcomed. The hiker is as much a part of the picture as the forester.

As of 1994, a complete renovation of the trail system is in progress, resurrecting old, forgotten trails, building a few new ones, and implementing a comprehensive system of trail signage. Be sure to pick up interpretive brochures and the free trail map, which shows much more than is discussed here.

When the gate is open to public vehicles, a straight-out car tour appeals to young and old, pausing for close looks, taking short walks. On weekends, the gate closed, Pack Forest becomes a de facto wilderness (except that bicycles are permitted on roads—but *not* on trail-trails) and hikes are therefore described from the gate.

Hugo Peak, round trip 5 miles

But first, look in on the Biosolids Interpretive Area, just up the entry road from the gatehouse, off to the left. A self-guiding trail demonstrates biosolid use for pastureland, soil reclamation, and the like.

Find the Hugo Peak trailhead on the right opposite the gatehouse, elevation 800 feet, and begin a gentle ascent through a recent plantation. In ½ mile pass the Hugo Peak Connector trail, going ½ mile left to the headquarters buildings through a 65-year-old stand of thinned Douglas fir. The Hugo Peak trail proceeds in a variety of forest stands, crossing the old grade of the Tacoma Eastern Railroad to Elbe and Morton, relocated when the Alder Dam drowned its original line along the Nisqually valley in 1944, and in a bit more crossing road No. 1000, elevation 1040 feet. In the 2 miles from this alternate trailhead to the summit, the way steepens to a crossing of road No. 1400 and enters a beauty of a forest—large cedar and smaller maples and fire-scarred old firs. Above a spring-fed meadow the way switchbacks on old roads-trails, levels out in a corridor of fir and hemlock, and goes up and down through spindly trees. Peek-a-boo views begin in a stand of young alder. The trail emerges from a rockpile off road No. 1081 to a sign, "Hugo Peak," pointing left to road No. 1080, where another sign leads to the highest point, 1740 feet.

Located at the exact abrupt front of the Cascades, since being partially clearcut in 1974 to salvage trees dying from fire damage, the summit plateau of Hugo has been the classic grandstand of Pack Forest. From the 1740-foot peak, and the 1720-foot peak, and the 1693-foot peak are views. Below is the Mashel valley, the Ohop valley joining from the north. Beyond are the Nisqually, Bald Hills, and woods and farms and lakes of the South Puget Plain, over which Nisqually and Deschutes Rivers run to Nisqually Reach and Budd Inlet, respectively. Beyond saltwaterways rise Black Hills and Olympics. The pulpmill steam plume marks Tacoma. The Issaquah Alps point to Seattle.

Road No. 1080 drops ¼ mile to Kirkland Pass to join road No. 1000.

1000 Loop, loop alone 7 miles, with all sidetrips 15 or more miles

The main road of Pack Forest, a grand loop around Hugo Peak, is Lathrop Drive, road No. 1000, a splendid "trail" (when the gate is closed) walk by itself, and a very full day for the long-leggity if all the sidetrips noted here are taken. But these are by no means all there is. Self-guiding nature trails are in place, under construction, or being planned for the vicinity of the headquarters conference center. Stop in and pick up all the brochures. Out in the beyond, new and restored trails are in the works, new signs to guide the walker, and new trail maps. The adventurous may even find some abandoned routes providing solitude, barked shins, thorn wounds, and sweat.

To do the loop in the direction preferred by clocks, walk left from the administration building, signed "Lathrop Drive, Murphy's Ranch." Pass above the millpond of the former sawmill and proceed along the road through forest experimentally treated with municipal sewage sludge in 1977, pioneer project in the system now being employed on forest lands throughout the region, and then a plantation of 1978. Cross 27 Creek and at 1½ miles from the administration building come to a sign on the right, "1050 Road."

Reservoir Trail, round-trip sidetrip 1½ miles

Turn right on road No. 1050 for ¼ mile to the 27 Creek Reservoir, intended by the CCC to provide water for fighting fires, but now an abandoned, moody, black pool. Here is the trailhead. The route ascends ¾ mile to Kirkland Pass and thus is another way to Hugo Peak.

From the trailhead cross the reservoir dam, turn left up the old road, and at a "Trail" sign go off right into a plantation featuring snags and masses of deer ferns. Views out left to Lookout Peak, down to Mashel and Ohop valleys. In ¼ mile the trail turns steeply up through fir 200 years old, most of the way beside a dry creek. Near the pass the forest crown opens and the ground is lushly green in spring-nourished grass and sedge.

Cross the dry creek to a cat track. This leads to road No. 1080; walk left down the road to Kirkland Pass. The trail also goes there, taking off across the cat road and paralleling it a ways.

Murphy's Ranch, round-trip sidetrip 1½ miles

Back on 1000 Loop, in a scant ½ mile from 27 Creek is a Y at the forest edge, 1160 feet, and the takeoff of two sidetrips, Murphy's Ranch and Litttle Mashel. Or maybe you'll want to bag the loop and spend the whole day here.

As soon as you've recovered from the impact of Rainier's huge whiteness, which here ambushes the eye, go left on road No. 1970 into the broad pastures of 650-acre Murphy's Ranch, which under the name of Flying M Ranch was famed in the 1960s for rock concerts, and in 1975 was acquired by Pack Forest.

In ½ mile, where the farmhouse used to be, is the former ranch entry road from the Alder Cutoff. Continue through fields to the two fish ponds, now devoted to floating ducks and providing foregrounds for photos of The Mountain.

Little Mashel Falls, round-trip sidetrip 1½ miles

Walk ⅓ mile on road No. 1970 to the far end of an experimental plantation of cottonwoods. At the end of a fence look left for a muddy track through the grass, start of the Falls Trail. The old road bends left, past a small grove of firs on the right and above a pond on the left. The trail winds around and down the hill. At the foot of the hill, ignore a path continuing straight ahead and down (a good exploration) and turn right into mixed forest. A flat stretch comes to a Y, an old road-trail straight right, the trail to the left. Now, on the descent, the roar of the falls grows loud and the way soon arrives at the top of Bridal Veil Falls (the middle and largest) and enchanting deep pools below the upper, or Tom Tom Falls. From Tom Tom, a path can be found upstream to a lovely little falls.

Return up the trail and watch on the right for an obscure track that drops down, down, down—slippery, slippery. Bridal Veil comes in view—wowee! Slip-slide on and down to a promontory ridge between the middle and lower falls. Turn right to the rock-slab pools at the base of Bridal Veil Falls. Walk behind the falls in a rock shelter. Roar, water, roar!

No safe safe route can be seen down to the lowest falls. Be satisfied.

Or not. The former road entry to Murphy's Ranch, dwindled to a trail,

Little Mashel Falls

crosses the river to the new (since 1944) grade of the Tacoma Eastern Railroad, which once upon a time was the primary tourist route from Tacoma to Elbe and The Mountain. On the far side find a path down the mossy, flowers-in-spring, rock slot the river has sliced to the uppermost falls. Carefully pick a slick way by potholes to the plunge basin.

Now for the real action. Return on the tracks 150 feet from the bridge and spot a dirt track up the cutbank. Follow the trail along the gorge rim. Rude paths go off left to poor looks down to the middle falls, but they're nothing much. The main tread leads to the top of the lower falls. There's something, okay. Arched over by maples, the stream flows on lichen-dark, water-rounded, exquisitely sculptured rock, down a small cataract into a black pool of foam-flecked mountain tea. There it gathers itself and hurls over the brink—to a preliminary drop, then out of sight in the forbidding chasm. Gracious. At one time or another Eatonville got water from here and toyed with a ridiculous hydroelectric scheme, but now the falls area is preserved in Pack Forest.

The bottom of the lower falls—actually a double falls totalling about 150 feet—can be reached by a perilous skidway. Not yet satisfied? In a ½-mile gorge the Little Mashel drops 270 more feet. That ought to do it.

Big Mashel Gorge, round-trip sidetrip 4 miles

Though the forest walk 1 mile upstream on the rail grade is pretty, downstream is the spectacularity. In a long 1 mile from the Little Mashel, the grade rounds a nose of lichen-black rock, a garden of alumroot, ocean spray, and goatsbeard. Ever seen a town nestle? That's what Eatonville does, in the Mashel valley, amid its hills. Look across to the fabulous Ohop Wall, turn around to see Hugo Peak, and gaze down to the moldering Eatonville sawmill that closed some 40 years ago but may still pose picturesquely, wasteburner and all, beside the ducky old millpond. Over lowlands are Bald Hills and Black Hills.

In 1 more mile is the Big Mashel River. Just before the bridge, skid down the embankment to river level and follow a woods road to the gorge. Lordy. Downstream the river widens to pools of what is merely a nice wild river. Upstream, though, it tumbles from a slot gorge through which mountain tea flows in black deeps as narrow as 4 feet wide under cliffs 200 feet high.

Newton Ecological Area, round-trip sidetrip loop 1 mile

Back on 1000 Loop, from the 1160-foot Y at Murphy's Ranch proceed upward on road No. 1000, passing road No. 1300 left to Bethel Ridge. Forest grown up since the 1926 and other fires abruptly yields to wonderful big trees of 1800 forest, plus a few older relics. Note fire damage to the big trees, many of which are nearing death—thus the salvage logging. In 1¼ miles, gaining 460 feet, is the Pack hub, Kirkland Pass, 1593 feet. Five roads come to the pass, all plainly signed, but pay attention. A mandatory sidetrip from here is to the 42-acre Ecological Area through 1800 forest, tall trees and deep shadows. In the heart of the area are relicts from a more ancient past. Walk the Trail of the Giants down the valley of usually waterless Newton Creek. The trail branches, forming a loop. Don't go fast, take your time—time to feel the dimensions of giant hemlocks and cedars and Douglas firs up to 9 feet in diameter, 250 feet tall, maybe 450 years old.

The Newton Creek Trail continues down the valley from the bottom of the loop, through a Douglas fir plantation to road No. 2000, there connecting to the Windy Ridge trail.

Pack Forest nature trail

And so home....

The way back on 1000 Loop is short and downhill. Descend on the middle road, No. 1000, signed "Highway." In ¾ mile leave the 1800 cathedral and enter "Nisqually Canyon Salvage, 1981." Views are smashing down to the drowned Nisqually Canyon and the La Grande Dam that done it. Shortly after is a plantation of exotics established in 1927, including Japanese red pine, redwood, Oriental cedar, Port Orford cedar, Korean pine, Arizona cypress, and big-cone spruce. Off left a bit on road No. 1500 are Ponderosa pines grown from seeds gathered in a dozen areas of the West. The Hugo Peak trail (alternative trailhead) is passed, and the administration area, and at 2 miles from Kirkland Pass the loop is closed.

2000 Loop, loop trail alone 5¼ miles, with all sideloops 10 miles

A loop off the 1000 Loop, and three loops off *that*. Kirkland Pass is the start-end. Set out on road No. 2000—which is *both* the roads to the left of No. 1000—take the one on the far left.

The way alternates between 1800 and 1926 fires, a textbook illustration of how fingers of fire follow natural flues up the slope. In ⅓ mile views open out to Eatonville and Rainier. In a scant 1 mile is Lookout Peak, 2034 feet, highest (?) point of Pack Forest's "island." The tower was built in 1929, pulled down in 1983.

Road No. 2000 bends around and descends to a junction with road No. 2040; off on the latter a short way is the summit of Windmill Peak, another claimant for the title of highest point of Pack Forest and site of a windmill and acid-rain gauge. The summit is cleared and views are superb.

At 1¾ mile is a junction with road No. 2500, signed "Bethel Ridge." At a long 2 miles, in fine stands of hemlock and fir, is a junction, 1700 feet, with road No. 2300. From here road No. 2000 ascends 1¾ miles to close the loop at Kirkland Pass.

Windy Ridge, loop trip 1½ miles

Directly across road No. 2000 from the Newton Creek trail is the Windy Ridge trail, ascending the ridge crest through dense, stagnated, 60-year-old fir, in ½ mile emerging on the ridge summit, 1990 feet, to a great big view of Mount Rainier. The way descends the steep north side of the ridge to the big trees of Newton Creek and ends at Kirkland Pass. The Trail of the Giants–Newton Creek trail completes the loop.

Lookout Trail, loop trip 2 miles

This new trail, completed in 1994, samples a variety of forest stands and wetlands, including demonstrations of experimental cut units and a meadow enhanced to provide habitat for elk, raptors, and wildlife.

The route starts near High Point (Lookout Peak), descends southerly, crossing roads No. 2000, 2500, and 2300, swinging east then north, crossing road No. 2300 again, and at road No. 2500 turning onto road No. 2080 to close the loop.

Canyon Peak, loop trip 1½ miles

From road No. 2000 walk road No. 2300, descending to a 1690-foot saddle between the main mass of Pack's mountain and the isolated jut of 1855-foot Canyon Peak. At a junction at the saddle continue straight ahead, soon intersecting road No. 2310, which circles the peak in clearcut views to Alder Dam and Reservoir, Stahl Mountain, and the Little Nisqually.

Other Trips

Fort Lewis. To explore the prairies in the spring flowering, plot alluring routes from the USGS maps, write an application for an "organized party," and send it, a month or more in advance of the desired date, to Headquarters, 9th Infantry Division at Fort Lewis, Fort Lewis, WA 98433. Attention: Public Affairs Officer.

Ohop Lookout. Mountain-edge views to Eatonville, looking like a Christmas card in the Mashel valley beneath the Bald Hills. Nearby is the Eatonville Rim, where the Big River eroded cliffs and potholes and channels in bedrock.

The Divide. Had the physical entirety (not to mention the Greater Ecosystem) of Rainier been put in the national park, America would come here to pay respects as it does to Paradise and Sunrise. A walker can pay

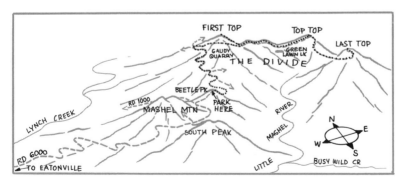

the Kapowsin meat-farmer the toll, drive to the gate at the edge of The Divide Foot-Only Zone, and readily follow logging roads a couple miles to the scalped 4100-foot top. A longer way is via the stumplands of Weyerhaeuser, if it hasn't gated the entry and gone into the meat business here, as it has on the White and Snoqualmie. A spur from road No. 6000 ascends to 3370-foot Beetle Peak, named for the vehicle which attained the summit at the venerable age of 105,926 miles, many spent surveying the four *Footsores,* and now in deserved retirement on Cougar Mountain. An elk trail connects ⅓ downhill mile from one company's scalping roads to the other; in 4 miles from Beetle Peak the Top Top is reached.

Busy Wild Mountain. Forest Service road No. 59 climbs from Highway 706 to the edge of the Kapowsin Tree Farm at 4200 feet. In 1 mile on Champion roads is Copper Knob, 4850 feet, nary a bush left to anchor the slimy volcanic soils sloughing off this way to the Nisqually river, that way to Busy Wild Creek, tributary to the Mashel. In ¾ mile more are two little lakes in cozy little subalpine cirques. In 1½ more miles of satanic beauty of yellow-white mush from which the last trees were stripped in the early 1980s, the summit of 4850-foot Busy Wild Mountain gives views of The Mountain close enough to watch the goats leaping crevasses. Another 2½ miles lead to the summit of Thing Peak, 4930 feet, once the site of Puyallup Ridge Lookout, now the boggling-big Thing, apparently the Bell System relay to the rings of Saturn.

Stahl Mountain. An unfamiliar south-of-the-Nisqually view of Rainier from the site of an old fire lookout. Drive the Little Nisqually Road and spurs to the clearcut frontier on the ridge crest. In 1978 forest trail led 1 mile to the cliff-edge summit and may remain. (Who's kidding whom?) A trusty native guide reported that in 1982 the Little Nisqually River trail— the veritable original trail—still existed, in virgin forest dating from an 1830 fire. Any volunteers to compose the requiem?

La Grande Canyon. The most spectacular section of the Nisqually

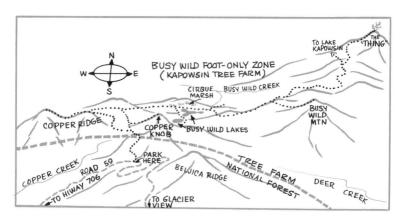

Looking north from Stahl Mountain

between glacier and delta. But Tacoma City Light got there before us and drowned it. Then, perhaps after *Footsore 4* enormously increased the number of walkers come to see La Grande Dam, built in 1912, rebuilt in 1944, and finger-narrow La Grande Reservoir, the canyon it desecrated, and the 840,000 tons of concrete, 330 feet high, 1500 feet long, of Alder Dam, built in 1944, the electricians got busy and fenced off all public accesses. Perhaps what stirred them to action is that licenses of the two dams expired December 31, 1993. Final application for relicensing was supposed to be in federal hands by the end of 1991 but was not, thanks to recent legislation which made use of public water no longer totally free. Tacoma City Light, in regional bad odor for its destruction of not only the most spectacular stretch of the Nisqually but also two canyons on the Cowlitz River, and one entire stretch of the Skokomish River, and its new desire to flood the Dosewallips River, was playing nice-nice with the Nisqually poo-bahs until Seattle City Light coughed up millions of dollars for "mitigation" of the evil it has wrought on the Skagit River. Tacoma apparently concluded the best bet was to say the hell with federal law and spend the next century in court. The public rights on the Nisqually be hanged. Bureaucracy *über alles*.

THE SOUTHERN FRONTIER

Ends. Whulge ends, and its feeder streams; here is a momentous hydrographic divide. From the Bald Hills flows the Deschutes, southernmost river of the Cascades to enter Puget Sound. Also from the Bald Hills flows the Skookumchuck, which turns south to the Rainier-born Cowlitz and thus the Columbia. But also from the Bald Hills flows the Chehalis, joined from the prairies by the Black, the two together nearly enwrapping the Black Hills and proceeding west to Grays Harbor.

Ends. Here ended the Puget Lobe of the continental glacier. A hiker from the north senses a peculiarity in the hills—they remind of the Western Cascades of Oregon, the Ozarks, or the southern Appalachians. The reason is that the ice rode up the north flanks (on the east side of the Black Hills, to about 1460 feet) but not over the highest tops; the terrain is not ice-shaped and youthful—as say, the Issaquah Alps—but mainly stream-sculptured, maturely dissected.

The Puget-Willamette Trough continues south, but here where it narrows between Bald Hills–Black Hills "portals" are the enigmatic prairies. What is Eastern Washington doing west of the crest? What are Oregon-

Bald Hills

like oak groves and western gray squirrels doing so far north? Tolmie in the 1840s remarked on the contrast with lush forests of uplands all around; declaring the prairies unsurpassed in elegance, he compared them to the open parks amid forests on artfully landscaped estates of English nobility. The art, of course, is Nature's (though prior to 1850 aided by regular burning done by Original Inhabitants to encourage the camas and the deer). The flats are the outwash plains of rivers from the front of the ice in its farthest advance toward Oregon. The soil is composed of river gravels with poor water-retention; no matter that the skies are Puget Sound-drippy—so far as plants are concerned the sites are semi-arid.

Ends. Here the Really Big River carried ice-dammed waters of the Cascades through today's Chehalis valley to the ocean, joined west of the Black Hills by the Really Big River from the Olympics.

Ends. On prairies and their upland counterparts, the "balds," and in adjoining woodlands, are the northern limits of some plant species. And the southern limits of others.

USGS maps: Bald Hill, Lake Lawrence, Vail, McKenna, Yelm, Maytown, Tumwater, Tenino, Rochester, Shelton, Malone

For a free map of Capitol State Forest, write Department of Natural Resources, Olympia, WA 98504

Bald Hills

Drive Highway 507 south from McKenna to the Four Corners intersection of highways from Yelm, Vail, McKenna, and Lake Lawrence. Go southeast on Bald Hill Road, marked by a large "Lake Lawrence" sign, 9.5 miles, to 1 mile past Single Tree Estates on Clear Lake. Turn left on Weyerhaeuser's road No. 1000, a great wide mainline haul road from the Vail Tree Farm. In 0.2 mile turn right on an unsigned, double-entry road.

At the absolute mountain front, on the tip of the ridge jutting into the angle between Nisqually and Deschutes Rivers, lies an ecological community—or better say, community of communities—that may best be introduced in the words of the surveyors' (and just about everybody else's) expert guide, Ed Alverson: "... lake, cliffs, canyon, prairie 'balds,' old-growth forest, oak-madrona woodland, and marsh-swampland, in a compact area ... a wider array of rare and interesting wildflowers and plants than anywhere else in the Puget Trough ... spring is the ideal time."

Man has done such things here as make a person ashamed of his species—groves of outstanding ancient forest reduced to stumpage, bald meadows ravaged by motorcycles. Yet latterly man has done something to redeem himself. The Nature Conservancy and the state Department of Natural Resources have combined to establish a Bald Hill Lake Natural Area Preserve. Be warned: boots, too, are the enemy of fragile terrain; most of the preserve is closed to public entry, protected for botanical research.

However, adjoining the closed area, both on the lake and hills above,

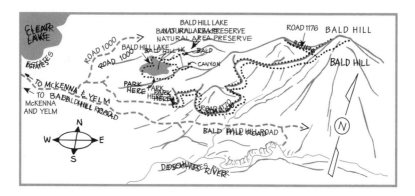

the walker can encounter all or most of the plants in the preserve. And on the hills there are views, too.

Bald Hill Lake Natural Area, round trip with sidetrips 1½ miles

The history of the area over the centuries was one of repeated fires, creating and perpetuating the "balds." Nooks of ancient forest survived the flames. But not the loggers, who in 1976 clearcut the shores of Bald Hill Lake, one of the crimes for which the Bottom Line someday will be made to answer. Nature Conservancy managed to save some 337 acres, including the unlogged canyon and the balds, here only lightly grazed. The area now is managed by the state DNR as a Natural Area Preserve. Some thirty-five grasses have been found, half of them native. The display of ferns includes a number of the unusual and rare. More than 300 plants have been identified. Many are at their northern limits and remind of Oregon; many "don't belong" on this side of the Cascades and remind of Eastern Washington. The flower show changes completely every few weeks. The April beginning is the little *Synthyris reniformis;* the July ending is farewell-to-spring.

So says Ed Alverson, so it must be true.

Now, about the significance of "natural area." Though the set-aside is for the ultimate purpose of enriching the human experience, the experience in question is not of the kinetic variety. The area, in order to be kept natural, must be protected from motors, wheels, and *too many feet*, assuredly, *all* swift, hard-stomping, aggressive feet. Lest the pedestrian come here for exercise of the muscles rather than the mind and spirit, we have eliminated discussion of accesses to the lake and paths that may or may not exist. Find your own way. If you fail, take it as a judgment by the Great Spirit that you are not worthy. Do proper penance, elsewhere, then try again.

Bald Hill East, round trip 8 miles

Drive 0.2 mile from road No. 1000 to a Y. Turn right a scant 1 mile to a second Y, elevation 830 feet.

It is possible to drive onward and upward, but since one of the two reasons for the trip is plants, the foot is the only fitting machine. Walk the left fork, road No. 1170, dodging lesser spurs and climbing steadily, then dipping to a creek valley. At several spots, due to the combination of repeated fires (set by the Original Inhabitants for "camas farms"?) and the dry sites resulting from near-surface, glacier-smoothed conglomerate bedrock, are prairie-like balds. Groves of Oregon white oak grow amid fields of common camas, poison camas, seablush, monkeyflower, buttercup, paintbrush, shooting star, strawberry, large bittercress, serviceberry.

At 1¾ miles the main road rounds a ridge tip at 1420 feet and the views begin and continue without a break in clearcuts of the middle and late 1970s and early 1980s. Below is the odd cliff of Fossil Rock, another trip in itself. In 1 mile more is a saddle at 1700 feet. To the right is the 2026-foot summit of Bald Hill, one of the viewpoints. For others, turn left on road No. 1176 a final scant ½ mile, over the tops of two 1740-foot bumps.

From pieces here and there assemble a 360-degree panorama. East beyond the Nisqually River are Ohop Lookout, Hugo, Dobbs, Wow, and Rainier. To the north spot nearby lakes—Kreger, Silver, Cranberry, and Rapjohn—and Ohop Valley, Kapowsin Scarp, Spar Pole Hill, Carbon Ridge. South over headwaters of Deschutes River are Bald Hills—and more of them west, Clear and Elbow Lakes at their foot. Farms and villages and woods dot the enormous sprawl of the South Puget Plain; out there boom Fort Lewis cannon. On a clear day see Olympia, Whulge, Olympics.

Capitol State Forest

Another name for Black Hills is Capitol State Forest. From 1901 to 1941 several cut-and-get-out companies operated here—the Bordeaux brothers' Mason County Logging, Vance Lumbering, and Mud Bay Logging. They advanced from bullteam to "lokie" logging and built more than 100 miles of railroads, the basis for today's road and trail systems. In the mid-1920s a far-sighted State Forester, Ted Goodyear, and his assistant Mike Webster, purchased 33,000 acres of logged, burned lands for 50 cents an acre, supplemented these with gifts, and assembled them with trust lands managed by the state for the common schools and counties. Some of the earliest tree-farming was here, seedlings set out by the CCC, then by Cedar Creek Youth Camp.

Since the 1960s the successor of the State Forestry Board, the Department of Natural Resources (DNR), has been authorized by RCW Chapter 79.68 to practice multiple-use sustained-yield forestry. Capitol Forest has some 75 miles of management roads, mostly gravel, suitable for ordinary automobiles; there are excellent campgrounds, picnic areas, and vista points, accessible by approaches shown on the excellent, free DNR map.

But pedestrians beware. Since the 1960s the Forest has gained an evil reputation. Some 90 miles of ATV routes have been developed, attracting sales and service outlets, rental agencies, and "staging areas" of private clubs. The DNR sought to eliminate conflict by splitting the Forest into an ATV Zone and a Hiker-Horse Zone, the deadline being the Black Hills Crest. A good idea. Unfortunately, ATVs are permitted on all roads and from them readily trespass on trails officially banned to wheels.

Capitol Forest often is cited as a model of how tree-farming, automobile recreation, and backcountry trail-hiking can coexist amicably. We wish we could be more enthusiastic about the walks in deep valleys by small streams in second-growth wildwoods. Walks on moor-like broadview heights in breathtaking vistas from Olympus to St. Helens to Rainier to Baker, from Puget Sound and Hood Canal to the Pacific Ocean. But the DNR said it all in a brochure of the late 1970s, "Trailbiking is the single most prevalent use of Capitol Forest." (Motorcycles, they meant.) Is it, still? In the late 1980s arrived from California the fat-tire bike. The March 1991 *Sunset Magazine* headlined an article, "South of Olympia, 200 miles of trails for mountain bikers." So be it.

We recommend a family-car tour, with family, on the 75 miles of recreational roads. We particularly call attention to Chehalis Valley Vista. Ascend the short path to a cleared knoll, 1150 feet, on the brink of the plunge to the floodplain 1000 feet below. You are standing on the absolute southern boundary of the Whulge world, beyond the limits of ancient ice, looking to Oregon, to the ocean, and a goshamighty more. See Rainier, Adams, St. Helens, and the hamlet of Rochester out in Baker Prairie, and Willapa Hills beyond the Doty Hills, and the enormous plume rising from the Chehalis Steam Plant, where stripmined coal is burned to generate electricity. Directly below, the Black River meanders at the foot of the Black Hills scarp. Across emerald pastures 2½ miles, the Chehalis River meanders at the foot of the opposite scarp. But they didn't dig this valley—that was done millennia ago by the Really Big River, several times the size of today's Columbia, the sum of all the rivers of the Cascades and Olympics dammed from more direct routes to the sea by the wall of Canadian ice.

Drive to the summit of Rock Candy Mountain. This northernmost of the three highest peaks of the Black Hills gives the choicest views straight down to petering-out saltwaterways of Puget Sound. Directly below is the site of Hollywood, the name given by brushapes who lived in Hollywood Camp, from the 1920s to 1947 site of Mason County Logging Company's Camp 4. After a day in the cold rain, rassling big sticks, the dry and warm railroad-car bunkhouses may actually have seemed as sybaritically magnificent as the entertainment capital of the world. The mountain honored the hobo's dreams of bulldogs with rubber teeth and cops with wooden legs, cigarette trees and hens that lay soft-boiled eggs, and a lake of booze where you can paddle around in big canoes. These hobo loggers brought civilization hereabouts to its zenith. Then came a lower order of apes.

However, let it be noted that wheel-travelers are notoriously lacking

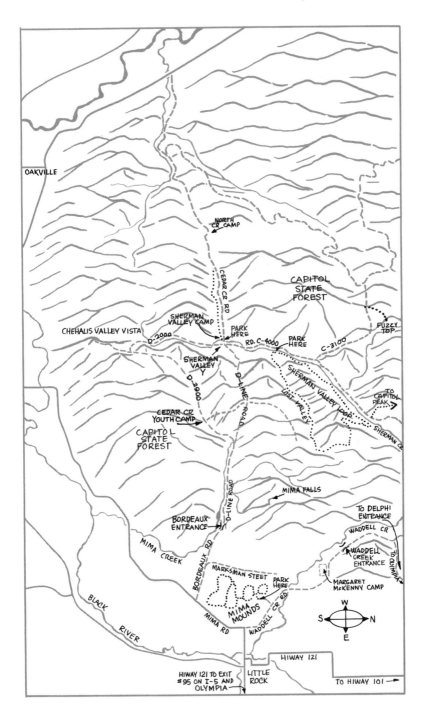

in the clever department. Local hikers know trails, even build them, which are not found by the folks with eyeballs spinning to keep pace with their wheels. Locals also know the seasons and days and hours to walk or ride horses in peace. However, as a regional amenity, appealing to visitors from a distance, the Black Hills lie in the future. Or if there is none, the past.

Still, we cannot omit three walks, two wheelfree and the third sampling the high country to show what we are missing, having been driven out by a surfeit of wheels, motor-powered *and* muscle-powered (which is to say, *gravity*-powered).

McLane Creek Nature Trail, round trip 1 mile

Go off I-5 on Exit 104 in Olympia and drive US 101 west 2 miles. Turn south at the exit signed "West Olympia, Black Lake," on Black Lake Boulevard 4 miles to a T with Delphi Road. Turn right 1 scant mile to the DNR sign and access road leading to the trailhead parking area, elevation 150 feet.

Beaver ponds, beaver dams, beaver lodges, and—if you're quiet and lucky—beaver splashing about their business oblivious to the audience. And an encyclopedia of woodland plants and marsh plants and swamp plants, on a mere 41 acres of DNR land that seem ten times that.

A self-guiding pamphlet and interpretive signs aid understanding of sights along the way, the most spectacular of which are three beaver ponds, the centerpiece broad and strewn with lily pads and wiggling with salamanders; view platforms are comfortable spots to lie in wait for the beaver. The path proceeds on plank walks through marshes and swamps, on bridges over McLane Creek. Partway along the 1.1-mile outer loop is a shortcut connector along an old railroad grade, passing close by one of the two beaver lodges. There are skunk cabbage and devils club, alder and fir—including at least one monster "wolf" disdained by the loggers. Ancient cedar stumps nurse young cedars. A two-legged maple arches over a trail "tunnel." Picturesque snags house bird families.

Mima Mounds Natural Area, round trip about 5 miles

Go off I-5 on Exit 95 and drive Highway 121 west to Littlerock. Proceed straight through on the road signed "Capitol Forest." Go right on Waddell Creek Road 0.7 mile and turn left to the parking area and trailhead, elevation 240 feet.

A traveler in 1841 wondered at the pimples and at last declared, "In utter desperation I cease to trouble myself about their origin and call them the 'inexplicable mounds.' " Geologists took a try at explaining them as the result of freezing and thawing. Biologists compared them to "prairie mounds" of the Great Plains, and the "hogwallow country" of California. In 1991 Victor Scheffer and associates conclusively (insofar as anything in science ever is) established them as the work of pocket gophers now gone from this scene but still at their labors elsewhere west of the Mississippi and north of Mexico.

Whatever, of the nearly 1,000,000 mounds originally scattered over

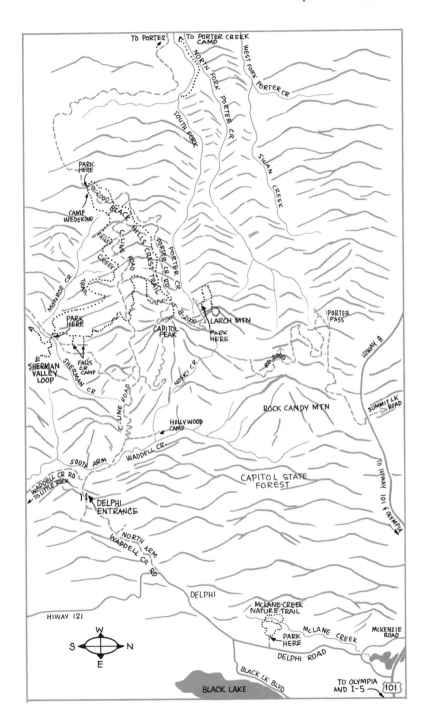

30,000 acres of prairies, most of those not already leveled by plows and cows and bulldozers were, in the 1960s, being ravaged by motorcycle hoodlums. The Nature Conservancy, the National Park Service, and Evergreen State College stepped in; in the 1970s the state Department of Natural Resources assumed protection and management and interpretation.

Begin at the dome of the interpretive center. Study the displays, then walk the paved ½-mile self-guiding nature trail, consulting the pamphlet that explains the evolution of the plant community.

Next, wander the 3–4 miles of less formal trails any old way, any old how. The Natural Area Preserve, 445 acres, is thoroughly sampled—fields, forest, and clumps of shrub-like firs pioneering the fields. The cessation of regular burning by the Original Inhabitants, done to perpetuate their "camas root farms," has resulted in

Aerial view of the "pimpled plain" of the Mima Mounds

expansion of forests. The spring flower show is famous—the grassland turns blue with camas blooms. In summer come the bluebells, wooly sunflowers, oxeye daisies. Even late October usually has a profusion of blue-bells-of-Scotland amid the golden grass and the airy balls of yellow-green lichen. Birds: little flitterers in the grass seeking seeds and bugs, raptors patrolling above on the lookout for little critters in the grass.

And mounds. Some in the woods, covered with moss and ferns. Some in the prairies, covered with grass and herbs. Contrast those seen from highways, low bumps nearly or completely flattened, to those here, in full original relief.

Don't rush. Take your time. Feel the vibrations. Watch out for Ancient Astronauts.

Black Hills Crest, round trip 8 miles

Drive Delphi Road–Waddell Creek Road (see McLane Creek Nature Trail) past the Delphi Entrance to a Y junction. Take the right fork 1.4 miles to a split. Go left on the C-Line Road, signed "Capitol Peak, 9 miles." Stay with the C-Line Road 7 miles to a junction on the ridgecrest, 2150 feet. Turn left on road No. B-2000 for 1.5 miles to Camp Wedekind, site of the 1947–65 planting camp from which better than 10,000,000 seedlings were set out amid the stumps. Park in a field atop broad-view Wedekind Pass, elevation 1896 feet.

Capitol Forest is most wisely and peacefuly visited on a rainy Tuesday morning in February. But for the high views unique in Whulge country, wait for a wet storm to wash the atmosphere and then (Tuesday morning in October) hie thee to the Black Hills Crest.

The five-star scenic supershow of the Black Hills ends atop Capitol Peak and has all those views. But in addition are kaleidoscopes from the trail along the crest of the range's longest, highest ridge, between the valleys of Sherman and Porter Creeks. Stroll for miles in bilberry and bracken and alpine-seeming shrubby firs, the sky-surrounded crest eerily moor-like. Enough to make a Scot homesick. Or an Ozark Mountain boy.

Walk Porter Creek Road a couple hundred feet and turn right on road-trail signed "Trail No. 30, Trail No. 6, Capitol Peak 4 miles." In another hundred feet diverge right toward a quarry on a still lesser track signed "Fall Creek Camp 9.4 miles, Porter Creek Camp 6.5 miles, Capitol Peak 4.1 miles via Trail No. 30 or Greenline #6." Ascend to the quarry top and a sign, "Capitol Peak 3.8, Porter Creek Camp 5.1." Ascend gently a long ½ mile to the crest at 2150 feet and a y. Go right, signed "Capitol Peak 3.5."

Now, stroll. On wings, almost, liberated from heavy Earth. A little up, a little down, from one "moor" to another. Grass and salal, huckleberry and salmonberry, old stumps and young firs, including plantations of alpine-appearing nobles. Lumps of weathered basalt columns poke through thin soil. In season the way is colorful with alpine-seeming flowers. Moors fall off right to Sherman Valley and Chehalis Valley draining to the ocean, left to Porter Valley and lacework of blue inlets and green peninsulas of South Sound and the Great Bend of Hood Canal. Ahead are the stump ridge of Big Larch and the surreal summit decorations of Capitol. (To paraphrase Descartes, "We communicate and therefore we exist.") Rainier looms whitely beyond.

Twice the road is crossed and twice more can be briefly glimpsed, but mostly the walker is totally unaware of wheels, so skillfully is the trail placed. The second crossing can confuse. This is at the 2150-foot saddle where the C-Line Road tops the ridge (see above). Take a few steps right from the junction along the C-Line Road and go left on a lesser road obscurely signed "Trail." In a couple hundred feet the trail indeed takes off up left to the crest. After a final grassy, rocky, meadow-like knoll at 2450 feet, the trail drops the short bit to a final 2150-foot saddle, that of Capitol Forest Vista, there meeting the upper end of the Capitol Peak trail from Sherman Valley. The final ¾ mile is on the road to Capitol Peak, 2667 feet.

One of the two tippy-tops of the Black Hills, Capitol commands a grand sweep of horizons. The vista from adjacent Big Larch Mountain is the approximate equal. The elder surveyor is prejudiced in Larch's favor because he came there on a crystalline day of late October and for the first time in all his travels of Whulge country saw, ice-chiseled in the depths of the Olympics, none other than Olympus. And by golly, out west was none other than the really-truly ocean. Not salt haze but the actual water, the waves shining in the low sun. Boy.

From whichever peak, sweep those horizons. South: the big valley of Sherman Creek, prairies (Mima, Baker, Grand Mound, and other), Chehalis valley, Doty and Willapa Hills. Easterly to northerly: the big valley of Waddell Creek, South Puget Plain, Bald Hills, St. Helens, Adams, Rainier, Glacier, Baker. Northerly: the big valley of Porter Creek, Big Larch and Rock Candy; Totten, Eld, Budd, and Henderson Inlets and Nisqually Reach, Black Lake and Olympia, Issaquah Alps, Green and Gold (Blue) Mountains, Olympics. West: what that Spanish chap saw from a peak in Darien.

Other Trips

Deschutes Falls. Is this glory spot of a slot canyon and an ancient forest and a homesteader's pasture preserved in a park or is it not? Are public officials smart or what? These questions, repeated over and over again to the beating of drums, led at long last to the state Wildlife and Recreation Fund enabling a Yes and a Yes. Thurston County Parks acquired 150 acres, a mile of Deschutes River frontage, the 75-foot-deep slot gorge, the waterfalls 15 and 35 feet high, grassy meadows, and riverbank ancient forest. See out-of-print *Footsore 4* for full description and praise. See the next edition of this book when details of public access are worked out.

Porcupine Ridge. The 50-yard line of the Bald Hills game, the royal box of the scenery opera. From a 1970s clearcut the scarp plummets to the South Puget Plain and views to just about the whole world. Follow the Weyerhaeuser Mainline to the locked gate of the Vail Tree Farm and climb to a window in the new-growing even-age monoculture (yawn) bottom-line forest.

Bloody Ridge. From plantations of the westernmost heights of the Bald Hills, look down to where the Canadian glacier halted in its Oregonward rush and died. Beware of the treacherous Weyerhaeuser gates. Loop on logging roads around Miller Hill and Bald Hill West, above the Skookumchuck Reservoir and Bloody Run.

Skookumchuck Falls. Walk past the closed gates, cross the divide from the Deschutes to the Skookumchuck, proceed up the latter, and discover a splendid stretch of wild river tumbling over a series of cascades to a mini-canyon of mossy bedrock bright with columbine. Which parks department has this treasure, a mere 25 miles from downtown Olympia, on its list? None? Then let's get some new parks departments.

Grand Mound Prairie. We supposed the whole prairie was securely in the Scatter Creek Habitat Management Area. Then all but the streambank was platted in 5-acre homesites.

KITSAP AND OLYMPIC PENINSULAS

~~~~~~

Kitsap Peninsula has beaches beyond praise—see our companion book. The terrestrial trails of greater than local interest are concentrated on the Tahuya sub-Peninsula, a disaster area, but not for that reason to be forgotten. It will have a happy future—if our society does. If it doesn't, in such combat zones as this we will witness the final victory of the savages. A science-fiction writer who frightens us by an Apocalypse of cities gone mad might well entertain readers with tales in which it is the madness in near-city wildlands that brings civilization tumbling to the abyss.

Olympic Peninsula has the beaches of the Strait of Juan de Fuca (again, the other book) and the trails of national park and national wilderness. Enough justification for being in the peninsula business, surely. The travel time tends to be lengthy, but much of it is ferryboard, not a minus in calculating a journey's rewards but a plus. Further, since the original motive of the surveyors was to inventory, in addition to beaches, rivers, and in-urban forests, the mountain fronts, perspectives from the Olympics are necessary to complete the tour of inspection that proceeded south from Chuckanut Mountain, along the Cascades and Issaquah Alps to the Bald Hills, turned west through the Black Hills, to end going north from South to Zion.

USGS maps: Vaughn, Longbranch, Burley, McNeil Island, Fox Island, Gig Harbor, Olalla, Bremerton East, Bremerton West, Duwamish Head, Suquamish, Belfair, Lake Wooten, Holly, Wildcat Lake, Potlatch, The Brothers, Seabeck, Brinnon, Poulsbo

Tahuya State Forest

The Tahuya ("oldest people") Peninsula, sub-peninsula of the Kitsap, undulates in a plateau up to 600 feet in elevation over some 120 square miles of second-growth wildland. Hundreds of lakes large and small, broad-view or moody-isolated, ever birdy, and myriad marshes and peat bog and swamps and meadows are the legacy of the Canadian glacier, as are the gravel soils which rapidly drain away the 40-inch annual rainfall, resulting in vegetation communities that "don't belong" on the wet west of the Cascades. The abundance of pine—western white, lodgepole, even Ponderosa—is striking. So are the creekside groves of quaking aspen. Startling are the stands of Oregon white oak. The understory also is un-

Tahuya River, Tahuya State Forest

Whulge-like, often dominated by evergreen huckleberry and manzanita and rhododendron. In the meadows during the spring flowering, a walker shakes his/her head in wonder at having been magically transported to alpine elevations.

The logging that commenced in bullteam shows near tidewater advanced inland via railroad, finishing before War II, skipping only "long corners" of ravines and ridges. Cut-and-run loggers let the land go for taxes, and thus came about the Tahuya State Forest of 33,000 acres, intermingled with private lands, managed by the Department of Natural Resources. Clearcutting of the long corners continues, as well as commercial thinning of second-growth, which on these stingy soils doesn't grow well at all, except in miles and miles of Christmas trees (fertilized to be shrubby). The most prominent economic activity is brushpicking for the florist industry.

The use is genuinely multiple, due emphasis given recreation—interpretive signs, vista points, and thirteen campgrounds. In the exciting dawn of legislative authorization to practice multiple-use, the DNR envisioned a trail system of more than 50 miles, continuous walks from saltwater of Hood Canal to the big sky of Green Mountain, trips in winter for solitude, in November to see the dog salmon spawning, in May and June for the showy bloom of rhododendron and mountain-like meadows.

Most of the "all-purpose" trails rarely see a foot or hoof. When is "multiple-use" not? When one use drives the others out. The wheels got the upper hand long before 1980, when the voters installed reason in the head office of the DNR, and no solution has yet been found to the mess inherited from the era of laissez faire tolerance. The DNR trails have willy nilly been integrated into the hundreds of miles of single-use razzerways on old rail grades. The noble trail scheme of the DNR has been put on hold. The Overland Trail to link the Tahuya River and Green Mountain has not been completed. The Connection Trail west from Powell Lake to Aldrich Lake has not been begun. Neither has the Aldrich Lake Trail, the path to the lake which in the 1920s served as a holding pond for logs waiting to be sluiced down a flume to tidewater for rafting to the mills, nor its extension, the Bald Point Trail down to Dry (Rendsland)

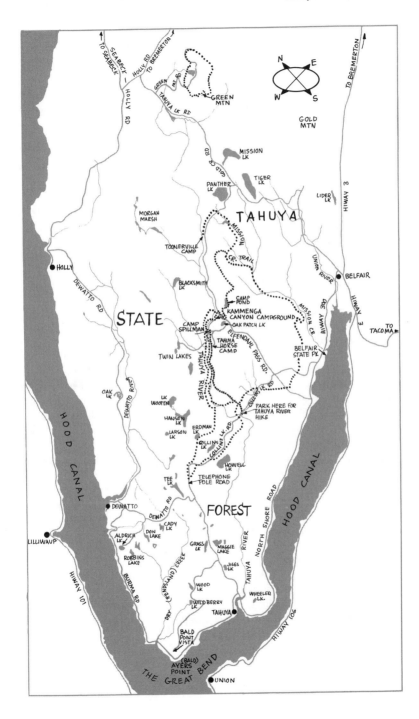

Creek and Bald (Ayres Point), jutting into the Great Bend of Hood Canal.

We are as shocked as anyone by our omission here of the 1700-foot apex of the Tahuya, of the Kitsap Peninsula, Green Mountain, but the scene became so dangerous that the DNR warned the public away. (Late note: In the summer of 1994 the help of citizen volunteers enabled the DNR to conditionally open Green Mountain, and if the yahoos are indeed under restraint, the trails will be discussed in the next edition. Until then, see *Footsore 4* if you can find it.)

The Tahuya will be reclaimed, as have been the Issaquah Alps. Until then this book, aimed at a regional audience, cannot encourage walkers from Seattle to expect a nice day there.

One sample must be presented, that the regional audience may get some notion what has been embezzled by the wheel freaks and scofflaws.

Tahuya River Trail, recommended round trip 5½ miles

From Belfair drive Highway 300 west 3.7 miles and just past Belfair State Park turn north on a blacktop road with a bundle of signs, including "Tahuya River." In 1 mile is a major intersection, Elfendahl Pass Road going left and right; go straight on Collins Lake Road. In 3.7 miles, as the road descends toward a valley bottom, spot an obscure trail on the right, just across from a two-car parking shoulder. (If you cross the Tahuya River you've gone a tad too far.) Elevation, 200 feet.

Where are we? Surely not a ferry ride and an hour's drive from Seattle. Some wizard has whisked us to a valley 8000 feet up in the wilderness of Montana. The modest river rattles in gravel meanders through meadows dotted by small pines, bright in alpine-like flowers. The trail ascends from riverbank to forest plateau, passes still ponds in circles of reeds. No, we're not in Montana after all, but home—a room in our wild mansion home we never suspected.

Crucially, *when* are we here? Never on weekends. Never in summer. Yet not in February because the flowers aren't out. Look to the weather. The walker wants to be here in blue sky, but not after a long spell of sunshine which has stirred up the wheels like hornets. Watch for a spring storm, the middle of May or thereabouts. The satellite photos on TV predict cloud masses moving on overnight, bringing a sparkling morning. Strike fast. Tuesday, Wednesday, or Thursday. Early morning. Best, dawn. Get away before Bremerton schools let out.

The way climbs a bit, then goes upsy-downsy along dry gravel drumlin ridges in rhododendrons and spindly firs and linear-pond bottoms in cool alder, partly on old logging-railroad grade. Razzer trails confuse; stay with the main track, and when there are two "mains," go left, where runs the Tahuya River, your goal.

After 1½ miles, something different, something wonderful. The trail drops off the plateau scarp to alder bottom, crosses a beaver-dammed slough into copses of spirea, and emerges in broad, big-sky meadowlands of young pines and huckleberry-topped stumps. Sidepaths lead to the river, where ducks swim off, herons flap up and away. The clear stream delights. One wants to choose a gravel bar, take off boots and wade. In fact, one has a Great Notion of coming here in shorts and tennis shoes on a warm spring day and doing the Long Wade for miles along the Tahuya. The stream, scarcely a "river" except in the monsoons when floodwaters roar, has plenty of banks neared by trail or road. Just you and the birds, and the fish, and the deer, squirrels, and coyote, maybe a bear, even a cat.

But, back to the trail. Through fields it winds, in columbine, meadow rue, fairy bells, blue-eyed Mary, and strawberry, and by hellebore bogs and groves of cottonwood and quaking aspen, sometimes climbing the 20–50-foot valley wall, in pines and twinflower, vanilla leaf, ginger, and coolwort. After 1 enchanting mile—the best the Tahuya has to offer—the trail enters Tahuya River Camp, elevation 250 feet.

The 2¾ miles to here, a 5½ mile round trip, is unique in Whulge country, well worth the complications of wheel-evading. The Tahuya River Trail goes on and the walker may well be so infatuated he/she devises a strategy to do the entire 12 miles to the Green Mountain Loop. The Oak Patch Natural Area Preserve, dominated by what may be the largest stand of Oregon white oak on the peninsula, is near the trail. At 1¾ miles from Tahuya River Camp is Kammenga Canyon Camp and in a scant 1 mile more, ecologically amazing Camp Pond. The forest ringing the shore includes lodgepole pine and oak. There are calypso orchids! The little meadows are lush in beargrass (really!) and other out-of-elevation plants. Note old ditches dug by homesteaders to convert meadow-marshes to pastures.

In another 1½ miles or so is the northern terminus of Mission Creek Trail. Ponds, marshes, creeks, forests. Another crossing of Elfendahl Pass Road, then of Tahuya River. Just before the river, pass Toonerville Camp, named for the Trolley in the funny pages of 1920s–30s newspapers. Here in the long ago was a logging-railroad reload, the grade later used for the "Lost Highway" that came from tidewater at Dewatto Bay and deadended here for many years, before modern county roads tied it eastward to civilization. Recross river and road. Recross road, cross Gold Creek Road, then Gold Creek. Along Gold Creek pass the falls, then ascend the hill to join the Green Mountain loop.

The Olympic Front

Given his way, President Franklin Delano Roosevelt would have extended Olympic National Park farther east. Had it been done then, the view from Seattle would not be of moths chomping what was, in Roosevelt's day, virgin green. It was not done. For ancient forest the walker must go to national park and national wilderness.

However, for airplane-wing panoramas of Whulge lowlands, summits of the Hood Canal front of the Olympics are well worth the extra-long travel they require.

South Mountain, round trip (both peaks) 9½ miles

Drive US 101 to 0.7 mile south of the Skokomish River and turn west on Skokomish Valley Road. At a Y in 6 miles go right on road No. 23, signed "Dennie Ahl Seed Orchard." In 2.2 miles, where road No. 2202 turns right, continue straight on road No. 23, signed "Brown Creek Campground." In 0.2 mile turn left on road No. 2199. Round a promontory (look down to pastures at the upper limit of the Skokomish floodplain), drop to cross Vance Creek. In 3.3 miles from the turn onto road No. 2199, road No. 2254 (not signed) and the railroad grade join in from the right. At 4.5 miles from road No. 23 is a T at Bingham Creek; go right and stay on the main road. At 2 miles from Bingham Creek is a sideroad right, perhaps inconspicuously signed "South Mountain 820." Turn up it, immediately starting to climb. In 0.5 mile is a big switchback. Park here, elevation 950 feet.

On the crystal-air November day of the first survey, five volcanoes were seen and one ocean, plus a Canal and a Sound and Three Fingers, Index, Phelps, Daniels, Chimney Rock, Goat Rocks, Green and Gold, Issaquah Alps, Doty and Bald and Black and Willapa Hills. Yes, and Olympics too. Rising abruptly from lowlands where the Canadian glacier petered out, South is the absolute southernmost peak of the Olympics, a unique viewpoint giving novel perspectives on the full length and width of the Puget Trough.

The road is perfectly drivable beyond—all the way to the summits—but the views from the near-naked slopes start almost immediately and demand constant attention. On an early-melting south slope, the route makes an excellent snowline-prober, the views richly rewarding long before the summit. Winding into valleys, out on spurs, crossing saddles, cutting through walls of rubbly basalt and harder pillow lava, the busy, entertaining way ascends in panoramas uninterrupted by the shrub plantation. Flower gardens on lava walls and in creeklets compete for attention—fields of lupine and beargrass especially striking. In 3 miles, at 2750 feet, is a saddle in the summit ridge, adding views north. Left ½ mile is West Peak, 3125 feet, formerly a lookout site, now bare and lonesome. Right on an up-and-down ridgecrest 1¼ miles is radio-towered East Peak, 3000 feet.

Here on the scarp that without prelude leaps up 2000 feet are views

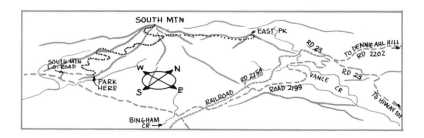

Olympic Mountains from South Mountain

that demand large-area maps and long hours. Close at hand, of course, are Olympics: a foreground of ridges and valleys denuded of trees, one of the most surrealisic scenes of clearcutting in all the Northwest; footstool peaks, Dennie Ahl and Dow; and the rugged heights, The Brothers, Washington, Ellinor, Pershing, Copper, and Cruiser. The East Peak (this is the one you see while driving up the Skokomish) gives the classic look down to the pastured floodplain of the valley curving around to join Hood Canal at the Great Bend. The West Peak (whose basalt surprisingly is capped by conglomerate) gives the dramatic vista to Grays Harbor. Below south is the forest plateau of the glacier terminus. Beyond this gulf where the meltwater streams flowed, including the Pretty Big River of ice-dammed rivers from the east side of the Olympics, rise the Black Hills, beyond which rolled the Really Big River from the Cascades; beyond that valley (now the Chehalis) are the Doty and Willapa Hills. Close enough below to see the house the Spring twins grew up in is Shelton, mills pluming.

Then, saltwaterways, cities, Cascades. For purposes of this book Ira Spring spent the night on the summit, viewing lights from Aberdeen to Olympia to Everett, and was so knocked out he forgot to take a picture.

Mount Walker

Drive US 101 to the Mt. Walker Viewpoint road, No. 2730, at Walker Pass, 5 miles south of Quilcene. Elevation, 727 feet.

The absolute easternmost summit of the Olympics, zapping straight up from Hood Canal, sitting out by its lonesome, cut off from neighbors by a deep glacier trough, Walker is, apart from skyline peaks, the most prominent point in the range as seen from Seattle. It follows that from Walker one can readily see Seattle. And so one can. And all the other neighborhoods of Puget Sound City and everything in between. The only thing wrong is a road to the top. On second consideration, that's not so wrong. In winter (October through April), the road is gated at the highway and thus is a trail. In other seasons there is the other and veritable trail.

The Road-Trail, round trip 11 miles

The 1978 survey was in utter solitude on a crisp February Wednesday in four inches of overnight snow, plenty for animal tracks and tree decorations but not enough to hinder feet. Plan your trip to be so lucky. The narrow, steep road ascends virgin forest, passing basalt walls and windows opening to views this way and that. In 1½ miles, at 1300 feet, are a half-bridge across a cliff and the first exclamation-point view, east over the Big U Turn Gorge of the Big Quilcene River to Constance. The way circles the peak, passing small windows north; at 4 miles, 2300 feet, is Wow Window, east over Hood Canal to Seattle. In a scant 1 mile more the road tops the forested summit ridge at 2760 feet and divides.

Left a scant ¼ mile, at 2804 feet, is North Point Lookout, the tower gone but the basalt garden of rhododendrons and other shrubs intact and the views enormous over Walker Pass, up the Big Quilcene valley to Constance, Warrior, Buckhorn, Townsend, and their supporting cast of

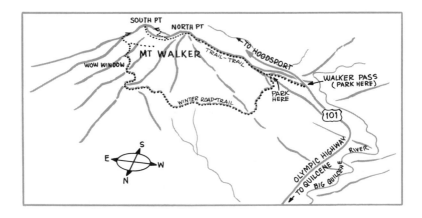

green ridges. Closer are clearcuts of Turner, Buck, and Crag. The Quilcene Range, Big Quilcene Lookout at the tip of the ridge, runs north toward Zion and Big Skidder Hill, and San Juan Islands and Canada.

Right a scant ½ mile, at 2750 feet, is South Point Observation, another garden and panorama. The foreground is saltwater at the foot of the mountain—Quilcene Bay off Dabob Bay off Hood Canal. The middleground is the Kitsap Peninsula. The background: Cascades from Baker to Glacier to Rainier to St. Helens; cities and towns from Everett to Seattle to Bremerton to Tacoma. Look at a map of Whulge country—whatever is on the map you probably can see from Walker. (Alternatively, as on the day of the 1978 survey, the east may be a shining cloudsea from horizon to horizon, only volcanoes poking above. But that's not bad either, on a winter day when the Olympics are carved from white ice and the forests are sugar candy.)

The Trail-Trail, round trip 5 miles

The trail was there before the road but for some years was lost in the brush before volunteers came a-whacking, after which, in 1988, came the younger surveyor. Views are less plentiful than on the road-trail. But the distance is less, by half. Wheels are banned. In June you may go blind from the color show.

Drive a scant 0.2 mile up from the highway to the clearly marked trailhead, elevation 775 feet. The path ascends steeply, unpleasantly so under a boot-depth of snow, and is so slippery when wet that many hikers then prefer to ascend the trail and descend the road. But in rhododendron time! As the feet move slowly up the trail, the nose is thrusting through masses of blossoms.

At 1½ miles, 2450 feet, is the only view comparable to those from the road. The trail switchbacks over a large rock outcrop. Off the trail, at the outcrop top, is a vista of Buck, Turner, Crag, Constance, Warrior, Buckhorn, and Townsend. The trail comes out at North Point, just west of where the lookout used to be.

Mount Zion, round trip 4 miles

From US 101 at 2 miles north of Quilcene, take the paved Lords Lake Loop Road. In 3.4 miles, just below the (Port Townsend) reservoir dam, go left on a gravel road signed "Mt. Zion Trail 7, Little Quilcene Trail 9." In 4.2 more miles is a triple fork; keep right, signed "Mt. Zion Trail 3," in views down the Little Quilcene valley to the end of Quilcene Bay. In 1.2 miles, at Bon Jon Pass, 2900 feet, take a right, contouring the northeast side of Gold Creek valley. At 2 miles from the pass, 11.2 miles from US 101, is the trailhead, elevation 2900 feet.

From a fragrant garden of rhododendron blossoms on a bald-rock knob, see mountains of Vancouver Island, waterways of Whulge far south on Puget Sound and north to the Strait of Georgia, islands and towns and cities of the plain, and Cascades from Rainier to Baker, and—but why go on? Especially since all the elder surveyor saw on a first assault was the

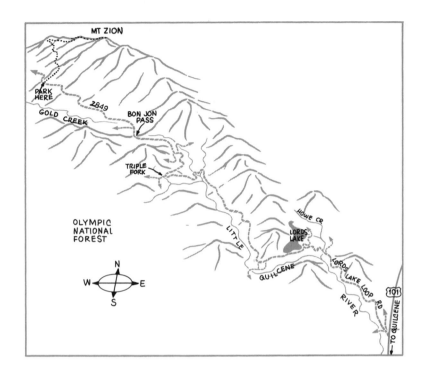

white insides of a cloud enwrapping a snow-white ridge. Returning the next day he found the cloud broken a bit, revealing to the west, over the valleys of Gold Creek and the Dungeness River, snowy peaks of Graywolf Ridge and, over Bon Jon Pass and the head of the Little Quilcene River, the white barrens of Mt. Townsend. But in the other direction the cloud remained, thinning just enough to reveal Port Discovery close enough below to see the fish jumping. Nevertheless, usually reliable sources declare Zion verily is the promised land for fans of the big picture.

In a corner of the Olympics with roads for fun-loving squirrelers everywhere, why the Forest Service should permit wheels on this last surviving scrap of trail is a mystery. Why these scant 2 miles cannot be reserved for feet is a question every hiker should ask the ranger. (Assuming the pose of the three monkeys, "See No Evil. Hear No Evil. Speak No Evil," he/she will blandly repeat the Official Incantation, "multiple-use.")

The summit ridge of Zion seems secure from logging; regrowth since the 1916 forest fire is so scrawny that not for generations will a log-exporter salivate here. The trail quickly switchbacks to the first windows out on Gold Creek valley and its clearcuts. Cliffs of rubbly basalt, then conglomerate, provide scenic rest-stop perches.

The summit is pleasantly open, all trees diminutive, if only a few are alpine-seeming, and in early summer the flower show brilliantly culminates in the rhododendrons. Sit on the site of the long-gone lookout cabin and enjoy the views. An "island mountain" cut off from the main range by deep valleys, Zion is a very high peak to be so far out. There's absolutely nothing to block the view from Seattle to Bellingham to Vancouver to Victoria. Unless, maybe, a cloud.

Other Trips

Green Mountain. The 6-mile loop from Green Mountain Camp, 1150 feet, circles the peak in forests, rock balds, marshes, and vistas south, north, west, and east, touching the 1770-foot summit, highest on the Kitsap Peninsula, an extension of the "Old Mountains" most famously surviving in the Issaquah Alps, which are in plain sight to the east, as is virtually every nook of Whulge from Admiralty Inlet south. No, we will not give up Green but until the ya-hooing ceases and the bullets stop whizzing and parked cars are safe from trashing we will stand at a secure distance and cheer on the DNR as it seeks to tame this mountain as it did Tiger. The January 1994 "declaration of war" by Land Commissioner Belcher put 6000 acres of Green Mountain off-limits to motorized vehicles. By July 1994 matters had improved. Those who dare may drive past the gate (if unlocked) at the Tahuya Lake–Gold Creek Road to Green Mountain Camp and the trail. An alternative start is a bit farther south on the highway at the crossing of Gold Creek. A 2¼ mile trail climbs to the summit, gaining 1100 feet.

Gold Mountain. The summit is a blabbermouth of towers and the fun wheels run wild, but the summit view encompasses Edmonds and Seattle and Tacoma and Olympia and Bremerton, and lakes and islands and saltwaterways and two mountain ranges, and that's a lot. The unique dazzler is a sight not to be seen from any other terrestrial point. Spread out close below as on a map are the "triplet fishhooks"—Hood Canal curling north from the Great Bend to its end in Lynch Cove, and the two terminal fingers of Puget Sound crooking north, Case Inlet to its end in North Bay, Carr Inlet to Burley Lagoon.

Lower Big Quilcene Trail. Bark Shanty Shelter used to be where

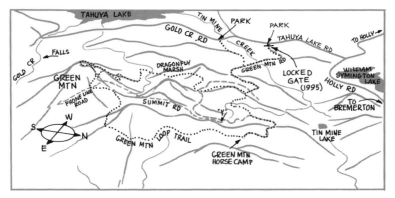

hikes started to Mt. Townsend and Marmot Pass. Then a logging road leapfrogged past Bark Shanty to a new trailhead to Marmot Pass, which the Forest Service placed on a motorcycle loop including Mt. Townsend. When the Buckhorn Wildernesss deprived the musclebutts of their razzerway, the kindly rangers felt that mercy required the provision of a new one, and thus the reconstruction of the Lower Big Quilcene Trail. On rainy Tuesday mornings in February, nostalgic Boy Scouts may savor such scraps of ancient forest as have survived. From the lower trailhead to the site of Bark Shanty is 2½ miles; from there to the upper trailhead at the boundary of the wilderness, 3½ miles.

Big Quilcene Lookout. The clearcut site of the lookout, 3450 feet, is close enough to Mt. Constance to see the mountain goats begging cookies from the mountain climbers, and Quilcene pastures are just a long moo away.

Webb Lookout. In a straight line with Green and Gold on the Kitsap Peninsula and the Issaquah Alps east of Seattle, this 2775-foot peak north of the Hamma Hamma River can be imagined to be a companion remnant of the Old (pre-Olympic and pre-Cascade) Mountains. The view is straight down to Hood Canal and out to everywhere.

Jorsted Point. The narrow, steep road to a 2300-foot helispot just south of the Hamma Hamma and close east of Washington and Pershing and hanging in the air above Hood Canal makes a fine and lonesome walk when the rowdies are still in school.

Dow Mountain. Cut off from neighbors by two deep valleys, the North Fork Skokomish drowned by Cushman Reservoir and a wind gap used in the long ago by ice and water, Dow is an island mountain, sensationally located close above Hood Canal beside the craggy mass of Washington. Do the road walk to the 2600-foot summit in winter, before blood stirs in the slugheads who come on sunny Sundays to racket on the mount.

Dennie Ahl Hill. On a crisp winter day when wheels are discouraged by snow, the walker can look out from the 2004-foot summit rising steeply above the Skokomish valley to the three volcanoes and half a dozen cities and towns, plus ice-chiseled crags of high mountains and sparkling waves of low waters.

Skokomish Delta. The largest delta of the Hood Canal side of the Olympics is the wildest, the lonesomest, and most scenic. The preserve of solitude, nearly 3 miles wide and up to 2 miles deep from saltwater to civilization, not counting a couple square miles of low-tide mudflats, give a walker plenty of space to commune with plovers and herons and clams and cows, and sniff the breezes blowing aromas of the saltmeadows that in spring are fields of flowers. Potlatch State Park lets feet on the beach ½ mile from the delta edge.

Twanoh State Park. A wild green gorge, a big-tree forest, and trails that loop from Hood Canal beaches to a valley that on a winter day, maples swollen in moss and draped in ferns, misty firs and cedars and hemlocks dripping giant drops, could be mistaken for a rain forest of the Queets.

SKYKOMISH RIVER

The Alpine Lakes Wilderness of 1976 and the Henry M. Jackson Wilderness of 1984 were monumental preservation works, yet while blessing the hearts of Congress and Presidents one cannot help note how careful they were to stay prudently distant from Highway 2 and whatever of Nature's bounty there, terrestrial or riparian, might be part of the inventory calculated into some corporation's Bottom Line.

In 1977 the kayakers, their long-accustomed put-ins and take-outs being year by year vacation-homed and fenced off, lobbied the Legislature into designating the Skykomish as first in a state system of Scenic Rivers, thinking thereby to guarantee a future of enhanced kayaking, walking, picnicking, and other quiet recreations. The hope still springs eternal, though the achievement is still fought off by the stubborn rearguard resistance of Privatizer selfishness and exploiter greed.

In 1978 *Footsore 2,* predecessor of this volume, proposed a Cascade Gateway Recreation Area which would, among other things, enormously enlarge Wallace Falls State Park to a superpark encompassing the May

Snohomish River from Lord Hill Regional Park

Creek watershed to the east. If any public official was listening, no response was forthcoming, not so much as a "We'll get back to you on that."

The 89-mile stretch of Highway 2 from Monroe to east of Leavenworth was classified a State Scenic Highway, and the 69 miles from Gold Bar to Leavenworth a National Forest Scenic Byway. The sign-making industry got a boost, as did revisers of highway maps. The benefit to land and waters has been as noticeable as "scenic river."

In 1990 another of this surveyor's 1978 proposals, for a Cascade Gateway Recreation Area centered on North Bend, was taken up and expanded into the concept of a Mountains-to-Sound Greenway along I-90 from Seattle to Snoqualmie Pass and east. Early in 1994 the other shoe dropped: a citizen group's proposal for a Stevens Pass Greenway from Everett to Wenatchee. It's gotta happen. It's gonna happen. Because it is there.

Scholars of the history of guidebooks may therefore be startled to find in this book a radical shortening-up of *Footsore 2* attention to the Skykomish.

The I-90/Snoqualmie River concept newly has its own book, *Hiking the Mountains-to-Sound Greenway*. The very few hikes in this volume, and especially the short shrift given "Other Trips," underline the necessity of an early task for the Stevens Pass people. Get a surveyor. Publish a book. Meanwhile, pedestrians, don't throw away your copies of the out-of-print *Footsore 2*.

USGS maps: Snohomish, Maltby, Monroe, Index, Sultan, Mt. Si, Baring, Grotto, Monte Cristo, Snoqualmie Lake

Lord Hill Regional Park

Go off Highway 522 west of Monroe on the exit signed "164th." Drive 124 Street SE northwesterly along the base of the highland 3.8 miles and turn south on 127 Avenue SE. At 1.6 miles turn left on 150 Street SE to the water towers, parking area, ranger headquarters, and trailhead, elevation 500 feet.

Two valleys connect Monroe and Snohomish. In one, a narrow slot, the Snoqualmie and Skykomish Rivers join to form the Snohomish River. The other, a wide floodplain, has no river at all anymore, which hardly seems fair. Between them a curious little highland rises to an astonishing apex of 737 feet, prominent from miles away, the highest point so far west. A further uniqueness for that locality, it is not glacial drift but has a heart of volcanic rock. Dissected into steep little peaks and deep little vales, little rock walls growing gardens of moss and flowers, ponds and marshes and swamps in little bowls, it is altogether enchanting to wildland travelers on two feet or four, or two wings. The beaver continue their engineering, bear harvest the berries, coyote crop the rabbits, deer browse the brush. The great blue heron roosts and may nest, as may (now or in future) bald eagle and osprey and other raptors. Ducks quack and swim,

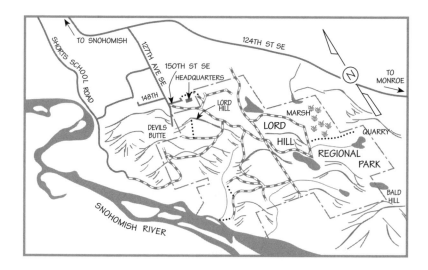

owls hoot and nest, frogs and redwing blackbirds racket—this and more wildlife, and all the wildland paths, are within minutes of Everett and satellite cities and the proliferating subdivisions of south Snohomish and north King Counties.

Residential subdivisions have crept steadily upward and inward on the highland, two quarries long have been gnawing into its vitals, and generations of loggers have come at it with bullteams, donkey engines, chainsaws, and cats, but Nature never quits, the trees grow back and the animals and birds never go away, and the island of "wildness within" is wilder by the year. In 1985 a portion of the area came together as Lord Hill (Snohomish County) Park, 200 acres donated by the Seaholt family, 160 acres of county trust land "reconveyed" to the county for park purposes by the state Department of Natural Resources. Further such reconveyances have brought the size up to some 1400 acres and other acquisitions may be possible, such as the two highly controversial quarries, and unbuildable slopes dropping steeply to the valley. An ultimate area of 2000 or more acres is possible, sufficient to guard the interior from an excess of sights and sounds of surrounding civilization.

The planning for the park is in progress at this writing. The formal opening was October 27, 1995. The informal opening occurred decades ago. The people who know the park immensely better than anybody else are its neighbors, Wayne and Loretta Albin. This is a walking family, early and late, in every season, over many a year, and Mr. Albin has assembled their routes, short and long, in a highly detailed and completely comprehensive inventory. Prepared to assist County Parks in its planning, *Lord Hill Regional Park Walking Paths* can be obtained by the public by sending a check for $5.00 to Philco Printing, 221 SW 153 Street, Suite 265, Burien, WA 98166. The 32-page guide, and a map and current-conditions sheet, is supplied in a plastic bag ready for carrying.

The hours spent in the park by the surveyors don't match up against Mr. and Mrs. Albins' years. We therefore have asked him to recommend a single good sampler. Following, slightly condensed but otherwise little modified, is his "Walk to the Snohomish River," 5¼ miles round trip, cumulative elevation gain in the ups and downs about 600 feet.

The looping route follows shaded logging roads through trees up to a half-century old to the Snohomish River and back along the higher and more open maintenance road for the natural gas pipeline. Mud in places. Look there for tracks of bobcat, cougar, coyote, and deer, as well as dogs, horses, llamas, and people.

From the parking lot (0.0 miles) a new trail soon enters the park (0.1) and connects to an existing logging road and trail system previously accessible only to nearby residents (plus a scattering of trespassers from afar). Do not venture on unknown roads or trails; except for the recently acquired official entrance, the park is entirely surrounded by private lands, private roads, and large, unfriendly, private dogs.

The trail joins an old logging road (0.2) in an early 1980s clearcut. A small wetland is passed, formed by loggers dumping slash in a creek. Listen for frogs in the skunk cabbage. Go uphill to the right on a slightly better road (0.3). Look for a large old stump on the right, notched for loggers' springboards 100 years ago. Turn left on the main park road (0.4), entering a mixed forest last logged about 50 years ago. This is the high point of the road, 500 feet above the river.

A road to the right (0.7) leads to the warmer and drier west side of the park. The road uphill to the left (0.9) reaches the largest lake in the park in about 0.6 mile and continues on a 4-mile loop, a good trip for another visit. Observe on the left (1.0) a beaver pond, signs of current beaver activity, and a beaver dam built at the road edge in 1991.

On a sharp turn to the right (1.6) ignore the shortcut across a rock outcrop. Stay on the road, note two roads going off to the left. The first is the return route of our loop. The left branch of the second road goes to a nice meadow, a good turnaround for a short trip; the right branch descends to the river but is grown over and best bypassed via the main road.

The main road drops into the canyon of the stream from the beaver dam. At the last switchback before the stream (2.0) look for a path continuing ahead and down. Follow it to the river road (2.1). Turn right and descend to just above the river (2.4). Cross the (currently dry) channel to a former island. Follow any path to the beach. The stream from the beaver dam enters the river on the right. Across the river cars can be seen on the SR 522 bridge, which crosses the Snohomish River just below its beginning in the confluence of the Skykomish and the Snoqualmie. Enjoy lunch.

Return to the rock outcrop (3.2). For a 4.8-mile day the road can be walked the 1.6 miles back to the parking lot. For the full tour, take the second right to the 80-foot-wide natural gas pipeline right-of-way (3.5). Turn left, steeply uphill, to the high point (3.8); views ahead to Mt. Baker and back to Mt. Rainier. At the first flat area (3.9) the road to the large lake crosses the pipeline and a short, steep road climbs to a view of The Brothers and Constance in the Olympics. Farther down (4.2) a large, shallow beaver pond is to the right. After going up a little and then down, note the tree-lined outlet stream ahead (4.5). Cross diagonally to the left side of the pipeline just before the stream and follow the trail up into the woods. At the top (4.6) it becomes a road; the area on the left also was logged in the 1980s. The third road to the right (4.9) is the way back to the parking lot (5.2).

Mr. Albin informs us that the name of the hill is from the Lord family, still in residence nearby. He guesses Devil's Butte was named that to give equal time. The highest point of the upland, just outside the park, is 737-foot Bald Hill; it was so when logged but not anymore and now surprises the traveler driving across the river bridge by a glimpse of mansions high in the wildwood.

Wallace Falls State Park

Drive Highway 2 to Gold Bar and turn north, following state park signs a long 1 mile to park headquarters, picnic ground, and trailhead, elevation 300 feet.

Spotted from down in the Skykomish valley, the white line slicing the

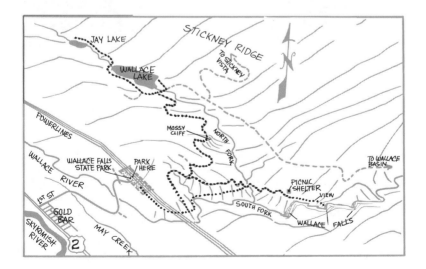

Wallace Falls

green cliffs high above long has attracted explorers. Since the trail improvements that came with the 1977 dedication of the state park, a hiker needn't be an adventurer to experience the spray-billowing gorge and earth-shaking thunder of Wallace Falls. Moreover, though the eleven separate plunges in a single awesome white-water canyon are drama sufficient for an exciting day, there are quieter beauties in the park forests, grown up since railroad logging in the World War I era and now well advanced into the stage of deep shadows, green moss and ferns, and woodland flowers.

The trail follows a powerline swath ¼ mile to the edge of a bluff down to the Wallace River, broad views to Baring, Index, and Persis, and turns into the woods to a split. From here it is 2¼ miles to the falls via the Woody Trail, 3¼ via the Old Railroad Grade Trail. Each has its merits; the neat plan is a loop.

Woody Trail

The path begins close by the river, boulder bars for picnicking, pools for chilling hot feet. The valley narrows and steepens to a gorge and the trail switchbacks high above the stream, then returns to it in 1 long mile, joins the Old Railroad Grade Trail; the two, united, drop to the rustic bridge over the North Fork Wallace River, 650 feet.

Old Railroad Grade Trail

The trail—an old logging railroad grade—ascends steadily and moderately, switchbacking twice. It enters a valley and at 1 mile from the split crosses a creek. Note remnants of an old trestle. Just beyond is a Y. The left goes to Wallace Lake; go right. Nearly flat and straight, the old grade swings out on a steep sidehill above the Wallace River. As it nears the gorge the trail leaves it, descending steeply right to rejoin the Woody Trail at 2 miles from the split.

Onward Together

The North Fork bridge is so pleasant a spot that many hikers, especially those with toddlers in the party, are content to picnic by the tumbling river and return. However, the falls call.

The wide, safe trail climbs steeply in handsome forest of mixed conifers, not as big as the stumps left by the 1920s logging, but getting there. The happy thought is that this forest will not again be logged, but decade by decade will move toward cathedral quality. Moreover, being in a park rather than a tree farm, it will exemplify Nature's Forests—fir, hemlock, cedar, and other conifers and a variety of hardwoods mingling, in contrast to the monotonous single-species monoculture of Man's Forests.

Crossing a ridge to the gorge of the South Fork Wallace River, the one with the falls, the trail ascends to a picnic shelter, 1200 feet, and railing-guarded overlooks of falls directly below and a vista of the main 250-foot falls farther up the gorge. Continuing on, mostly up, the way passes Middle Viewpoint, an impressive close look at the main falls. Finally, at 1500 feet, 1 mile from North Fork bridge, the trail ends at Valley Overlook. The brink of the main falls is below, a giddy sight. Out the slot of the gorge is a broad view of the Skykomish River, the villages of Gold Bar and Startup, Mt. Sultan and the High Rock Hills, the Olympics.

Wallace Lake

Neither a lowland nor truly a mountain lake, yet indubitably a lake. Actually, though, the walk's the thing, not the endpoint.

At 1¼ miles on the Old Railroad Grade Trail, turn left on a road-become-trail. In ¼ mile is a T with the old road to Wallace Lake, now closed to the public by private property owners. Turn right. Not much happens—just a succession of old stumps and continuous dense second-growth. At about 3 miles, 1300 feet, a mossy cliff rises 100 feet above the road. Beat through the trees on the backside for a view over screening trees to Mt. Sultan. In the next 2½ miles the road twice comes alongside the whitewater North Fork, the second time while nearing Wallace Lake.

Here is a T with a private, gated road maintained by a timber company, used by park staff for maintenance, but closed to the general public. Two directions present themselves, right and left.

Turn right on the lakeshore road, cross the outlet (1844 feet), and in a short bit reach a Y. The right goes ¼ mile to a second Y, the right here sidehilling into Wallace Basin, the left climbing the side of Stickney Ridge. Back at the first Y, turn left into a large campground beside a creek entering the lake. A nice spot for lunch.

Back at the T, turn left on the lakeshore road ⅓ mile to a Y. The left is the private (gated) road up from the Sultan River; go right on a narrow lane leading in ¼ mile to an inlet creek at the north end of the lake and the best picnicking of all, on a gravelly shore with fine views of the lake, Stickney Ridge, and Ragged Ridge. Across the inlet stream a grownover green tunnel of a road leads in 1 mile to Jay Lake, 1900 feet, which only fishermen and birdwatchers could get really excited about.

Mineral City

From Index Corner on Highway 2, drive North Fork Skykomish River Road 8.8 miles, to just past Howard Creek, and turn left over the river. At 0.2 mile from the bridge, turn right on a road signed "Road closed 1.3 miles ahead. No turnaround." Pass a sideroad right to the site of Galena, founded in 1890. At 1.6 miles from the bridge the Silver Creek road is barricaded by large boulders and, if that weren't enough, 1000 feet of the road has suffered the terminal slide-out that has been impending since the 1890s. A foot trail has been built by volunteers but is liable to go any minute. Park at the barricade, elevation 1500 feet.

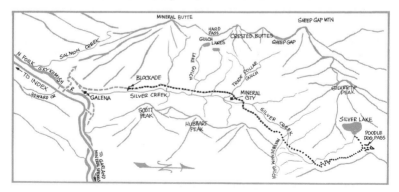

The Silver Creek valley reeks of history. Little remains to be seen. However, much can be felt, especially if the hiker is equipped with *Guide to Monte Cristo Area,* by Harry Majors and Richard McCollum, published in 1977 and now out of print (see a library), and *Mining in the Pacific Northwest,* by Lawrence K. Hodges, published in 1897, another library-only treasure. With one or both on library loan, a person can breathe the atmosphere of two major settlements, 2500 mining claims and hundreds of holes in the ground, and major trails over several passes to Sultan Basin and Monte Cristo.

The first prospector arrived in 1871, and by 1891 some seventy-five diggers were at work between Galena and Mineral City. A flood that washed out much of the trail along the North Fork Skykomish, and completion of the railroad to Monte Cristo, pretty well depopulated Silver Creek, and the subsequent rushes to the Yukon and Alaska pretty well depopulated the North Cascades. However, hiking up the valley in the spring of 1942 the elder surveyor passed a cabin of very great age. Peering from a window was a very aged and very shy man who evidently hadn't rushed anywhere, except here, and that very long ago. Returning downvalley next day, the surveyor found displayed on a roadside log a row of magnificent quartz crystals; the shy smile in the window showed they were meant as gifts which were accepted with a smile. Because of the exchange of smiles the surveyor feels somewhat connected to the olden days of the valley.

Mineral City

The barricade is quickly explained by a cliff of rotten rock where keeping the road open to wheels would cost more than anyone currently cares to spend. (This was true, too, in 1942, when the surveyor parked his Model A and hoisted Trapper Nelson at the same spot.) One hopes the trail-only erosion of the recent slide is not improved, or at least not to admit the two-wheelers and three-wheelers that in the recent past have pretty well ruled out the hike on summer weekends, at least as far as Mineral City.

On weekdays at least, and perhaps for now on weekends as well, there is no lovelier and more peaceful walk in the area. Though loggers entered the valley in the mid-1940s and by the end of the decade had slashed their way virtually to the meadows of Silvertip Peak, and periodically have returned, most recently in the early 1980s, much of the lower creek flows in so deep a canyon the virgin forest has been let alone—Douglas fir and hemlocks up to 4 feet in diameter. There are trees, and there is water.

But interrupt your reveries to wail at the wreckage left by a savage logging show in the very canyon, inaccessible to trucks and thus done by helicopter, and not a murmur of protest from Forest Service or state because it was on "private" land. Scattered logging of this sort has gone on and will continue until the value of these scraps of ancient forest amid canyon cliffs is recognized and protected. Look not to the Forest Service. To Congress?

When a hiker isn't tiptoeing to the road edge to look down into white-roaring slots in the rock, he/she is pausing to exclaim at the waterfalls that splash down Pole Gulch, Moore Gulch, Lockwood Gulch, Cascade Gulch, and Lake Gulch—this latter the route of the miners' trail over Hard Pass to Sultan Basin. Springs ooze from cliffs, their drippings followed down by lines of saxifrage and hanging ribbons of twinflower. Several holes in the ground are passed, and a rotting cabin, and a rotting Seattle bus ("10 Capitol Hill").

At 3 miles, 2180 feet, the road enters the wide sidevalley of Trade Dollar Gulch, route of the (gone) trail over Sheep Gap to Sultan Basin and site of Silver City, founded in 1873, reestablished in 1890 as Mineral City, and in 1896 boasting two hotels, two saloons, two stores, and five other buildings. Nothing of these was visible in 1942, but there were several buildings of later vintage—occupied, in fact, until the draft or high-paying jobs in the shipyards called the miners away. The surveyor camped in the main house, borrowing a can of peaches for his dessert, and explored the mine, gathering crystals of brilliant-red, glassy-transparent arsenic pyrite. Nothing was to be found of houses or mine on the surveyor's next visit, in 1985.

Poodle Dog Pass

In summer the best walking is beyond, where rude creeks turn back wheels and almost boots and subalpine beauties begin to compensate for the barbaric logging done in the 1940s and after. Until the railroad was completed from Barlow Pass, this was a main supply route for the heavy action at Monte Cristo—and in fact was the way by which that area's vivid mineralization was discovered in 1889. Again, most of the history is in the books. But there are flowers.

Trade Dollar Gulch lacks a bridge and the creek is a mean wade in early summer. The road dwindles to trail as it crosses Silver Creek—on a truck bridge—and climbs in alder, then avalanche brush, but partly, too, in patches of virgin silver fir. The waterfall of Molybdenum Gulch is as pretty as they come, and the views grow of Sheep Gap and Silvertip and other peaks. A mine can be seen across the valley in Red Gulch. In 1942 the surveyor saw several buildings high on that wall. On the trail (the road then ended at Mineral City) he passed an old cabin that had been occupied and a mine that had been worked very recently. Scores of ore sacks were piled beside the cabin, chalcopyrite, galena, and sphalerite, the fruits of years of "high-grading"—hand-cleaning the ore with a rock hammer—the only practical way to mine these thin seams, and only worth a man's time in a Great Depression.

At 2850 feet, 1½ miles from Mineral City, the logging road-trail crosses Silver Creek—without a bridge. By late summer the wading or boulder-hopping is no longer life-threatening. Having plowed straight up in snow in 1942, and having turned back in 1985 due to a cowardly dog who felt her life was threatened, the surveyor can report of the route beyond only that the last of the clearcuts is reached in ¾ mile, at 3200 feet, and the abandoned trail, maintained by fishermen's boots and draped with plastic ribbons, then switchbacks 1 long mile to Poodle Dog Pass, 4380 feet. From the junction here the historic trail descends to Monte Cristo. The path left leads to Silver Lake, 4260 feet, set in a cirque scooped from the side of Silvertip.

West Fork Miller River

Drive Highway 2 east from Index Corners 10 miles and turn right, to a sign for Money Creek Campground, on Old Cascade Highway. At a Y in 1 mile turn right on Miller River Road 3.3 miles to an unsigned and undrivable sideroad right. If you come to the West Fork bridge, you've gone several hundred feet too far. Park here, elevation 1291 feet.

Along the valley of the West Fork a long finger of "Management Zone" thrusts deep into the Alpine Lakes Wilderness. Presumably the boundary was drawn to exclude the patented mining claims that have been intermittently worked by one generation of fools after another, each convinced the next stick of dynamite may blast through to the Mother Lode. The valley ought to be Wilderness because it surely is wilderness. The road that was drivable by ordinary vehicles until the era of World War II has been let go, unmaintained, and—unless reopened by the "miners" in Coney Basin, they having found some new money from "investors" not yet placed under court guardianship—too discouraging for even the wheels of witless prospectors or amateur archaeologists come to plunder the middens of nigh onto a century of witless prospectors.

This is the best valley in the area to study old idiocies, old middens,

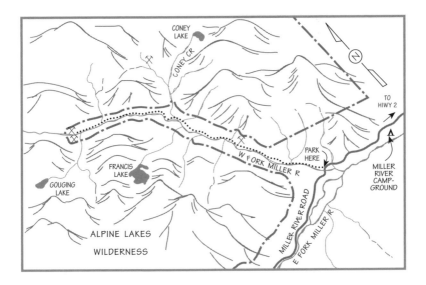

and old junk. In addition there are miles of ancient forest—fortunately not extensive enough to be worth logging (one prays), due to the steep walls and narrowness of the valley and the swaths cut by avalanches and alluvial fans. The river is a steady delight, the water sometimes sheeting over granite slabs for all the world like the High Sierra, sometimes quietly flowing through limeade swimming holes.

Watch for miners' garbage here and there, remnants of camps and cabins. At 1½ miles a Monarch kitchen range marks the site of the Silver Dollar Mine, located up the slope in the brush. In 1944 the surveyor surveyed the tunnels, then only recently abandoned, the miner having been drafted. The way continues past a 7-foot cedar, deep forests of 5-foot hemlocks, fields of bracken opening views to ridges of Cascade Mountain. At 2½ miles, 2050 feet, a sidetrail takes off right up the valley of Coney Creek; the map shows it going to a nameless mine at 3100 feet. At 3¾ miles, 2200 feet, is "Cleopatra City." The surveyor didn't spot the map-shown "jeep trail" climbing to the Cleopatra Mine at 3400 feet, but in the broad field are ruins of two cabins and many rusty or rotten artifacts; the star attraction is a truck some 50 years old. A bit beyond here the road-trail, the whole distance never more than ¼ mile from the Alpine Lakes Wilderness on both sides, at last enters the Wilderness and at 4½ miles, 2400 feet, ends in a final flurry of holes in the ground. Somebody has been busy rather recently, evidenced by an elaborate privy in the woods above a mine tunnel. Somebody or other has been busy here for decades—the rotten logs of a cabin must date from the turn of the century.

Special note: For a miles-long glory of meadow flowers in bloom, do the trip in late spring or early summer.

Other Trips

Thomas Eddy. "The last really wild section of the Snohomish River," this 300-acre portion of the Moon River Ranch, abandoned and going back to nature, is being studied for acquisition by Snohomish County Parks. Enclosed in a meander, the site includes a mile of riverbank, gravel bars a favorite of fishermen, swimmers, and picnickers, wetlands, beaver dams, eagle nests, and a close view of Lord Hill. The county plans to keep the proposed park in a natural state.

Buck Island Park. The pride of Monroe, a floodway tanglewood up to ⅓ mile wide and nearly 1 mile long between the converging waters of the Skykomish River and Woods Creek. When the river is up and the sloughs are full, the peninsula becomes an archipelago, traversed on high by the abandoned grade of the Milwaukee Railroad, which proceeds across the river on the abandoned bridge.

Cow Vista (Barr Hill). A perch an abrupt 1000 feet above the Skykomish River. Razzers and even family cars drive to the top, ignorant of the old saying, "To make the world bigger, go slower," and the self-evident truth that the swift-moving eye sees only a fraction of what there is to see, and that mostly road. Walk it. In early morning before school lets out.

Blue Mountain. From Olney Pass on the Sultan Basin Road, a supersteep logging road climbs to the scalped ridge at 3000 feet and tightropes along the crest 2 miles, in 360-degree panoramas every step of the way.

Stickney Ridge. Stickney, though only 5367 feet high, is among the most prominent peaks on the Cascade front as viewed from Everett and Seattle. An abandoned, unsigned woods road from the Sultan Basin Road climbs to 3150 feet on the west ridge and views to Everett and Seattle and a large portion of the rest of the world. Beyond a 3700-foot saddle, the road drops to Wallace Lake for a one-way-trip exit via Wallace Falls State Park.

Wallace Basin. Proposed, along with Lake Stickney, for addition to Wallace Falls State Park. But also subject of an older and conflicting (in part) proposal for a new Ragged Ridge (national) Wilderness.

Lake Isabel. The 2842-foot cirque lake is in de facto wilderness and must be placed in a Ragged Ridge Wilderness. A favorite trip for doughty explorers who don't mind the approach through miles of the notorious Reiter Razzerland, such a scandal that for years nobody would confess to ownership (it's a lot of mismanagers, including the state, which let the situation get out of hand in the old, pre-1980 days). However, in 1993 the DNR took a bold step, politically enabled to do so by destruction of $500,000 worth of timber on common school trust lands. *Motor vehicles have been banned from 8200 acres, which works out to some 13 square miles.*

Mount Sultan. Rising as high above the town of Sultan as Si does above North Bend, the vistas from the Cascade front so enormous that a flank was site of the Haystack Lookout, this was as rich a climb of old logging roads as the Weyerhaeuser tree "farms" offered. But then Weyco instituted a new gate policy, shutting off razzerboy wheels at the McCoy Creek gate. That was good. But the walking trip was stretched from a former car-assisted easy walk to a 20-mile round trip likable only by the long-leggity, what with an elevation gain to the 3590-foot summit of 3500 feet. But the gate shut out the racketeers and just about assures solitude (unless it is opened as a "fee gate," and the $55 license would exclude all noise except that of the meat-hungry).

Mount Sultana. Closely adjoining Mt. Sultan on the south, its 4206-foot companion was freshly scalped in the late 1970s. For a while it was an easy stroll but the gate now makes it a sweaty job of work for the longest-leggitiest of pedestrians.

Tomtit Alps. At the foot of Mt. Sultan nestles a miniature mountain range—steep little peaklets with startling rock walls, intimate little valleys coiling around them, little lakes that have an alpine feel despite the little elevation. It ought to be inhabited by the little people. But the accesses, once upon a time freely open to walkers, have been closed off by (1) housebuilders and (2) a little logging company which loathes birdwatchers and rejoices when it can make them unhappy. However, we can remind parks departments that they ought to do something useful here.

Tomtit Vista. The logging road that climbs from Cedar Ponds Lake onto the scarp at the Cascade front reaches prodigious views down to the Alps and out to the Skykomish and the cities of Whulge. Higher still, logging roads permit a complicated but shortcut route to Mt. Sultan and Mt. Sultana. But the surveyor won't go back because on his last trip he unwittingly drove over a clever little trap which so flattened two of his tires they had to be destroyed. These natives definitely are restless.

Haystack Mountain. The (gone) Haystack Lookout was on Mt. Sultan, not Haystack Mountain, located to the east. A sharp sleuth can ferret out logging roads to the summit views.

Skykomish River Rail Trail. The classic low-valley views of jaw-dropping peaks. Plus the best riverside walk the Skykomish has to offer. The living railroad can be walked from Everett to the mouth of the tunnel under Stevens Pass, the last part on the Iron Goat Trail, the former rail grade that was the site of the Wellington Massacre. This 4½ mile stretch of rail grade is an easy day and provides intimacy with the river and views of the Index Nordgipfel that ought to dissuade you from becoming a mountain climber. The trip starts where Highway 2 comes to the river east of Reiter Road, follows abandoned rail grade, then living rails to the town of Index.

Jumpoff Vista. From a perch high on craggy Jumpoff Ridge, above the North Fork Skykomish River, the views extend out past Index and Persis to Whulge and the Olympics.

Schmidt Beer Can Trail. Starting from the North Fork Skykomish Road just beyond the 11-mile bridge, a 1-mile road choked by brush ends at mine tunnels blasted from rock so solid no shoring was used. Remains of a privy (a 50-gallon barrel) which has taken a swandive to the bottom of the tailings dump. Little other litter. Except pop cans and, in prominent abundance, Schmidt beer cans.

Money Creek. A white-water creek, virgin forests, old mining garbage and the bed of a narrow-gauge mining railroad, two subalpine lakes, and in season flower gardens or bushels of blueberries. When the miners get too gimpy to crawl around underground, or find other hobbies, the upper valley should be transferred from the Alpine Lakes Management Zone to the Alpine Lakes Wilderness and the road permitted to revert gracefully to trail. It does so now, just about every winter, and for some months is an excellent footroad. Later, when the boulders are cleared away and the floodwater gulches filled in, there are enough wheelfree sidetrips to fill out a day—including a brawl with the bushes in a genuine roaring wilderness (if not Wilderness).

STILLAGUAMISH RIVER

Of all the rivers within the close ken (an easy day's round-trip drive) of Puget Sound City, the Stillaguamish is the most varied. At Stanwood it meanders among cows into Whulge, the first stream north of the Nisqually to meet tidewater in pastoral rather than industrial mode. In the headwaters it flows from glaciers that hang high above farms, strikingly Alpine-like.

Between the two forks and their geometrically fenced floodplains lies the Boulder River Wilderness, established in 1984. Less known to hikers is the thrust of highlands west from the wilderness to tree-mining country. The summits of Olo, Blue, and Wheeler have been scalped almost to the last huckleberry bush and will not see chainsaws again until some century after the twenty-first. The broad views over the lowlands from near the Cascade front therefore will last almost that long. The scarp of the absolute front, 1770-foot Ebey Hill and 2240-foot Jordan Mountain,

Jordan Bridge over South Fork Stillaguamish River

clearcut (again) in the 1980s, has become a favorite family drive for picnicking and sunset-watching.

This lowland-invading peninsula of high country is parallelled by two others. South of the South Fork Stillaguamish is the ridge climaxing in Mt. Pilchuck. The grand old "Nanga," whose summit trail is described in a companion book to this, might be supposed to be totally tramped by boots. Yet the south slopes above the Pilchuck River (the River not the Creek; "pilchuck" is Chinook jargon for "red water," or as we call it, "mountain tea," and there's a lot of it around) are neglected. Why has no government agency been smart enough to reopen the south-slope summit trail, free of white slop months before the north-side trail is suitable for genteel travel?

North of the North Fork the highland peninsula splits in two, divided by the odd valley that accommodates Deer Creek, flowing south, and Lake Cavanaugh-Pilchuck Creek (the Creek not the River) flowing westerly. The valley cuts off an "island" of peaks—Frailey, Washington, and Stimson—opportunity for a city-close, mountain-edge, all-year trail system. North of the Cavanaugh valley are the Cultus Mountains, where logging long ago obliterated the trails, but to whose abandoned logging roads the boots are returning for snowline-probing and bush-roaming.

The thoughtful hiker is bemused by the reshaping of the landscape here by man. He should not overlook the reshaping by Nature. Visualize the Canadian ice overtopping peaks as high as 4000 feet, pushing from the lowlands up such valleys as those of Lake Cavanaugh and Jim Creek, and up the Stillaguamish North Fork nearly to Whitehorse, and up the South Fork far past Pilchuck, dumping all that gravel and clay and till. Visualize the Big River, carrying as much water as today's Columbia, fed by all the streams of the North Cascades, flowing along the ice margin, dodging this way and that, trying to find a way to Aberdeen.

USGS maps: Stanwood, Arlington West, Arlington East, Lake Stevens, Granite Falls, Silverton, Clear Lake, Oso, Fortson, Darrington

River Meadows Regional Park

Bus: 230

Drive Highway 530 east about 0.5 mile from the Arlington town-edge bridge and turn right on Jordan Road, signed "Granite Falls." In 0.8 mile more turn right again, again on Jordan Road. In some 2.5 miles more cross Jim Creek; 0.7 mile beyond is the park entrance. The entry road descends four alluvial terraces representing four periods in the river's history. From the highway on the topmost level, 209 feet, the way drops to a terrace featuring a barn and orchard, then to a forest flat, and then a broad field. At the field edge, 0.5 mile from the highway, the road ends at the last step down, to the water. Elevation, 100 feet.

"From this area north to Jim Creek was long ago, a settlement of the

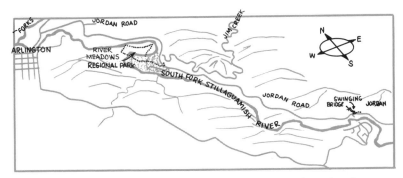

Stillaguamish tribe. The settlement was said to have three longhouses which served as a winter home for the tribe who hunted and fished along the south fork of the Stillaguamish River and Jim Creek." From the park introduction board.

Someday, if the dreaming goes well, a trail will traverse the 15 riverbank miles from Arlington to Granite Falls, connecting to the Monte Cristo Railroad. The Stillaguamish here is perhaps surpassed for wild excitement only by the Green River Gorge. A 200-acre Snohomish County Park is a sampler.

Walk downstream past the picnic area into alder-cottonwood forest. The road, closed to motorized vehicles, ends in ½ mile on a river bar across from a 200-foot wall of glacial clay and till. A fishermen's path continues another ½ mile, nearly to Jim Creek; where the terrace pinches out, a path ascends to the next level and the highway.

Now go upstream, close by the river in the narrowing pasture, ½ mile to the terrace end and park boundary. Trees and water and birds. A path continues and might be walkable another 2 miles or so. Or might not.

By no means ignore the gravel bars. In fact, perhaps it's best to ignore the terrace paths altogether, infested as they are by fat-tire bikes spinning back and forth under the benign smile of County Parks. The alternative to gravel bars is to come on weekdays before school lets out. Never in summer. Never on Sunday.

While in the vicinity, continue upriver on Jordan Road a scant 3 miles to Jordan's General Store. Park in the space provided and cross the Jordan Bridge, a swinging footbridge built in 1977 to replace the rotted-out historic structure. The span gives a bouncing walk (don't run) and fine river views; a path leads to a picnic-type gravel bar.

Monte Cristo Railroad

Drive Highway 92 east from Granite Falls 7 miles to where road No. 41, signed "Tupso Pass," veers off left. Park on the wide highway shoulder, elevation 1000 feet.

White water churning through a wild green gorge at the edge of the lowlands, close to Puget Sound City, open to walking the whole year. That's the South Fork Stillaguamish River.

Plus history! To bring out (imaginary) gold and silver "as rich as Monte Cristo," the railway was built through canyon and forest, reaching Granite Falls in October 1892 and Monte Cristo in August 1893. Winter floods quickly tore out the grade, as other floods did other winters. Rebuilt in 1902, when only the most vacant-eyed gullibles persisted, the line was traveled by gasoline-engine car (the "Galloping Goose") through the 1920s, mostly for tourists. A flood in 1930 ended that. In 1936 the track was dismantled and in 1942 an auto road was completed to Monte Cristo, occupying most of the grade from Verlot upvalley.

The 12 miles of rail grade from Granite Falls to Verlot have been partly left alone by man, partly not obliterated by Nature. Artifacts of the engineering feat—dating halfway back to inception of the Industrial Revolution—compete with scenery. Snohomish County Parks once had a grand plan for preservation and respectful recreation. Does State Parks have a plan? Anybody? Even now, when the sole guardian is Divine Providence, the route is prowled by buffs of history and wildland.

Best forget, for now, the rail route from Granite Falls past a mill and beside a quarry and beneath hillside clearcuts, though in the wild tangle are ruins to set the archaeologist's heart pit-a-patting. Best forget, for now, the stretch from a missing bridge over the river to Tunnel No. 3. Finally, forget the way from Old Rotary to the (missing) Rotary Bridge and through the swamp to what was, when first the elder surveyor came a-hiking with Troop 324, the Mt. Pilchuck trailhead, and onward to the bridge (not missing) to Verlot.

But do remember, and do walk, everybody's favorite tour, the long-famed classic. Tunnels and masonry preserve memories of the railroad. And the reason for the tunnels is that here the river is a white turmoil in a slot gorge of black walls and green jungles.

The trailhead is marked by a handsome brick structure, an Eagle Scout project. Signed "Tunnel 6 1.6 miles, Tunnel 5 1.8 miles," the trail crosses a plantation and descends a forested hillside to an alluvial terrace, at ¼ mile intersecting a woods road. Turn right and follow the road as it drops to a lower terrace, makes a u-turn upvalley, then a u-turn downvalley. Here the rail grade is joined.

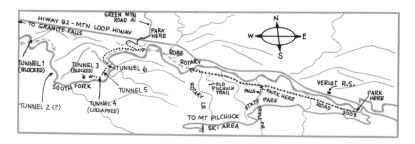

At 1 mile from the highway the woods road ends on the riverbank and the trail proceeds downstream along the edge of a wide, marshy alder bottom. In ⅓ mile the bottom ends and the grade slices the canyon wall. The river turns crazy white. Here began the blasting and concreting, the hole-digging and wall-building. At ¼ mile from the alder bottom is Tunnel No. 6, a spooky cavern 30 feet high and about as wide, 300 feet long, littered with old timbers, ties still set in rock slots.

Returning to daylight, a walker finds the river a tumult of cataracts, the grade narrow, the gorge wild, the ghosts pushy. A bit farther is Tunnel No. 5, 100 feet long, the downstream mouth partly blocked. The grade enters a debris-heaped cut (Tunnel No. 4, collapsed). Then, at 800 feet, ½ mile from Tunnel No. 6, comes a single concrete span arching over a chute plunging to the river. Crossing the chute demands a couple steps most folks won't care to dare. And anyhow, a few yards on is Tunnel No. 3, blocked, no way through and the exposed trail over the top of the ridge not something to discuss in polite society.

North Fork Stillaguamish River: Whulge to Wilderness

In the early 1960s, when the Literary Fund Committee set about furthering the purposes of The Mountaineers enunciated in 1906, placing particular emphasis on "To preserve by protective legislation or otherwise the natural beauty of Northwest America," it adopted as its key strategy the putting of feet on the land. Guidebooks. The *100 Hikes* series grew to five volumes, treating trails in "the wildness without" of the Cascades and Olympics. It was followed by the four volumes of the *Footsore* series (successor to the pioneering *Footloose Around Puget Sound*) covering the beaches of the Whulge and the foothills of the Cascades and Olympics, "the wildness within" the scenes of human "trammeling," which by definition of the Wilderness Act is excluded from the "without." The ganglia of the "within" are, self-evidently, the rivers connecting the saltwater and the glaciers.

In development now or planned or proposed are hitching-trails along the Nisqually, Duwamish-Green-White, Puyallup, Snoqualmie, and Skykomish. However, in those early 1960s when this sort of vision-spinning began, it seemed to us spinners that the easiest hitching corridor was from the mouths of the Stillaguamish River, emptying into Port Susan and Skagit Bay at Stanwood, to the river forks at Arlington, up the North Fork to Darrington, and thence across the Sauk River Valley to the Whitechuck River and onward and upward to its source in the ice of the Glacier Peak Wilderness.

The North Fork Stillaguamish "Trail" was described step by step in *Footsore 3* (1978) and again in the first printing (1995) of this book. However, the trains have quit running on the tracks from Arlington to

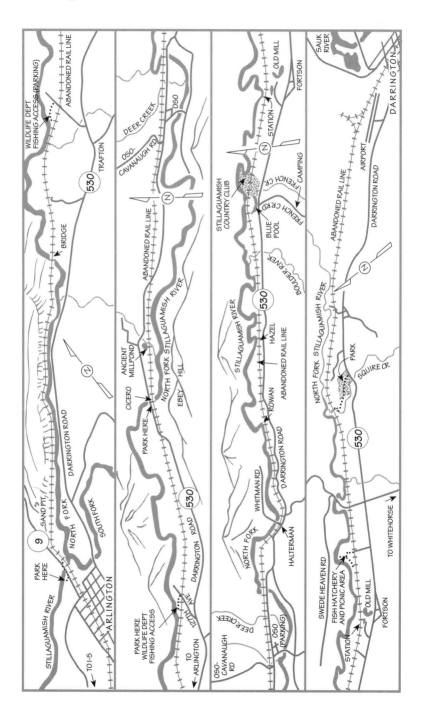

Darrington, and the Rails to Trails movement, which has had so many notable successes across the nation (in our area, the Burke-Gilman Trail of King County, the Foothills Trail of Pierce County, the Centennial Trail of Snohomish County, and the John Wayne Trail across the State of Washington) so far has not fared so well east of Arlington.

It is not the purpose here to point fingers at the obstructors and the faint of heart. But neither is it the intent to concede final defeat. The 27½ miles of the old rail grade from Arlington to Darrington are not officially or legally a "trail" and whenever a sign is encountered, NO TRESPASSING, the walker must obey. Nevertheless, a number of fully public accesses are open to the proposed trail route, giving good short walks on public lands—and good looks at the river and the peaks from which it flows.

The Forks

Bus: 210

Drive Highway 9 to the north edge of Arlington and park at Haller Bridge Park, elevation 40 feet.

River forks are geographically significant and ever-amusing. The feature here is a magnificent sandbar thronged in season with kiddies building castles, bigger folks swimming in the deep, brown-green, silt-murky pools. At medium-low water the bar is walkable downstream ¾ mile. The Dike Road takes feet another mile to a boggling-huge gravel mine. In a dozen miles more are Stanwood and the Whulge, the two mouths of the river emptying into Port Susan and Skagit Bay. Public roads give access to gravel bars and fishermen's paths on State Wildlife Department easements, samples of the superb someday trail.

To examine the upstream way, walk north over the highway bridge, climb the embankment, and turn left the short bit to what used to be Arlington Junction. Go right. The initial 1 mile past an enormous sandpit is unprepossessing, but the next 2 miles are the very best part of the whole route to Darrington. The lonesome grade, made so by cliff on one side and river on the other, is sliced in hanging-garden walls of rotten sandstone and conglomerate dropping to green pools and white rapids of the wild river, a bird avenue nearly arched over by alders and maples.

Trafton Fishing Hole

Bus: 230

Drive Highway 530 east 0.3 mile from Trafton Road (Jim Creek Road) and turn north on 127 Avenue NE, which in 0.5 mile crosses the old rail grade. Just beyond on the left is the unsigned Wildlife Department public fishing access, elevation 98 feet.

Beyond fields abruptly rises the front of the Cascades—Washington, Stimson, and "Little Ridge" north, Ebey Hill south. Cows in pastures, herons in sloughs, splendid old wooden barns, graceful old farmhouses, wild river flowing through wildwoods.

Cicero Bridge

Bus: 230

Drive Highway 530 east 3.5 miles from Trafton to Cicero Bridge. Turn right before the bridge on Monty Road to "Public Fishing." Park here, elevation 125 feet.

The gravel bar is a favorite ol' swimmin' hole. Nearby upstream are visions of America Past, including rotting artifacts of a lumber mill, mossy concrete footings and old pilings and a collapsing wooden bridge, presumably from the millpond. Frailey dominates the view north.

Oso

Bus: 230

Drive Highway 530 to the major metropolis between Arlington and Darrington, quaint old Oso, elevation 200 feet.

Another old millpond. The historic, picturesque Oso School. A bridge whose graffiti proclaims, "Welcome to Oso, Partytown USA." Frailey falls to the rear, Wheeler walls the valley to the south; up the valley can be glimpsed glaciers. East of Oso the exposures of gravel in hillocks identify the terminal moraines of the glacier from Canada. Rising above the valley on the north is a centerpiece of really terrific geology: the textbook folding and faulting of Higgins, horizontal strata separated by a faultline from folded, dipping strata, one of which forms the great naked slab known as the Roller Rink.

Fortson Mill

Drive Highway 530 east 9.5 miles from Oso. Turn left on Fortson Mill Road to the vanished mill, elevation 400 feet.

It ought to be a State Historical Site. But if signs forbid, do not poke about concrete and timbers of the mill, rotting pilings and plank bridge of the millpond.

Fish Hatchery

Drive Highway 530 east o.6 mile from Fortson and turn left to ponds and picnic area of a public fish hatchery in a bulge of forest enclosed by a meander of the river.

Swede Heaven

Drive Highway 530 to 0.5 mile past Whitehorse Store and turn left on Swede Heaven Road. Park the car and walk the road north, over the river, to pastures and barns of the venerable community of Swede Heaven. Views of Higgins geology to the north. To the south, the glaciers of Whitehorse, a gasper of a mountain leaping more than 6000 feet above cows chewing cuds, very Swiss-like.

Squire Creek County Park

Proceeding east on Highway 530, turn off into old-tree forest of a dandy little picnic park by the creek that flows from headwaters amid the peaks of Whitehorse, Jumbo, and Three Fingers. Rude paths lead ½ mile through woodland to the abandoned rail grade and the river.

Darrington Airport

Continue on Highway 530 through beautiful downtown Darrington and follow signs to the Darrington Airport, elevation 549 feet. Stupendous views of Jumbo and the glaciers of Whitehorse. Muse on the oddity of the fact that the valley continues eastward as wide as ever, but the Stillaguamish River doesn't come from there. The valley ahead is that of the Sauk River, a tributary of the Skagit, which in the geologic past captured the headwaters of the Stillaguamish River, which once flowed from Glacier Peak. When the elder suveyor began climbing, he knew Mountaineers who in earlier years had gotten off the train from Seattle in Darrington, hoisted pack, and hit the trail to Glacier. No major ingenuity would be needed to reinstitute a footpath from Darrington to the Sauk to its tributary, the Whitechuck, and on into the Glacier Peak Wilderness.

Lake Twentytwo

Drive Highway 92 for 0.6 mile beyond the east edge of Verlot and turn right to the trailhead parking area, elevation 1100 feet.

The younger surveyor's little sister was much impressed, at a certain age, by white-foaming torrents plunging down cliffs—as she called them, "wow-fows." The climb to Lake Twentytwo ends in a cirque where waters ripple and cliffs beetle, and that's all very pretty. But this really is a walk for wowfows. And wow trees. Set aside in 1947 to permit comparison of virgin systems with managed (logged) ones, the 790-acre Lake Twentytwo Research Natural Area is among the most-visited, most-loved wilderness forests in the Cascades. (No camping, no fires, walk softly.)

The trail begins in an arboretum of giant trees and tiny flowers and sidehills the forest downvalley ⅓ mile to a junction with the old trail. The loitering ends here—the way is now straight up the hill. Tree-gawking continues, the crown canopy of 3-foot hemlocks and 9-foot cedars high above the steep slopes of moss and ferns. In ¼ mile, at 1400 feet, is a bridge over Twentytwo Creek and the first of the falls; on hot summer days many walkers never proceed past the green pools and chill spray. But a bit farther is a sidepath to a sensational falls, and soon another. Now the way leaves the creek and ascends an avalanche slope in views over the valley to Green, Liberty, and the tip of Three Fingers, and up the valley to Big Four. Also in sight are clay banks—silt deposited in the lake dammed by the Canadian glacier, from which the Big River flowed over the divide east of Pilchuck.

Twentytwo Creek

Switchbacking over the top of the avalanche slope and a rockslide, the trail reenters ancient forest, crosses any number of sipping creeks, passes another terrific falls, and at last flattens in a little valley to the lakeshore. A solemn spot, avalanche snow lingering most of most summers beneath the cirque headwall. But if snow prevents reaching it, as it well may in spring, the trip is still a huge success at the third wowfow. Or second. Or first.

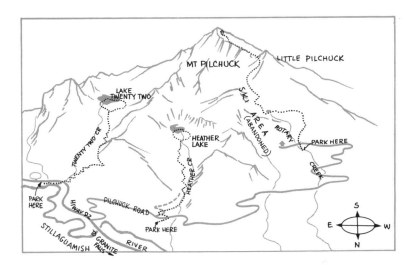

Other Trips

Pilchuck Vista. When the summit trail on the north side of Nanga Pilchuck is up to your hiking shorts in snow, as is normally the case until July, the undrivable logging ex-roads of Kelly Creek on the sunny south give the feet an easy climb to 3550 feet. Old maps show a trail continuing to the summit. Not a bad idea.

Little Pilchuck. A jaunty footstool peaklet, prominent for miles around. Trimming of its greenery opened a viewpoint easy for boots when the high country is sloppy white. From the Granite Falls–Monroe backroad highway, Scotty Road leads to a gate. Feet follow the nose through clearcuts to the 2320-foot summit.

Heather Lake. A cathedral forest and a 2450-foot cirque lake at the foot of Mt. Pilchuck, whose heights are hidden by the cirque walls. The 2-mile trail has been among the most loved in the Cascades for much of a century. In early winter, after hard freezes but before deep snows, ice-skaters throng.

Bear Lake and Pinnacle Lake. From Highway 92, road No. 4020, then No. 4021, take the car to the trailhead. Bear Lake, 2775 feet, is a short stroll on fancy turnpike. At 2 miles, 3800 feet, is Pinnacle Lake, forests and meadows and cliffs.

Ashland Lakes and Twin Falls Lake. Behind the ice dam of the Canadian glacier, a huge lake filled the mountain valleys. The Big River was its outlet, and to make its way south overtopped the ridge east of Pilchuck. The moody little Ashland Lakes (marshes) lie in the forested trough. Twin Falls Lake occupies the plunge basin of the ancient falls into the valley of the Pilchuck River. Logging roads and timber sales continuously confuse the route. Drive as for Bear Lake and watch for signs and cross your fingers.

Trout Lake and Olo Mountain. Logging roads from Highway 92 lead through the stumps and the bushes to a pretty little low-valley lake infested by fishermen and a 3400-foot summit which will have views to the Mukilteo ferry until the bushes become trees. If the gate is closed the walking is pretty peaceful. If not, perhaps not.

Wheeler Mountain. Tired of the everyday world? Want to get away from it all? At the far west end of the ridge running out from Whitehorse is a 3700-foot summit that was flattened by the Canadian glacier and scalped to the last twig. The elder surveyor walked Canyon Creek logging roads 10 miles through tens of thousands of stumps to see the sun set over Whulge and Olympics and howled with the coyotes as he ran all the way home.

Whulge-to-Arlington Trail. Accesses provided by Snohomish County Parks and the state Fish and Wildlife Department allow a walker to sample the Stillaguamish River from its outlet to the forks. Railroad tracks are the route 6 miles from Stanwood to Silvana. From the public river access there, it's 8 river miles to Arlington. Gulhaugen Road and Strotz Road, off Highway 530, let the feet on 1½ miles of riverbank. Haller Bridge Park, at the edge of Arlington, features the union of North Fork and South Fork, a momentous spectacle, and a glorious sandbar, thronged with little bodies in season, and giving pedestrians a start on nearly 2 miles of riverbank walking downstream.

Snohomish-Arlington Way. The "Snohomish County Burke-Gilman," a 17-mile "rails to trails" triumph, yclept Centennial Trail. Worth coming from a distance with a bike, or rollerskates, or skateboard. Otherwise, delightful for close neighbors but not a "regional" amenity. Excellently walkable (horse-ridable) in the odd hours of the off day. Eventually will be extended north to Mount Vernon (and Bellingham?), perhaps south to Monroe (and Duvall?). As long as rails are in place, the contemplative walker who finds himself in Arlington will do better to head for Darrington.

Stimson Hill. A logging road climbs to the 2850-foot summit, whose views have become cluttered by new trees.

Mount Washington. Old logging roads climb obscurely and intricately to the summit, which is now very hairy, but has open views along the way.

Frailey Mountain. The 2666-foot summit can be attained by three road routes, one from Lake Cavanaugh (four-wheel-drive logging road), another from the North Fork Stillaguamish (crosses private property, "No Trespassing"), and the third a rude logging spur from the Cavanaugh-Oso Road across the east ridge of Frailey. Washouts and slides may promote quiet, or may not. Seek a time-window of peace amid the uproar of four-wheelers, motorcycles, hang-gliders, and fat-tire bikes. If you succeed, the views of Whulge, the cows in the valley, and the glaciers on Whitehorse are very fine. Carry a good supply of tranquilizers in case you fail.

SKAGIT RIVER

~~~~~~

Draining a third of the north–south length of the Washington Cascades, and a share of British Columbia, the Skagit is far and away the largest stream of Whulge. Big river. Big country. The delta-floodplain is so broad a walker there feels at sea in the green. The come-ashore San Juan Islands and those still awash, the fault-block mountains and valleys, the handiwork of the Canadian glacier, nowhere so impressive as here near the sources of the ice, and the startling bulge of the Cascades west to saltwater—it's almost more geology than the dilettante can handle.

The Cultus Mountains, south of the Skagit, have been and still are the uncontested empire of loggers and gunners and machine-riders, unfit for habitation or even more than fleeting visitation by pacifists. Fire Mountain, however, gives the walker a look in on a more humane future, as well as a look out to almost more scenery than the brain can absorb without a boggle. North of the Skagit the combined 10,000 acres of Larrabee State Park and Department of Natural Resources holdings on Chuckanut and Elephant are the state's largest wildland outside the inner sanctums of the Cascades and Olympics and incomparably the largest footed in the saltchuck.

Nation-wide fame among hikers lies ahead. The summit views of the delta and San Juans are sensational. Turn your head and the immediacy of the Great White Watcher can set your legs to jittering. Though geologists and journalists ran off in a pack to St. Helens when that's where the headlines and grants were to be got, Baker continues to leak steam as it has for lo these millennia and one of these days, pow, right in the kisser.

USGS maps: Conway, Mount Vernon, Clear Lake, Wickersham, Alger, Bow, Bellingham South

Fire Mountain

Drive I-5 to Exit 221 and go off east on Highway 534 to Highway 9. Turn north to Big Lake and at Milepost 46 turn east on Walker Valley Road. Drive the blacktop a twisting 2.2 miles through pastures and woods to a gravel sideroad right, signed "ORV park 1¼ miles." Continue ahead on the county road 0.5 mile to the end, elevation 400 feet. The road beyond is private, entry to the Fire Mountain Scout Reservation. Opposite the ranger's residence is a shoulder with space for two or three cars. If it's full, drive back to the ORV park road and park on a shoulder of it—not of the county road, which must be kept freely open for Scout use.

The maps call it "Cultus," Chinook jargon (it was not a language, but a

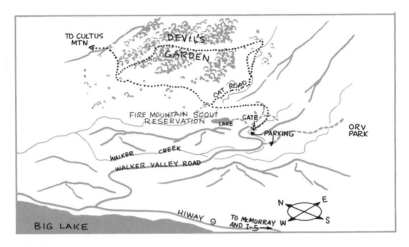

hash jumbled up by the Chinook-speaking people and the English-speaking Europeans to facilitate exploitation of the former by the latter) for "useless." The name for the great huge hulk of mountain mass standing guard over the entrance of the Skagit valley translates from the language of the Original Inhabitants here, the Skagit, as "Fire Mountain," lightning rod that it has always been. Passage through the Scout reservation is entirely dependent on hospitality. That depends on good manners of guests. Happy to say, the mutual courtesy since the route was first publicized in the 1978 predecessor of this volume has been a paradigm of wilderness-edge peace and friendship. To begin any of these trips, obtain permission from the ranger, readily granted except in fire season, when no entry can be allowed.

The Devils Garden

Residents of hot lands envision Hell as a furnace, and cold-land folk as an icebox. It follows that for Whulgers the lair of the Devil is gray, twilight-gloomy, green-oozy, dank and clammy, slimy and slippery. Yet if it is to be the Enemy's garden, it must suit infernal notions of beauty, which is to say it must be frightening as Hell.

Well, something bloody awful happened here. The ranger speculates a gas explosion—a burp from His furnace beneath. The surveyor hypothesized a cataclysmic landslide, a huge piece of Cultus busting loose. The entire mountainside clear down to Walker Valley is littered with monster boulders, mostly hidden by trees. Here in the Garden they are nakedly open, some 50–100 acres of rocks as big as houses—a chaos—a catastrophe frozen in the moment of its conclusion. The chilling fact is, this was no slow talus growth of millennia, this happened all at once, in minutes— and not in the remote past but, as geologists measure time, just a tick ago of Earth's clock. When the elder surveyor climbed above, seeking an absence matching the presence of the landslide, none was to be found. Louis Reed put forth a convincing theory. Not far north is the Big Hole in the side of Cultus. It seems almost self-evident that when the Canadian glacier was slowing down, melting down, its surface lowered from the summit of Cultus nearly to the foot. A chunk of ice-oversteepened mountain collapsed onto the glacier, which maintained motion south even as the front was melting north. The landslide got only this far before the glacier stagnated, then melted away beneath the boulders.

Devils Garden

Where the driveway goes right to the ranger's house, and a gated road left to the camp, take the road straight ahead. In about 250 steps is a Y; the right is NO TRESPASS-ING; go left on the main road, along the edge of a pasture adjoining the reservation. At the far end, elevation 500 feet, as the road is starting an ascent into forest, note on the right a cat road partly blocked by a heap of gravel. Just before this cat road is a cropped-off cedar. Just beyond the cat road is a wood sign on a fir tree, "Devils Garden"—impossible to see except when descending the main road. So watch where you're going.

Turn right, uphill, on the cat road. At an elevation of 1750 feet cross an ancient railroad grade. The cat trail here splits in two pieces which later rejoin. For simplicity, take the left and proceed up a swale. At about 925 feet, ¾ mile from the pasture, spot a flagged trail taking off left.

The Alpine Scramblers first(?) flagged the route in 1976, marking the way to "towlders" (tower-boulders) they named Whalehead, Church Tower, Camelback, Blockhouse, etc. However, the 1988 survey found no flags beyond the first boulder field and no evident route. The younger surveyor of 1988, as had the elder surveyor of 1978, crossed a hump from the first boulders to—horrors! The Garden! How to describe it? With a catch in the breath, a prickling of the skin. Extending some ¼ mile ahead along the slope, and nearly that much up and down, is a "talus"—but no cliff in sight above, just forest all around. Boulders the size of watermelons and suitcases, and bales of hay, and Volkswagens, and Winnebagos and summer cottages, and apartment houses, strewn in disorderly ridges of rocks separated by valleys of rocks, 50-foot towers stirring the blood of a cragger standing above black clefts only a caver could love.

Progress is less walking than scrambling, using the hands and the seat of the britches, bewaring of moss-and-lichen slip-and-slide disasters. How far to go? How much time to spend? A person easily could devote a day to exploring trogs and pinnacles. Or could be content to spread a picnic lunch on the green moss table of a boulder and admire the devilishness.

Donkey Vista–Hugeview Corner

Eye-widening, breath-stopping views from Seattle to the Olympics to the San Juan Islands. A donkey engine peacefully rusting at the landing where the logger walked away from it a quarter-century ago. The Big Hole.

From the reservation entrance, elevation 400 feet, set out as for Devils Garden but stay on the main road, past a sideroad to Scout cabins. In a scant 2 miles the way levels at 900 feet. Ahead a loud creek is heard and in bushes to the right is a white survey post. To save walking a long way around, go off right on a Scout-built shortcut trail that links old cat tracks and climbs steeply, crossing a branch of Nookachamps Creek, and in 1¼ miles rejoins the road at 1800 feet.

To the right, the road leads 3½ miles to Split Rock Meadows or in about the same distance to a 3970-foot peak of Cultus. For the trip here in hand, go left, lose 100 feet to a plank bridge over tumbling Nookachamps Creek, then contour to a Y at ½ mile from the shortcut trail. The road left is the long-way-around-home; go right, climbing again. At a junction in ½ mile the main road proceeds straight ahead. Take a sidetrip along it the short bit to the Big Hole, where an enormous chunk of mountain slid out, creating this scoop prominent from the lowlands—and also creating Devils Garden.

Returned, turn uphill on grassy-grown S-W-J-1000. Impassable to wheels, the old road ascends eastward in mostly alder forest screening a very big picture. In 1 mile, at 2400 feet, a grade obscurely continues ahead; instead, switchback left a final ½ mile to glory. At 2758 feet, 5½ miles from the ranger's house, the road emerges from alders on a landing. Zounds.

The vista is plenty to keep you wheeing and wowing through lunch. But buffs of logging history will be equally enchanted by the donkey engine left here in 1954 or so by Toughy Boyd when he finished salvage-logging and snag-falling after still another of Fire Mountain's fires.

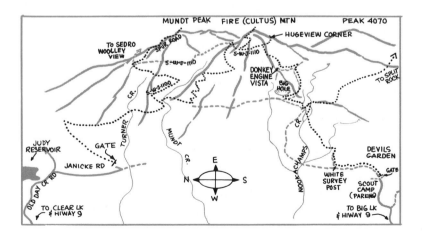

On a day when the brush is dry and you're feeling nimble, try the Scout "trail" upward. Just before the landing, note ribbons leading up a cat track. When the track ends at a draw, a rude path continues in a vertical gymnasium, a snarl of fallen logs and a jungle of young greenery, fun for limber youths but very rude indeed to middle-aged trail-trampers. The acrobatic log-walking and clambering soon yield to easier going and in ½ mile, at 3400 feet, a higher road is reached that leads in ¼ mile to Hugeview Corner. Having fainted and fallen down and revived and gotten up, while the echoes of your bleats reverberate, sit and gaze: South to Stimson and Frailey beyond Pilchuck Creek, Wheeler beyond the North Fork Stillaguamish, Pilchuck beyond the South Fork, Sultan and Si beyond the Skykomish, Rattlesnake and Issaquah Alps beyond the Snoqualmie, and Seattle and Rainier. Southwest and west—down to the Scout camp and green pastures of Walker Valley, Big Lake and Lake McMurray, Devils and Little, Everett and Possession Sound, Camano and Whidbey Islands, Port Townsend and the Olympics. Northwest—the shining Skagit winding through green floodplain and delta, Craft and Ika Islands in Skagit Bay, Erie on Fidalgo Island, the other San Juan Islands, Vancouver Island, Strait of Juan de Fuca, Whulge. East—over headwaters of Nookachamps Creek into the maze of the Cultus Mountains.

Split Rock Meadows

The southwest salient of the Cultus Mountains, jutting into the angle between the graben of Big Lake and the trough of Pilchuck Creek–Lake Cavanaugh, has enough curiosities to choke a geomorphologist: Big Hole, Devils Garden, Bald Mountain, Table Mountain, "Bumpy Ridge." Most features are explained by the glacier from Canada riding over the Cultus crest, smoothing here, plucking there, dumping everywhere. But certain chunks and clefts seem to speak of fault blocks and earthquakes and cataclysms. What about Split Rock?

At the 1800-foot point 3½ miles from the ranger's residence, where the route to Donkey Vista crosses Nookachamps Creek, don't cross, stay right, and continue upward 3½ miles, along and sometimes near the creek, to the Nookachamps–Lake Cavanaugh divide. Here sits a great naked hunk of rock that doesn't grow out of the mountain but alienly sits atop, split by giant cracks, shedding a talus of boulders. Its 250-foot front wall rises vertically from a bog-meadow ¼ mile long, coursed by a creek flowing from one tea-dark, spookily deep pool to another. In June the bog flowers bloom. For big views, scramble up the forested backside to the summit, 3260 feet.

Elephant Mountain—Oyster Dome

Drive Highway 11, Chuckanut Drive, to Milepost 10, 1 mile north of Chuckanut Manor Inn, 0.3 mile north of Oyster Bar, to a pair of turnouts spacious enough for several cars, and a sometimes-signed trailhead. If you come to Oyster Creek bridge you've overshot. Elevation, 200 feet.

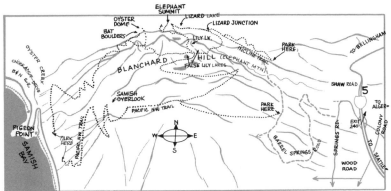

From the Samish section of the Skagit delta, lift your eyes and see the elephant. Why government mapmakers ignored the local name in favor of innocuous "Blanchard Hill" is not known. So far as the Oyster Dome is concerned, nobody seems to have felt the inevitability of the name until the elder surveyor, recently returned from Yosemite domes, happened by. As the elephant is the dominant feature of the landscape from below, the dome is the supreme feature on high.

"Hill," even "mountain," fails to do justice; more properly it's a range that rises abruptly from the north edge of the Skagit-Samish delta and sprawls over a dozen square miles between the glacier troughs of Oyster Creek and Friday Creek–Samish Lake. Railroad-logged in the 1920s–30s (or 1911?), in the 1990s it's a spacious second-growth wilderness. A second clearcutting has begun on the 8000 acres held by the DNR, but provision is being made to preserve foot trails. Adjoining, across Oyster valley, are the 2500 acres of Larrabee State Park; lands of Whatcom County Parks are contiguous. When the interagency trails plan is completed and implemented, the pedestrian will be able to walk from Whulge to two summits, to Cedar and Pine Lakes, to ancient Douglas fir forest, to scenic overlooks, and right into downtown Fairhaven.

The shortest way to the summit of Elephant Mountain is a trail from the east. The shortest way to Oyster Dome is a trail from the west. The two trails are the same one, actually, but the west is far and away best.

From the highway the path ascends a gully ¼ mile to a woods road. Turn left on it to where a sign, "Trail," points to the right. Elevation, 475 feet. The way climbs steeply a scant ½ mile and at 625 feet levels out to an alder bottom. From here, up up up you go, ½ mile to a lovely rock-slab waterfall at 900 feet; at 1125 feet, cross the creek. In another ¼ mile, at 1325 feet, hit a ridge top, leave alders for big cedar, fir, and hemlock. Hearing a gurgle, sidehill to cross the creek. Looking up through the treetops, see a looming cliff. Continue climbing, listening to Lily Creek on the left, dodging paths that go there.

At a scant 2 miles, 1825 feet, the major sidetrail (look for a fir tree with orange arrow) crosses Lily Creek and its waterfalls to a heap of gigantic boulders at the foot of the slabs, trogs, ribs, cracks, and chimneys rising vertically to the top of Oyster Dome. The Bat (talus) Caves appeal to some tastes—though apparently not to bats, which haven't been seen in recent years. Neither have the domestic goats which in the early 1980s were released here—to become coyote suppers? Rock climbers are abundant but harmless.

The best is yet to come. Return to the main trail and climb a steep ¼ mile to the junction at the leveling-out, 2000 feet. Lily Lake lies ahead. Turn left, cross Lily Creek, cascading over rock outcrops, and ascend ¼ mile on a path through scraggly trees and mossy boulders to the glacier-polished slab of Oyster Dome, 2025 feet, 2½ miles from Chuckanut Drive. Gasp! Walk carefully! The slab is slippery when wet and the brink hangs a giddy 350 feet above the Bat Boulders. Wind-tortured pines and hemlocks and a picturesque weathered snag cling to the edge. The views? Skagit delta, Skagit Bay, San Juan Islands, Olympics, Rainier, China.

The trail continues (as part of the Pacific Northwest Trail, to Montana, actually) and a sidetrail ascends to the top of Elephant, but compared to Oyster Dome the views are inferior.

Chuckanut Mountain (Larrabee State Park)

Drive Highway 11, Chuckanut Drive, to Larrabee State Park. A bit north of the highway-side garages and ranger's house is a parking area, elevation 130 feet. A trailhead sign says "Viewpoint 0.9 mile, Fragrance Lake 1.9 miles."

For the other trailhead recommended here, on Chuckanut Drive 0.2 mile north of Milepost 14, Fragrance Lake Road takes off uphill from a gravel turnout, elevation 170 feet. The sign reads, "Fragrance Lake Road. South Logging Road 1 mile. Lost Lake Trail 2.1 miles. Fragrance Lake Trail 2.2 miles. Road end 2.2 miles." The gate is open all year, 6:30 A.M. to dusk. Drive to the permanently gated Lost Lake road-trail, elevation 1050 feet.

In the hundreds of miles from California through Oregon and Washington, the Cascade Mountains sit far back from saltwater. But here at the north edge of the Skagit delta the range juts to the very shore and dives to the beaches. Spectacular. Maybe a geologist would say these aren't the Cascades at all, but an extension of the drowned range that forms the San Juan Islands. Certainly here is the most dazzling view out to that archipelago.

Put this splendid lump of mountain—Chuckanut Mountain—together with lakes fragrant of wildness, lakes lost behind the ranges, wave-swept shores of Whulge, and what have you got? Larrabee State Park, some 2500 acres of glacier troughs and glacier-streamlined ridges, deep forests and sky-open, wide-view rock balds, and saltwater beaches. Put that together with some 8000 acres of adjoining DNR lands and you've got—well, something very, very good. Something unique.

Several walks sample the park. One is on the shore—the Whulge Trail described in a companion book to this. Another climbs to big views and a secluded lake. Two others go higher on the mountain, to bigger views. A last goes over the mountain to no view except those into the heart of solitude.

Fragrance Lake, round trip 4 miles

When all roads are loud with machines, all beaches hectic with childish laughter, when all Larrabee State Park seems groaning under weight of deserved popularity, there is yet a haven, a foot-only trail through deep forest to a gem of a lake in a quiet green bowl. And on the way is a superb view over Samish Bay to the San Juan Islands. What's the fragrance? Peace, it's wonderful.

Switchback steeply a short bit up to a powerline-woods road on the grade of the old Mount Vernon–Bellingham Interurban Railway, become the 6-mile Whatcom County Interurban "Trail" linking Larrabee State Park to Fairhaven City Park in Bellingham. The route is a joint endeavor of Whatcom County, Bellingham Parks, and State Parks. A nice bikeway/backyard stroll it is; hikers coming from Puget Sound City, though, will pass it up in favor of more exciting park paths.

Turn right a few steps to a resumption of trail. The good trees begin— and get better. The trail switchbacks up through noble specimens ¾ mile to a saddle. The trail ahead is "Fragrance Lake, 1.1 miles."

First turn left to "Viewpoint 0.2 mile." In gorgeous forest, firs up to 5 feet thick, proceed to a railing-guarded cliff brink, elevation 650 feet.

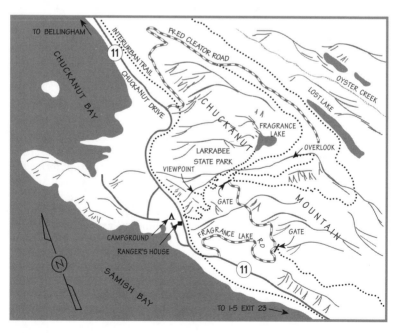

Samish Bay, Anacortes, and San Juan Islands from Oyster Dome

Survey the horizon of islands and waters from refineries of March Point on Fidalgo to Guemes and Cypress and Orcas and Samish and Lummi and the rest. Look straight down to the highway and the shores of Wildcat Cove.

Return to the junction, follow a creeklet down a bit, then again switchback steeply up to another saddle. Here a sidetrail climbs right a few steps to Fragrance Lake Road—the short route to the lake. The main trail drops gently ¼ mile along a small vale in tall-tree forest of cedar and hemlock, a lush understory, to the lake, 1030 feet.

Good-to-meager path circles the lake, over creeks, through groves of 8-foot cedars and 6-foot spruces, under gray rock walls half-hidden in greenery. All is silence. Then—"splash!"—a fish leaps. The fragrance? Sniff and sniff and you'll inhale many fragrances, but not the "Fragrance," which is how local Anglo-Saxons misheard the name of a foreign feller (French, most likely) who had a cabin at the lake.

Lost Lake, round trip 5 miles

The Fragrance Lake Road gives access to four hikes. One, of course, is to Fragrance Lake—the short way. A second, taking off at 657 feet, 1 mile from Chuckanut Drive, is the (unsigned?) "Logging Road," which heads south into lands added to the park by exchange with the DNR in the late 1980s after logging of whatever trees were left after the Chuckanut Burn of the mid-1960s. The semi-naked slopes of South Chuckanut Mountain give the best views of the San Juans. (How many islands can be counted from here? About 20, 25? Would you believe 35?) A third is the 1-mile Overlook Trail, climbing left from the gate, 1050 feet, to Chuckanut's summit, 1940 feet, and dropping a bit to Cyrus Gates Overlook, 1800 feet, on the side of North Chuckanut Mountain.

The story on the fourth hike is not so much views as solitude. Lonesomeness is the attraction of the over-the-hill province of the park. Lonesomeness and geology. The sedimentary structures strike northwest-southeast, dictating alignment of valleys and ridges, and the shales-sandstones-conglomerates differ so greatly in resistance to erosion as to form prominent trenches and ribs and cliffs. Here in the second-growth wilderness myriad ponds and lakes and marshes dribble together to form Oyster Creek, which exploits a line of weakness to cut between Chuckanut Mountain and Elephant Mountain to saltwater. Occupying one trench in the rocks is Lost Lake. And lost a walker may well feel in these faraway depths where once the Canadian glacier gouged.

In big fir, maybe-virgin forest, then alders, passing a great window to the San Juan Islands, Skagit delta, and Olympics, at 1 long mile from Fragrance Lake Road the way reaches a 1577-foot saddle in the ridge of Chuckanut Mountain. Here is a T. The left is the way to Lost Lake. Descend an aldery ravine, in looks over Oyster Creek to 1870-foot "Cedar Peak" and 2300-foot Elephant, and I-5 and Samish Lake, and Cascades beyond.

The road bottoms out and levels beneath an imposing cliff. Lost Lake is glimpsed below in big firs. At 1 long mile from the saddle is a T. The left, formerly the local favorite razzers' mudrun, now is gated shut. Take the right a few yards to a mucky trail which proceeds ¼ mile to the head of the black-bottomed, weak-tea lake. Ducks take off, scaring a walker half to death. Bald eagles nest hereabouts. Where a shore trail goes right, turn left and follow the sandstone-hearted rib downlake to an excellent mossy slab tilted steeply into the lake, elevation 1182 feet. This is the lunch spot. By all means continue a bit farther to where lake water pours over a rock sill and sheets foaming-white down black cliffs. Skid down a path for close looks. Below is a beaver pond in another long valley, contained by another long rock rib. The ranger once saw six beavers in a day. The bottom of the Oyster valley is still a couple hundred feet below, with more lakes, marshes, and a maze of old logging roads. You could get lost without hardly trying.

Other Trips

Little Mountain. Little it is, the summit 980 feet, not counting the lookout tower, but the Skagit delta is so close below a person can see leaves of the grass beside the concrete swath of I-5. The 250-degree arc of view sweeps over the emerald plain, silver meanders of the Skagit, sparkling waters of Skagit Bay, and peaks of the drowned mountain range that form the San Juan Islands. A road climbs from Mount Vernon to the top. A 1½ mile trail from the south is nicer. The trailhead sign on Hickox Road says "Hiker Trail Only." The first ½ mile is private property, open to the public by owner benevolence.

Devils Range. Isolated from the true front of the Cascades by a fault-block valley, the Devils Range is the false front. Scott Mountain, 1620 feet, trail access only, is the champion for views. Devils Mountain, 1727 feet, has a summit road and no views. Ten Lake sits in a cozy cirque-like bowl at a mere 1200 feet yet has the look of an almost-subalpine cirque lake. Something ought to be done about all this. And it is, by loggers and quarriers and platters. Local folks can keep up with the pace of change and find loopholes in the barriers but visitors from afar are liable to get yelled and barked at and lost. Pity. Due to Privatizers, the 25 square miles of exciting wildland at the edge of pastoral civilization have been omitted from these pages.

Skagit River Dikes. The diking and ditching of the Skagit delta is called "reclamation," implying that Man was here first and Nature was the transgressor. Walkers who recognize this as a typically anthropomorphic reversal most enjoy the walks when the sky is full of TV cameras and the delta roads are a gridlock of hardhats and CB radios and Red Cross doughnuts and hot coffee. The dikes along Fir Island, up the South Fork from Conway and up the North Fork from Skagit Bay to where the two distributaries separate at the site of long-gone Skagit City, are wide-open to cows but rather inhospitable to foreigners. Sandbars and public parks provide free-and-easy walking across the river from Mount Vernon and on the city side upstream to the Big Bend. As the river nears the mountain front, mean-it barb-wire fences become troublesome. East of Burlington the dikes end and the explorer must take to the boats.

Wickersham-Woolley-Lyman Mountain. With Fire (Cultus) Mountain, this is one of the matching pair at the gateway from the Skagit delta to the Skagit valley. The 50 square miles of the behemoth lump 4257 feet above floodplains barely higher than sea level. The entirety has been skinned once and is being re-skinned wherever trees have grown larger than fence posts. The 1978 survey from Wickersham has not been repeated, the way made dangerous by gypos' fierce trucks and dogs. The route from Lyman, via Pipeline Road to a chain, foot travel beyond, is friendlier.

Pacific Northwest Trail. The route is envisioned as running from the Continental Divide in Montana to Capa Alava on the Pacific Ocean. Ribboning and whacking-out has been underway for well into a second decade, entirely by volunteers, to a chorus of few if any official blessings and a number of muttered oaths. The way is expected to be opened in the mid-1990s from Dock Butte at the boundary of Mt. Baker–Snoqualmie National Forest the 80 miles west across Josephine, Wickersham-Wooley-Lyman, Anderson, and Elephant to the saltchuck at Samish Bay. For the guidebook, write Pacific Northwest Trail Association, P.O. Box 1048, Seattle, WA 98111.

INDEX

THE MOUNTAINEERS, founded in 1906, is a nonprofit outdoor activity and conservation club, whose mission is "to explore, study, preserve, and enjoy the natural beauty of the outdoors...." Based in Seattle, Washington, the club is now the third-largest such organization in the United States, with 15,000 members and five branches throughout Washington State.

The Mountaineers sponsors both classes and year-round outdoor activities in the Pacific Northwest, which include hiking, mountain climbing, ski-touring, snowshoeing, bicycling, camping, kayaking and canoeing, nature study, sailing, and adventure travel. The club's conservation division supports environmental causes through educational activities, sponsoring legislation, and presenting informational programs. All club activities are led by skilled, experienced volunteers, who are dedicated to promoting safe and responsible enjoyment and preservation of the outdoors.

The Mountaineers Books, an active, nonprofit publishing program of the club, produces guidebooks, instructional texts, historical works, natural history guides, and works on environmental conservation. All books produced by The Mountaineers are aimed at fulfilling the club's mission.

If you would like to participate in these organized outdoor activities or the club's programs, consider a membership in The Mountaineers. For information and an application, write or call The Mountaineers, Club Headquarters, 300 Third Avenue West, Seattle, Washington 98119; (206) 284-6310; e-mail: clubmail@mountaineers.org.

Send or call for our catalog of more than 300 outdoor titles:
The Mountaineers Books
1001 SW Klickitat Way, Suite 201
Seattle, WA 98134
1-800-553-4453 / e-mail: mbooks@mountaineers.org